WILD
guide

Devon, Cornwall and the South West

Hidden Places, Great Adventures
and the Good Life

Daniel Start, Tania Pascoe and Jo Keeling

WILD
guide

Contents

Regional overview... 6

Introduction... 9

BEST FOR...
Secret beaches 16
Canoe adventures 18
Lost ruins and ancient stones 20
Night walks and sunsets 22
Caves, caverns and grottoes......................... 24
Ancient woodlands 26
Meadows and seasons 28
Wild camping 30
Food and foraging 32

THE COUNTIES
Cornwall.. 36
Devon..108
Somerset...172
Dorset 220

Co-ordinate conversions............................254
Acknowledgements 256

Regional Overview

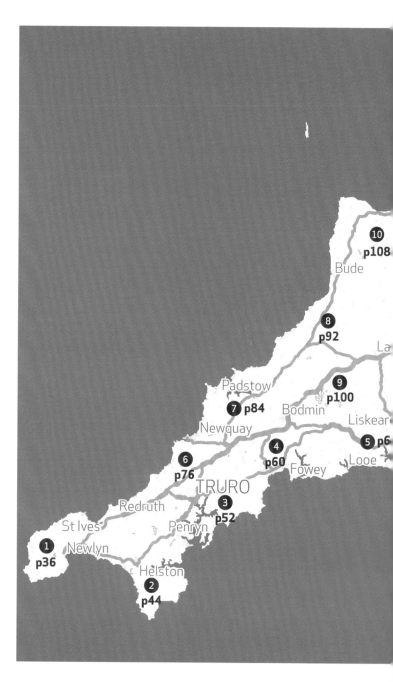

Cornwall

1 Penwith & Scilly	36
2 Lizard & Helford	44
3 Roseland & Veryan	52
4 Fowey & St Austell	60
5 Tamar & Looe	68
6 St Agnes	76
7 Padstow & Bedruthan	84
8 Tintagel & Bude	92
9 Bodmin Moor	100

Devon

10 Hartland & Torridge	108
11 North Devon	116
12 Southwest Dartmoor	124
13 Northwest Dartmoor	132
14 Northeast Dartmoor	140
15 Southeast Dartmoor	148
16 South Devon Coast	156
17 East Devon	164

Somerset

18 Central Exmoor	172
19 Quantock & Blackdown	180
20 Somerset Levels	188
21 Mendip Hills	196
22 Somerset Avon	204
23 East Somerset	212

Dorset

24 East Dorset	220
25 Dorset Purbeck	228
26 Dorchester & Portland	236
27 West Dorset	244

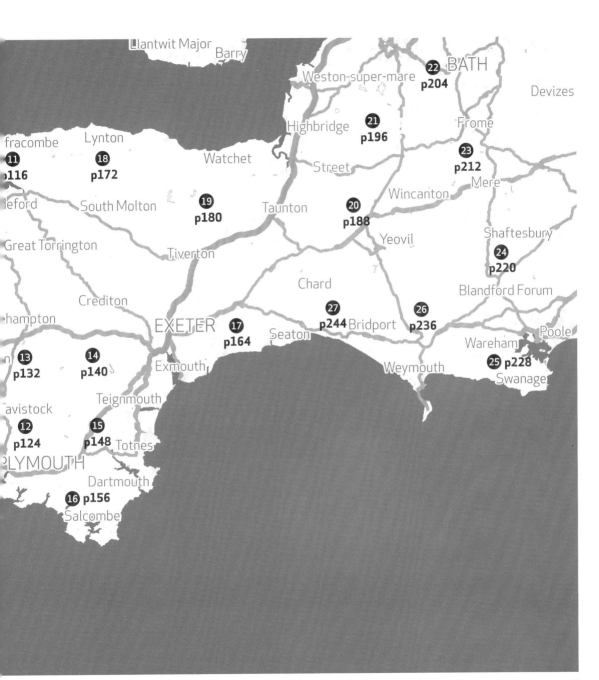

Llantwit Major
Barry

Weston-super-mare

22 BATH
p204

Devizes

Highbridge

Frome

21
p196

23
p212

Mere

fracombe

Lynton

Watchet

Street

Wincanton

11
116

18
p172

Taunton

20
p188

Yeovil

Shaftesbury

leford

South Molton

19
p180

24
p220

Great Torrington

Tiverton

Chard

Blandford Forum

Crediton

27
p244 Bridport

26
p236

Poole

hampton

EXETER

17
p164

Seaton

Wareham

13
p132

14
p140

Exmouth

Weymouth

25 p228

avistock

Teignmouth

Swanage

12
p124

15
p148 Totnes

LYMOUTH

Dartmouth

16 p156

Salcombe

Introduction

Discover lost ruins overgrown by ancient forests; clamber down to a secret cove and explore sea caves; picnic in a meadow of orchids and rare butterflies; watch the sun set from an Iron Age hill fort; search for glow worms in the dusk then wait for the sky to turn deep indigo and fill with stars.

The *Wild Guide* is a celebration of the wild places that lie hidden, just off the beaten path. It's your guide to a lifetime of joyful exploration and simple pleasures. And these special places are on your very doorstep, if you know where to look.

Great adventures

In our modern digital world, much is made of our new-found freedoms – to work remotely, be contactable anywhere and always be online. Yet we remain tethered to our technology and busier than ever.

Our children, deprived of beneficial wild experiences during their development, can suffer so-called nature-deficit disorder.

Our remedy is a big dose of simple adventures of the most natural kind – exploring the wilder places that lie on the edge of everyday life and throwing yourself into new experiences. There are rivers for swimming or canoeing, moors and meadows to camp in, ancient pathways for night-time walks, woods and ruins to explore and subterranean worlds to discover. Straying out of your comfort zone is not without risk, but new adventures can bring an enormous sense of freedom and well-being.

Hidden places

Think of the South West in summer, and queues of traffic on the A30 and tiny lanes jammed with caravans may spring to mind. Yet, once you know where to look you'll find a region of extraordinary secluded beauty, its remote coastline indented with tiny coves, its vast moorlands fringed by ancient woodland, crossed by babbling streams and watched over by sacred stones.

Our formula for getting away from the crowds is based around the magic of some key locations:

Wild coast: The intertidal zone is perhaps the greatest wild area in the UK today, a no-man's land continuously covered and then revealed by the great ocean. Secret coves and caves await the adventurous, while precipitous cliffs and rugged smugglers' trails offer a challenge that rewards and invigorates in equal measure.

Rivers and lakes: The beautiful, natural waterways that have shaped our verdant landscape, especially where their courses are not followed by roads, offer wonderful wild corridors that are ideal for swimming, canoeing, fishing and embracing a slower pace of life.

Sunset hill forts: To watch the sun set is to squeeze the very last juice from the day. It's a unique opportunity to feel the subtle changes around you as birds roost, dusk settles, and nocturnal creatures begin to stir. Hill tops provide an ideal vantage point and many are also rich in Iron Age history.

Ancient woods: These rich fragments of what were once great forests are not only places to wander in peace, but also allow admittance into a stimulating world of den building, camping out, tree climbing and foraging for wild food.

Lost ruins: There are so many relics of Britain's rich history to inspire us, from sacred stone circles to cliff-top engine houses, many overgrown and abandoned but with fascinating stories to tell. Ruins offer adventure and romance – the vital ingredients of every truly picturesque location.

Meadows and wildlife: To be surrounded by wild, unspoilt beauty, from carpets of divinely scented bluebells in May to the uplifting sight of a falcon swooping overhead, is to be reminded of the power of nature. It can help to reconnect us and reawaken our sense of wonder.

The good life

For a truly wholesome feel, travel to the locations in this guide by walking, canoeing, cycling, swimming or horse riding, and then eat hearty local food of known provenance, created with care. Some light foraging is satisfying too, especially of the most abundant treats, including wild garlic, mussels and maybe a line-caught mackerel, all cooked up on a little driftwood fire. After some stargazing camp on a beach or by a waterfall or stream where you can wash in the morning.

We chose to write our first *Wild Guide* about the South West because we wanted to celebrate simple adventures close to home. The South West is a place we know, love and live in, so the idea of an intimate local guide, filled with secret destinations and special places, appealed. Along the way, we have met so many people living a simpler, richer life, such as artisan producers making delicious traditional foods and smallholders who tend to their pigs and chickens alongside guests.

The end result is a compendium (longer than intended) of wonderful adventures and wild places. It is packed full of memories of wild campsites, night walks, foraging missions, sunset surfing, canoe trips at dawn and countless dips into moorland tarns and Somerset rivers. And all without flying, or queuing, or paying very much at all. We hope the book inspires many wild and wonderful escapades – do write and tell us how you get on.

Dan, Tania and Jo

wildguide@wildguide.net

Finding your way & access

Most places listed are on a public right of way, permissive path, open-access land or benefit from long-use rights. However some places, usually marked ?, may not have such clear rights. **You will need to make your own judgment about whether to proceed or seek permission from the landowner.**

An overview map and directions are provided, but the latitude, longitude for each location, provided in WGS84 decimal degrees, is the definitive reference and can be entered into any online map site, such as Google, Bing or Streetmap. The latter two provide Ordnance Survey mapping overlays, which show footpaths. OpenStreetMap increasingly shows paths, too. Print out the map before you go, or save a 'screen grab'. Map apps such as ViewRanger or Memory-Map are useful, and you can also enter the co-ordinates into your smartphone GPS or car sat nav (enable 'decimal degrees'). Postcodes are provided for convenience, but only provide a rough location. If you have paper maps, look up the equivalent National Grid reference in the conversion table at the back of the book. If a parking place is mentioned, always make your own judgment and be considerate. Where two places are named in the title, the focus of the text is always the first. Walk-in times given are one way only, allowing 15 mins per km, which is quite brisk. Abbreviations in the directions refer to left and right (L, R); north, east, south and west (N, E, S, W) and direction (dir). There are also: National Trust (NT), English Heritage (EH), Royal Society for the Protection of Birds (RSPB), National Nature Reserve (NNR), Youth Hostel Association (YHA), National Cycle Network (NCN) & Camping and Caravanning Club (CCC).

Wild & responsible

1. Fasten all gates and only climb them at the hinges.
2. Keep your dogs under close control, especially around livestock and in nature reserves.
3. Take your litter home, and gain good karma by collecting other people's.
4. If you wash in streams or rivers, use only biodegradable soap, or none at all.
5. Take special care on country roads and park considerately, to allow room for a tractor or truck.
6. Take map, compass, whistle and waterproof clothing when venturing into remote or high areas.
7. Always tell someone where you are going, and do not rely on your mobile phone.

Best for
Secret beaches

Rocky, indented and often spectacular, the South West coast has some fantastic secret coves. Access isn't always straightforward and some are difficult to find, but that's half the fun. There's almost always a path down, sometimes with the help of a rope or some rough steps, so take great care and you'll enjoy a refreshing plunge away from the crowds.

Before setting off, check the tides times carefully, as many hidden coves only reveal their perfect white sand at low tide. Remember also that tides are much more extreme during full and new moons – the so-called 'spring' tides that occur every fortnight. In the South West, low tide tends to be around lunchtime during spring tides. This is a great time to be on the beach and there will certainly be more sand to sit on, but the risk of being cut off may be greater, so try not to lose track of time.

Pedn Vounder, Treen (Penwith 5)

Veor Cove, Zennor (Penwith 8)

Lankidden, Kennack (Lizard 2)

Crook Point Sands (North Devon 8)

Cellar Cove, Portholland (Roseland 5)

Man Sands, Woodhuish (South Devon 15)

St Gabriel's Mouth (West Dorset 1)

Smugglers' Path, White Nothe (Dorchester 3)

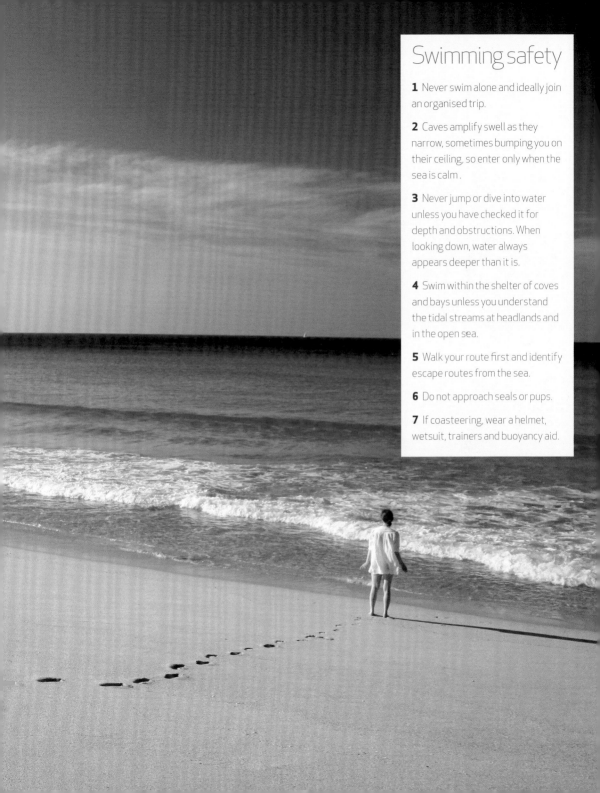

Swimming safety

1 Never swim alone and ideally join an organised trip.

2 Caves amplify swell as they narrow, sometimes bumping you on their ceiling, so enter only when the sea is calm .

3 Never jump or dive into water unless you have checked it for depth and obstructions. When looking down, water always appears deeper than it is.

4 Swim within the shelter of coves and bays unless you understand the tidal streams at headlands and in the open sea.

5 Walk your route first and identify escape routes from the sea.

6 Do not approach seals or pups.

7 If coasteering, wear a helmet, wetsuit, trainers and buoyancy aid.

Best for
Canoe adventures

More people than ever now own a canoe or kayak, thanks in part to affordable new designs. The safest are the 'sit-on-tops' made of hard plastic, which are unsinkable and self-draining. If you capsize, just get back on and keep going. The easiest to transport are the inflatables, with various thicknesses of skin. Make sure you buy one with multiple chambers and don't use inflatables if you plan to venture far from the shore.

Everyone has the right to canoe on tidal waters, so if you are a beginner head for the sheltered estuaries and creeks common along the southern coast of the South West. If you time your trip carefully you can head upstream with the flow and return with the ebb. Be aware that the estuary mouth, where the river meets the sea, can be subject to swell and breaking waves. If you plan to canoe on non-tidal, inland waters, check out access arrangements and always be respectful to fishermen.

Bosahan Cove, Helford (Lizard 11)

Fal-Ruan upper creeks, River Fal (Roseland 27)

Pont Pill Creek, River Fowey (Fowey 10)

Erme ria estuary (South Devon 17)

Kingsbridge ria, South Pool (South Devon 19)

Staverton, River Dart (Southeast Dartmoor 7)

Fremington Quay, River Taw (North Devon 18)

Ladram Bay (East Devon 1)

Swimming safety

1 Never swim alone, and keep a constant watch on weak swimmers.

2 Cold water can dramatically decrease swimming ability, create cold shock and cause drowning through panic. Know your limits, enter slowly and stay close to the shoreline.

3 Never jump into water unless you have thoroughly checked for depth and obstructions.

4 Avoid strong currents, such as those directly under large waterfalls or weirs, or those found in river rapids during floods: they can drag you under.

5 Always make sure you know how you will get out before you get in.

6 Wear footwear if you can.

7 Avoid direct contact with blue-green algae, and be wary of water quality in lowland areas during droughts and heavy rain. Cover cuts with plasters if worried, and if you develop flu-like symptoms tell your doctor you have been in a river.

Best for
Lost ruins and ancient stones

Concealed in woods and covered in ivy or standing open to the elements on a remote cliff top, the South West has many ancient stone monuments, follies and industrial relics. Such places are often richly atmospheric and well worth seeking out.

The most recent ruins are the remnants of once-thriving industries, including engine houses, processing mills, railway tracks, tunnels and quarries. The tin-mining areas of the north Cornish coast have their own stark beauty and the lunar landscape of clay pits to the south, many filled with aquamarine water, is unique and extraordinary. Going further back in time, it is still possible to see the fascinating traces left by Roman lead mining, as well as the remains of an amphitheatre, in the Mendips.

This region is rich in Bronze and Iron Age remains, from hill forts to standing stones. Some of the most sacred are the ancient stone circles of West Penwith, Bodmin and Dartmoor, set in wonderfully wild locations. You can explore mysterious underground burial chambers or 'fogous', wander around lost village settlements, or visit ceremonial stone rows, some many miles long.

Boscawen-un Stone Cirlce (Penwith 19)

Wheal Trewavas, Rinsey (Lizard 21)

Scorhill Stone Circle (Northeast Dartmoor 16)

Merrivale Stone Row (Southwest Dartmoor 20)

Rame Head Chapel (Tamar 17)

St Luke's Chapel (West Dorset 11)

Nunney Castle (East Somerset 15)

Fussell Iron Works, Mells (East Somerset 16)

Best for
Night walks and sunsets

The golden hour before sunset is a magical time of day when heat still lingers in the air and the light bathes the landscape in a warm glow. Find a high vantage point and experience the glorious, grand finale of the day. And if you are looking out to sea, you might even see the intriguing 'green flash' that occurs in those last few seconds before the sun disappears.

As dusk descends, wrap up and settle down to watch and listen under an indigo sky. At night, the landscape shows its true wild character: familiar outlines blur, nightjars call, glow-worms shine and overhead the stars begin to glitter. For stargazing choose a clear night and a remote spot, such as Exmoor. Plan night walks on moonlit nights and pack a torch but try not to use it. Let your eyes adjust to the dark – it can take about 20 minutes – then start walking with slow, careful strides, taking high steps to avoid tripping on uneven ground. Retrace ancient routes and think of all the people who have travelled the same path over hundreds of years.

Zennor Quoit sunset (Penwith 21)

Lych Way, Corpse Road night walk (Northwest Dartmoor 11)

Bolt Tail Cliff Castle sunset (South Devon 21)

Dunkery Beacon star gazing (Central Exmoor 14)

St Aldhelm's Chapel sunset (Dorset Purbeck 22)

Maiden Castle sunset (Dorchester 13)

Sutton Wick hill fort sunset (Somerset Avon 19)

Pildson Pen hill fort sunset (West Dorset 5)

Best for
Caves, caverns and grottoes

Sculpted by natural forces and long used as shelter by people and animals, the caves and caverns of the South West offer a glimpse into the underworld. The caverns below Cheddar Gorge in the Mendips were formed from huge flows of meltwater, when glaciers retreated at the end of the last ice age, while those those higher on the plateau were eroded by the powerful action of water on rock. In some places many thousands of animal bones have been found, including those of hyena, mammoth, lion and buffalo; in others archeologists have uncovered the remains of our cave-dwelling ancestors. Sea caves, scoured out by pounding waves, also offer a fascinating insight into the world beneath our feet.

Most of the places recommended have large, safe openings, but if you venture further into the interior, you will need specialist equipment. In all cases, we would suggest wearing a cycle helmet, old clothes and wellington boots, and carrying a torch. Sea caves should only be explored in calm seas and in a group, with everyone wearing helmets, life jackets and wetsuits.

Nanjizal Arch, Polgigga (Penwith 2)

Holywell Cave, Holywell Beach (Agnes 15)

Wheal Coates sea caves, Porthchapel (Agnes 6)

Merlin's Cavern, Tintagel (Tintagel 13)

Pridhamsleigh Cavern (Southeast Dartmoor 17)

Monster Cavern, Cheddar Gorge (Mendips 9)

Goatchurch Cavern, Burrintgon Combe (Mendips 7)

Blue Grotto, Stair Hole, Lulworth (Dorset Purbeck 2)

Best for
Ancient woodlands

Ancient forests are a precious remnant of the vast primordial woodland that once covered the UK. Some trees, such as yew, are the oldest living creatures on earth and some of those found in churchyards predate Christianity. Oaks can live to be thousands of years old, becoming hollow over time and with massive boughs that are perfect to climb. As a rough guide, an oak with a girth of 12 feet is about 170 years old.

Discovering such venerable trees, climbing up and into them and imagining their history can be a memorable experience. Older woodland, too, can offer excellent trees for climbing freestyle. Experienced climbers bring ropes and harnesses to penetrate higher into the canopy of tall trees, and some even string up special night-hammocks to sleep among the boughs.

If you bring your own rope, you can easily set up a tree swing. Use a smaller string with a stone to hoist a larger rope up over a branch, then tighten with a lasso knot. Or try den-building, which is the perfect activity in any woodland, and guaranteed to keep older children amused for hours.

Tremayne Wood, Helford (Lizard 16)

Trelissick tree climbing (Roseland 15)

Dizzard Wood, Millook Haven (Tintagel 18)

Wistman's Wood (Northwest Dartmoor 6)

Black-a-Tor Copse (Northwest Dartmoor 7)

Yarner Wood (Northeast Dartmoor 10)

Holford Beeches (Quantocks 15)

Wyndham's Oak, Silton (East Somerset 8)

Best for
Meadows and seasons

Each season in the South West brings its own delights. Visit ancient woodlands in early spring for wild daffodils and wood anemones, and in late spring for bluebells. In April the rare snake's head fritillary transforms damp meadows, while in May and June exquisite native orchids emerge.

Look out for ponies and their foals on Dartmoor, Exmoor and Bodmin Moor in early summer, when grassland is dotted with wild flowers. At this season, many woodland glades are alive with butterflies, such as the marsh fritillary, and on a warm evening you might see glow-worms, too.

Dolphins and porpoises, drawn by the warm Gulf Stream currents, swim up the coast in the summer months, and Cornwall is a hot-spot for basking sharks. These huge but harmless plankton eaters turn up in springtime, often staying until the end of summer. The abundant life in the water also attracts many birds, including gannets, fulmars, puffins and seasonal migrants such as shearwaters, skuas and kittiwakes.

In autumn, the South West's ancient woodlands blaze with fiery colours, while enormous flocks of starlings, numbering tens of thousands, creating dazzling aerial displays as winter approaches.

West Pentire Head poppies (Agnes 19)

Enys and Park Lye bluebells (Roseland 17)

Holwell Lawn bluebells, Hound Tor (Northeast Dartmoor 15)

Dunsford Wood wild daffodils (Northeast Dartmoor 17)

Edford Woods wild daffodils (East Somerset 13)

Westhay Moor starlings (Somerset Levels 11)

Kingcombe orchids (West Dorset 13)

Fontmell Downs glow-worms (East Dorset 9)

Best for
Wild camping

Those of us who live in the South West are fortunate
that Dartmoor National Park not only allows but actively
encourages wild camping, because to camp in the open
landscape is the best way to get really close to nature

Whether alone or with a group, don't pitch your tent on
any lowland farmland (moorland enclosed by walls or
fences), within 100 metres of a road, anywhere within
sight of houses, in reservoir catchment areas or on
archaeological sites. If you are in a camper van, it's
also illegal to sleep in car parks, lay-bys or on moorland
verges.

In other parts of the region, wild camping by walkers is
often tolerated in more remote rural areas – typically,
more than a half-day's walk from an official campsite
or other accommodation. Keep your group small and
respect the site by taking litter home and leaving
the area as you found it. And if you are camping on a
secluded beach, wait until just before dusk to pitch your
tent and leave early. Any wood fires should be below the
high-tide line, so the sea can carry away the ash.

Vault Beach, Gorran Haven (Roseland 4)

King Arthur's Hall (Bodmin 18)

Kilmar Tor (Bodmin 10)

Piles Copse, Erme Valley (Southwest Dartmoor 14)

Huntingdon Cross (Southeast Dartmoor 38)

Black-a-Tor copse (Northwest Dartmoor 7)

East Porlock Bay (Central Exmoor 2)

Brig's Farm (West Dorset 23)

Wild camping

1 Camp above the highest fell wall, well away from towns and villages.

2 Leave no litter, remove other people's, and don't bury litter.

3 Do not light any fires, even if there's evidence that fires may have been lit by others.

4 Stay for only one night.

5 Keep groups very small – only one or two tents.

6 Camp as unobtrusively as possible, with inconspicuous tents that blend into the landscape.

7 Take away tampons and sanitary towels; burying them doesn't work, as animals dig them up again.

8 Perform toilet duties at least 30m (100ft) from water, and bury the results with a trowel.

Best for
Food and foraging

To get a real sense of a place, it's a good idea to explore its native food, and the South West offers one of the richest arrays of home-reared, freshly harvested, clotted-cream-smothered bounty that you will find anywhere on our island.

Provenance here can be measured in metres. Honesty boxes filled with overspill from veg patches line the little lanes of Devon and Cornwall, so fill your basket with shiny courgettes, pots of jam, eggs with deep-yellow yolks and some scented flowers for your camping table. Buy fish straight from the fishing boats in tiny harbours and head for the growing number of farmers' or village markets that offer a lifeline to rural, artisan food producers. Their hand-made, traditional foods, free from additives and made with love, will make you want to throw away your supermarket loyalty card.

You can always catch your own supper by standing on the shoreline with a hook and line (unlike river fishing you don't need a licence), or learn to forage for wild mushrooms in autumn. And if you want to get even closer to your food, sign up to one of the many courses on offer such as pig rearing and butchering or cheesemaking.

Trevellas cove mussels (Agnes 17)

Veryan Country Market (Roseland 33)

Heddon's Mouth bass fishing (North Devon 20)

Wildwise canoe foraging (Southeast Dartmoor 11)

Cider Brandy, Kingsbury Episcopi (Somerset Levels 14)

Quantock Common whortleberries (Quantocks 22)

Ethicurean (Somerset Avon 29)

River Cottage courses (East Devon 23)

PENWITH & SCILLY

Our perfect weekend

→ **Dance** barefoot around the Merry Maidens stone circle at dawn.

→ **Explore** the underground fogou at Carn Euny by candlelight and dip a toe in the holy well.

→ **Paddle** in the shallow lagoons at Pedn Voundner and sit on the offshore sand bar.

→ **Discover** the coralline sea caves at Nanjizal, as sun pours in through the great arch.

→ **Find** secret coves at Veor, then refuel with delicious Moomaid ice cream at Zennor.

→ **Swim** in the pool fed by springs, high on the wildflower moorland at Baker's Pit.

→ **Spot** dolphins and basking shark off the coast near Porthgwarra.

→ **Sleep** in a roundhouse, hobbit home, straw-bale cabin or safari tent, in one of the many quirky places to stay.

→ **Soak** up the atmosphere at Botallack Mine's cliff-top ruins.

→ **Clamber** through the Mên-an-Tol holed fertility stone, then walk to the Nine Maiden stone circle and Ding Dong mine.

Here on the very edge of Britain, sandy coves nestle between granite cliffs that are encrusted with ruined mine workings. The sacred symbols of ancient humans are everywhere, from stone circles overgrown by moorland heather to secluded holy wells by sheltered streams.

The mysterious monuments of this remote peninsula give Penwith an air of magic and mischief. Its special atmosphere may tempt you to dance around stone circles at sunrise, explore undergound fogous by candlelight, or just relax and watch the sun set from an ancient, hilltop fort.

Beyond the cliffs, the ocean stretches almost 30 miles to the exotic Isles of Scilly. Beneath these waves, according to Arthurian legend, is the lost kingdom of Lyonesse. If you can make time for a trip, head for the offshore islands and campsites on St Martins, Bryher or St Agnes and experience amazing beaches, organic food and an absorbingly slow pace of life.

The coves and beaches along Penwith's sensational, rocky coastline take some finding, but you will be rewarded with pure, white sand and clear water. Warmed by the Gulf Stream, it carries an abundance of sea life, from the harmless basking shark to dolphins and porpoises.

Nanjizal Bay, near Land's End, feels like the edge of the world. At the north end, three sandstone caves are hunched like gnarled dinosaur claws. At the south, a tall eyelet rock arch – Zawn Pyg or the 'Song of the Sea' – shields a low-tide plunge pool and an echoing sea cave. For the perfect beach, head for Pedn Vounder, a dramatic bay protected by towering granite outcrops. In summer, the sandbars and shallow lagoons that form between them warm up in the afternoon sun.

The area has always attracted artists, owing to its remote location and luminous ocean light, and the many unpretentious places to eat or sleep also have a relaxed and creative feel. Try living in a Celtic round house, or eat at one of the many artist's cafés, but for real gastro flair in a fantastic, wild setting, The Gurnard's Head is our absolute favourite, every time.

SECRET COVES

1 GREAT BAY, ST MARTIN'S, SCILLY

St Martin's is a low-key, organic-food-friendly island and Great Bay, on its NE sheltered side, is a long expanse of sand with a low-tide rock causeway to White Island. To the N of the beach find an ancient stone and turf labyrinth.

→ From St Martin's Hotel (excellent cocktail bar) walk 15 mins up road and at community hall/reading rooms turn L across moors and continue 5 mins down to bay.

20 mins, 49.9698, -6.2919

2 NANJIZAL, POLGIGGA

This is the real Land's End: wild and rugged with great caves that could hide sleeping dragons. The sands are variable, depending on the winter storms. The 'Song of the Sea' eyelet rock arch has a sandy plunge pool and astonishing sea caves, pink with coralline.

→ 1 mile S from Land's End or 2 miles N from Porthgwarra, on coast path. Or park on the Porthgwarra road (300m from B3315 Polgigga) and take footpath track on R for 10 mins, then turning R through gate after Bosistow Farmhouse (a great place to rent, see 37).

20 mins, 50.0536, -5.6926

3 PORTH CHAPEL, ST LEVAN

Path leads down pretty stream-valley path to sand cove. Local produce market at the chapel, first Monday of the month.

→ 1 mile walk W of Porthcurno on coast path or drive beyond Minack Theatre and park by church.

10 mins, 50.0391, -5.6579

4 PENTLE BAY, TRESCO

Empty, dazzling-white sands, E of priory.

5 mins, 49.9480, -6.3221

5 PEDN VOUNDER, TREEN

Superb tidal sands and lagoons between Logan Rock and Porthcurno. Semi-naturist. Tricky final descent down rocks.

→ Treen village and Logan Rock Inn (01736 810495) are off B3315 before Porthcurno. Follow track from café (see 28), past Treen Farm Camping (see 47) to coast path for 10mins, then straight over the coast path to headland and beach.

20 mins, 50.0440, -5.6423

6 PORTH NANVEN, COT VALLEY

Cove with low-tide sands at base of a pretty valley with parking. From Priests' Cove there

is an annual swimming race to the offshore Brisons islets every July.

→ From St Just school follow signs to find parking at valley bottom.

2 mins, 50.1188, -5.7004

7 PORTHERAS COVE, PENDEEN

Beautiful, lesser-known cove with excellent white sand at all tides and a pretty stream and waterfall.

→ Walk E from Pendeen lighthouse or down from Lower Chypraze Farm (turn L off B3306 2km after Pendeen, as you enter Morvah).

20 mins, 50.1643, -5.6564

8 VEOR COVE, ZENNOR

Lovely, secret low-tide beach, just W of Pendour Cove with legendary mermaids.

→ From Zennor make for coast path. Turn L down to stream and back up (100m) to find overgrown track on R. Continue from brow down to the next cove below.

25 mins, 50.1946, -5.5812

LAKE SWIMMING

9 BAKER'S PIT LAKE AND FOLLY

Open moorland spring-fed lake (once a china

clay pit) with ruins of old mining works and Roger's Tower folly. Walk on to find Chysauster ancient village.

→ Turn L off the B3311 from Penzance at Nancledra. After 1 mile turn L to Georgia and park at the road end and walk SW on track.
10 mins, 50.1667, -5.5295

10 CARN KENIDJACK

Impressive tor on on open moorland. To S is the 'dancing stones' circle and next to that a deep quarry pool, good for a dip on a hot summer day. Look out for several ancient holed stones. Bring map.

→ At the top of Trewellard Hill, near the junction where the B3318 splits into two, 800m E of transmitters, find track to tor then continue S for circle (50.1338, -5.6586) and lake to its W (50.1344, -5.6613).
25 mins, 50.1348, -5.6612

RUINS AND CAVES

11 PIPER'S HOLE, TRESCO, SCILLY

Descend into this large cavern in the cliffs and wade across the freshwater pool to find a beach and more tunnels beyond. More atmospheric by candlelight.

→ On the wild NE tip of the island, just above high-tide line, hidden at the top of an inlet. Take a look at the ruins of King Charles' Fort on your return.
30 mins, 49.9680, -6.3438

12 BOTALLACK MINE, PENDEEN

Well-known but spectacular cliff-edge engine house ruins. The mine tunnels ran miles under the sea in seach of Botallackite, a green mineral formed by the action of sea water on copper ore.

→ Walk 500m further S along the cliff to see the ruins of the arsenic mines.
5 mins, 50.1437, -5.6927

13 PORTHGWARRA TUNNELS

Two old tunnels lead down to the cove here. They were hand dug so horses and carts could load up with seaweed to fertilise the fields. Small tea-hut for refreshments.

→ Turn off the B3315 at Polgigga, just past Porthcurno, and continue to end of road.
3 mins, 50.0367, -5.6718

14 DING DONG MINE, MADRON

An atmospheric, ruined engine house, perched high on the top of wild moorland.

→ From Penzance follow the Madron road through the village, and turn off R after 1 mile at Bosiliak. If you reach Lanyon Quoit and tea-room you have gone too far. A short walk links to Nine Maidens stone circle (50.1606, -5.5937) and Mên-an-Tol (see 18) .
5 mins, 50.1542, -5.5928

ANCIENT AND SACRED

15 MERRY MAIDENS, LAMORNA

Well-known, and by the roadside, but a wonderful sight nonetheless, especially at sunset. These ten maidens were turned to stone for dancing on the Sabbath.

→ 1 mile W of the turning for Lamorna, on the B3315. Stones are in field to L.
1 min, 50.0651, -5.5887

16 CARN EUNY ANCIENT SETTLEMENT

One of the finest Bronze Age village-sites in the UK dating to 500BC. Lost among trees and more atmospheric than nearby Chysauster. Underground fogou passage and holy well in the woods at the source of Lamorna's stream.

→ Turn off A30 after B3283, signed Carn Euny. Continue 2 miles (turn L at T-junction), park at Brane and walk 600m. If you take footpath on L instead of R you will come to a

stream and the remains of St Euny chapel and holy well (50.1030, -5.6374). You can also walk here from Carn Brea (see 20).

10 mins, 50.1027, -5.6337 🚲🚶

17 ST CREDAN'S WELL, SANCREED

In a grove of holly bushes, stone steps lead down into a tiny womb-like chamber and pool. Its sacred tree is adorned with prayer flags and ribbons and there is a stone cross.

→ Follow path opposite Sancreed church.

2 mins, 50.1078, -5.6117

18 MÊN-AN-TOL, MORVAH

Famous fertility stone said to possess healing powers if you crawl through it.

→ 2 miles SE from Morvah on the Penzance moorland road, then 1 mile walk up track to L. Or approach across moor from Ding Dong mine ruins (see 14), or complete circuit via Nine Maidens stone circle (50.1606, -5.5937).

20 mins, 50.1585, -5.6047 🚲🚶

19 BOSCAWEN-UN STONE CIRCLE

More difficult to reach than the Merry Maidens, this is a wild and magical place.

→ On A30 half way from Penzance to Land's End. Pass the B3283, then 800m after the

Carn Euny & Sancreed junction (on R), find parking bay on L with wooden kissing-gate in hedge. 500m to circle.

10 mins, 50.0898, -5.6193

SUNSET HILLFORTS

20 CARN BREA, SENNEN

Breathtaking sea views from the first and last hill in England, with Bronze Age burial chambers at the summit. Keep watch for the elusive 'green flash' in the final moments of the sunset (use a filter to view).

→ Signed off the A30 on R, 3 miles before Sennen.

10 mins, 50.0946, -5.6562 📷

21 ZENNOR HILL AND QUOIT

Great pancakes of stacked stone mark this burial chamber, which looks out over the Atlantic from its high wild moorland vantage point.

→ Leave Zennor heading E and find footpath off road on R after 100m (leave car in village).

30 mins, 50.1882, -5.5475 🏔📷

WILDLIFE WONDERS

22 MARAZION MARSH STARLINGS

Watch thousands of starlings roost over the inland marsh in winter.

→ Find RSPB car park on the R, ½ mile W from Marazion (St Michael's Mount).

5 mins, 50.128, -5.484 📷

23 DOLPHIN SPOTTING & SEA KAYAKING

Penwith's waters, warmed by the Gulf Stream, are rich in basking shark, dolphin, porpoise, seals and sunfish. Try launching your kayak from the slipway at Porthgwarra, or contact Elemental Tours (who also run wild seashore foraging courses).

→ Elemental Tours 07971 540280

50.0744, -5.6225 🛶

LOCAL FOOD

24 THE GURNARDS HEAD, TREEN

Excellent upmarket pub in a 17th-century coaching inn at the wild and remote Gurnard's Head. Famous for its local, sustainably sourced food and comfortable, rustic-chic rooms. You might also like to try its sister property, the Old Coastguard Hotel in Mousehole (01736 731222).

→ Treen, Zennor, TR26 3DE, 01736 796928
50.1826, -5.5932

25 FAT HEN WILD FOOD

Professional ecologist and cook, Caroline Davey, teaches foraging and cookery skills, followed by a foragers' feast in her barns.

→ Gwenmenhir, Boscawen-noon Farm, St Buryan, TR19 6EH, 01736 810156,
50.0921, -5.6107

26 NEWLYN CHEESE & CHARCUTERIE

Home to all things unpasteurised, creamy and delicious. Deservedly popular. Good greengrocer opposite.

→ 1 New Road, TR18 5PZ, 01736 368714
50.1075, -5.5498

27 TINNERS ARMS, ZENNOR

Small, 700-year-old granite-built pub that is so cosy on a cold, mizzly day. Visit St Senara's church opposite to see the ancient chair with its intriguing mermaid carving.

→ St Ives, TR26 3BY, 01736 796927
50.1918, -5.5676

28 TREEN CAFÉ, PORTHCURNO

Selling locally made bread and delicious breakfasts, this small café is a real gem, especially if you are staying at the campsite.

→ Treen, St Buryan, TR19 6LF, 01736 811285
50.0493, -5.6419

29 APPLE TREE CAFÉ, LANDS END

Lovely rural community café and art gallery serving thoughtful homemade food. Good for refuelling after a walk down to Nanjizal.

→ Trevescan, TR19 7AQ, 01736 872753
50.0654, -5.6959

30 JELBERTS ICES, NEWLYN

Jelberts, once a family-run dairy business, is a local legend. It sells only a single flavour (with the option of clotted cream on top).

→ New Road, Newlyn, TR18 5PZ
50.10752, -5.54976

31 COURTHOUSE CAFÉ, GEEVOR MINE

You don't need to pay the entrance fee to visit the café and enjoy magnificent views and locally sourced lunches.

→ Pendeen, TR19 7EW, 01736 788662
50.1517, -5.6764

32 ST IVES FARMER'S MARKET

Thursdays, 9.30am - 2.00pm.

→ The Guildhall, Street an Pol, TR26 2DS
50.2116, -5.4798

33 MOOMAID OF ZENNOR

Luxury Cornish ice cream made on the farm at Tremedda. Try the sea salt and caramel flavour. Also available at the Wayfarers Museum in Zennor (next to the water wheel).

→ Zennor, St. Ives, TR26 3DA
50.1906, -5.5683

34 PEPPERCORN KITCHEN, MARAZION

Middle-Eastern cooking and the scent of wood smoke from their woodburner in winter. Eat in or take your tasty morsels to enjoy on Perran Sands.

→ Lynfield Yard, Perranuthnoe, Marazion, TR20 9NE, 01736 719584, 07907 691639
50.1138, -5.4432

35 GALLERY LATITUDE 50, CRIPPLESEASE

If you're after a herbal infusion and home-made cake, or a morning coffee, this art gallery and simple café will inspire with its wonderful views. For lunch or a pint of ale, pop over the road to the Engine Inn.

→ Nancledra, TR20 8NF, 01736 741052
50.1772, -5.5024

CAMP AND STAY

36 BRYHER CAMPSITE, SCILLY

Nestled in a sheltered valley on the breathtaking island of Bryher. Open April to September.

→ Jenford, Bryher, TR23 0PR, 01720 422886
49.9570, -6.3546

37 BOSISTOW FARMHOUSE, NANJIZAL

In a remote coastal location above isolated Nanjizal beach. Self-catering and with good winter discounts.

→ St Aubyn Estates, Nanjizal, St Levan, TR19 6JJ, 01736 710507
50.0520, -5.6813

38 COVE COTTAGE, GURNARD'S HEAD

Down a steep track, almost on the water's edge, with exquisite interior and two double rooms. Lie in bed and look out over the bay with views to the dragon profile of Gurnard's Head. Lovely, secret low tide cove and cave down to the left. Minimum two-night stay.

→ Zennor, St. Ives, TR26 3DE, 01736 798317
50.1889, -5.5932

9 BOSWARTHEN FARM, MADRON

Safari tents on the farm with sea views from every one. Sauna and hot tub in the meadow. Campfire lasagne served by Maddy. Farm shop with local produce.

→ Boswarthen Farm, Madron, TR20 8PA, 7731 776767
50.1423,-5.5815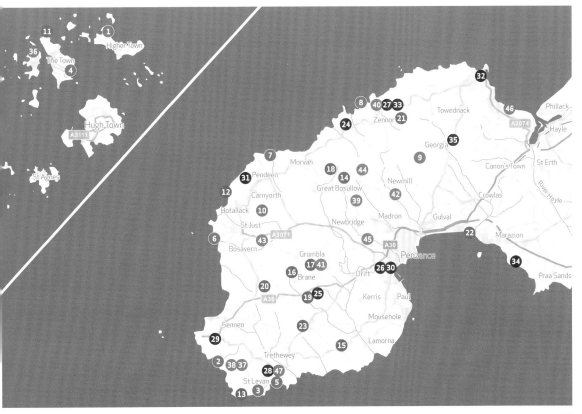

40 OLD CHAPEL BACKPACKERS, ZENNOR

Atmospheric backpacking hostel in an old chapel, with excellent café (10am – 5pm).

→ Zennor, St Ives, TR26 3BY, 01736 798307
50.1923,-5.5679

41 HOUSE OF STRAW & HOBBIT HOUSE

Two very organic structures: a straw-bale house and a round wood cabin with stained-glass. Sheepskins, woodburners, lanterns, composting loos and an edible garden.

→ Plan-it Earth, Chy ena, Sancreed, TR20 8QS, 01275 395447
50.1074,-5.6092

42 NOONGALLAS CAMPING

Good views of Mounts Bay. Campsite is on high ground, remote from main roads and town lights. Adjoins the little ancient Trevaylor woodland and stream. Campfires.

→ Gulval, Penzance, TR20 8UT, 01736366698
50.1466,-5.5485

43 BALLESWIDDEN CABIN, ST JUST

Simple, stylish writer's cabin, perfect for a cosy weekend away. Chesterfield sofa, clawfoot bath, walls of books and an open fire on the deck.

→ The Count House, Balleswidden, TR19 7RY
50.1189,-5.6602

44 BODRIFTY ROUND HOUSE

An Iron Age roundhouse reconstruction. Beautifully executed and styled. Egyptian cotton sheets and duck-down duvet. Handmade four-poster bed with flowers woven into the willow headboard.

→ Canopyandstars.co.uk, 01275 395447
50.1589,-5.5776

45 ORCHARD FLOWER FARM

Beautiful decked cabin with acres of wild gardens to explore; like living in a treehouse.

→ Madron, Penzance, (Boutique Retreats 01872 553491).
50.1222, -5.5707

46 THE CABIN, ST IVES

Accessible only by foot in secluded location and overlooking Porth Kidney Sands. Whitewashed floorboards and nautical touches. Sleeps 2.

→ Carbis Bay, St Ives, (Boutique Retreats 01872 553491)
50.1949, -5.4541

47 TREEN FARM CAMPSITE

Fantastic cliff-top family campsite with great views. Lovely walk down to Pedn-Vounder, Penwith's most spectacular sands. Local café, and pub in delightfully small hamlet. No booking so turn up from 8.30am.

→ Treen Farm, Saint Levan, TR19 6LF
50.0501,-5.6412

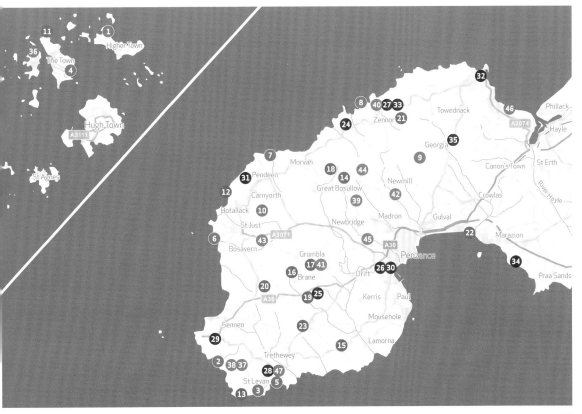

LIZARD & HELFORD

Our perfect weekend

- → **Swim** at remote Scott's Quay then stop for lunch at Potager kitchen-garden café.
- → **Adventure** into the Devil's Frying Pan, one of the UK's most dramatic sea caves.
- → **Snorkel** in the clear waters of Lankidden Cove and look for basking sharks.
- → **Watch** the sunset at Church Cove then enjoy a sundowner at the Barefoot Kitchen café.
- → **Descend** into the underground passages of the ancient Halliggye chamber by candlelight.
- → **Camp** by the estuary at Gear Farm and sample the gourmet wood-fired pizzas.
- → **Canoe** the Helford Passage at sunrise and explore mysterious Frenchman's Creek.
- → **Swing** from ropes and play in the maze at Glendurgan gardens.
- → **Explore** the ruined mines at Trewavas whose tunnels reached out under the sea.
- → **Skinny dip** at Porthcew Cove as the sun sets over the western ocean.

Tiny white coves with slopes covered in wild flowers nestle between rock pinnacles on the Lizard's breathtaking, rugged coastline. Yet to the north east, the landscape is gentler and there are wooded creeks and magical gardens to explore on the peaceful Helford estuary.

Perhaps the most spectacular destination is Kynance Cove, immortalised by the Romantic poets and painters, with clear, azure water for snorkelling and and extraordinary, serpentine-rock towers for dare-devil jumps.

To the west, dramatic Mullion Cove, and the giant open sea cave at Cadgwith offer more adventure swimming, but for family-friendly beaches head further up the coastline. Relax at sandy Church Cove or look for the ruts worn by smuggler's carts as they hauled up booty at Prussia Cove. At picturesque Rinsey, the engine houses of Wheal Trewavas cling to the cliffs, testament to the astonishing feats of engineering needed to extract copper from lodes stretching beneath the sea bed and reached by long tunnels.

On the east coast, around remote Porthoustock, more recent mining ventures are in various stages of abandonment with old quays, jetties and structures to explore. On the headland above, Roskilly's ice-cream farm is worth a visit and you stay overnight in a stylish Lovelane's retro caravan.

Just a little way south, a pleasant walk down a gentle, wooded valley brings you to the remote coves of Lankidden and Downas, sheltering beneath moorland along a stretch of virtually untouched Cornish coastline. These are perfect places to catch crabs and look out for basking sharks and dolphins.

Continuing up the coast to the beautiful Helford estuary, walk through ancient oak woods to find secluded Scott's Quay, or go back even further in time and visit the Iron Age underground chamber, Halliggye Fogou, on the Trelowarren Estate. Everywhere on this estuary there are mysterious tidal inlets: for a truly magical experience, glide in an open canoe on waters overhung by trees and explore Frenchman's Creek. There are several hidden coves with silver-shale beaches, and Bosahan is our favourite.

Delicious local food is always a highlight of this area. Gear Farm, at the head of the Helford, is a wonderful place to camp and eat kitchen-garden veg, home-cured meat and superb wood-fired pizzas. Potager café, Barefoot Kitchen and New Yard restaurant are also highly recommended.

SECRET COVES

1 DEVIL'S FRYING PAN, CADGWITH
Pretty fishing village with swimming cove. Peer down into the dramatic Devil's Frying Pan blowhole, or the seriously adventurous can swim around into it (calm seas only).

→ 300m W on coast path from Cadgwith.
10 mins, 49.9849, -5.1804 🏊📺

2 DOWNAS COVE, KENNACK
Tiny low-tide, sand cove on the most deserted stretch of the Lizard. Great for snorkelling. Keep a look out for basking sharks from the hillfort on Carrick Lûz headland above Lankidden Cove.

→ S from Ponsongath (near Coverack) via wooded valley (1 mile) or E from Kennack Sands via coast path (2 miles, passing Lankidden Cove on way 50.0072, 5.1320).
30 mins, 50.0084, -5.1221 🏊📺🐾🚶🏔️🐚

3 KYNANCE COVE & ASPARAGUS ISLAND
Popular, but spectacular NT cove with shiny, serpentine rocks. Deep plunge pools on low tide N beach with pinnacles from which dare devils leap. Good NT tea room and you can also rent the beach cottage (sleeps 3) and stay overnight (01326 290436).

→ Signed R off A3083, 10 miles S of Helston, dir Lizard. NT parking.
15 mins, 49.9755, -5.2309 🏊🚶📺🐾🍴☕

4 MULLION COVE
Dramatic cove and small harbour. Locals jump from the quay and snorkel among the offshore rocks. Wet-suited adventurers can swim 500m S to find hidden cove of Laden Ceyn, opposite Mullion Island. Or walk 1 mile N to sandy, beautiful Polurrian Cove.

→ 3 miles before Kynance, turn L (B3296), through Mullion to Mullion Cove (4 miles).
5 mins, 50.0155, -5.2574 🏊🚶📺📺

5 CHURCH COVE
Charming, sandy cove with shoreside church and parking. Barefoot Kitchen café nearby. Poldhu Cove is a short walk to S (10 mins).

→ Follow tiny lanes from Gunwalloe Fishing Cove (off A3083, S of Helston Down).
2 mins, 50.03788, -5.26700 🏊🍴☕

6 PRUSSIA COVE
Famous smugglers' cove, with grooves worn by the wheels of brandy-laden carts. Many houses and cottages are for rent from the Porth-en-Alls family estate (01736 762014).

Coast path leads W 600m to Piskies Cove with caves, or E 500m to Kenneggy sands.

→ From A394 turn R at Falmouth Packet Inn (Rosudgeon), 5 miles E of Penzance.
15 mins, 50.1010, -5.4176 🏊🐾📺☕

7 PORTHCEW BEACH, RINSEY
Beautiful west facing cove, set beneath ruined mine chimneys.

→ Rinsey is signed 1 miles S of A394 at Ashton. Beach is below cliff-edge car park. See also Wheal Trewavas (see 21).
5 mins, 50.0935, -5.3668 🏊📺☕

8 LEGGAN COVE, ST KEVERNE
Shingle and coarse dark sand falls away into crystal-clear waters. Hidden between two disused quarries, 1 mile E of St Keverne.

→ From St Keverne follow signs (dir Porthoustock) to small hamlet of Rosenithon. Turn R at post-box in wall and continue on footpath through fields down to Godrevy Cove (10 mins). Leggan Cove is just to N.
15 mins, 50.0501, -5.0641 🏊🏔️🐚

RIVER AND CREEKS

9 HELFORD RIVER BOATS

Self-drive motor boats, rowing boats, kayaks, sailing dinghies, all available to hire by the day or hour. Enjoy the quiet inlets and coves, fringed by woods with ancient oaks.

→ Kiosk at Helford Passage, on the beach in front of the Ferryboat Inn. For guided kayak tours, try Aberfal Outdoor Pursuits (07968 770756).

2 mins, 50.1006, -5.1282 🏊

10 SCOTT'S QUAY, NANCENOY

Remote stone quay on secluded tributary of the Helford. Great place for a swim at high tide. Rope swing.

→ Bear E down on lane from Trengilly Wartha pub, Nancenoy, (01326 340332) and find footpath on R after 300m. Walk 1 mile across fields, past mature beech woods down to quay. Potager café is nearby (see 24).

20 mins, 50.1027, -5.1644 🏊🍴🚻🚶

11 BOSAHAN COVE, HELFORD

Secluded shingle cove with boathouse, backed by woods. Easy destination on a kayak. The less energetic might prefer to stop for a harbourside beer at The Old

Shipwright Arms (TR12 6JX, 01326 231235).

→ 1 mile E of Helford village on coast path.
15 mins, 50.0950, -5.1143 🏊🚶🚻🍴

12 FRENCHMAN'S CREEK, HELFORD

Remote, deeply wooded creek made famous by Daphne du Maurier. Too muddy for swimming but perfect for canoeing.

→ 1 mile W of Helford village on shore path.
20 mins, 50.0851, -5.1467 🏊🚣

13 TREVASSACK QUARRY POOL

Spring-fed quarry pool on moor, ideal for a secluded freshwater swim on a hot day.

→ 1½ miles SE of Garras on B3293, turn R (opposite no entry gatehouse, and before St Martin's turning on L). Find rickety gate on L after ½ mile, opposite Trevassack.
1 mins, 50.0561, -5.1986 🏊

14 LOE POOL AND BAR

Cornwall's largest natural lake with a wooded path that leads down to the beach. Those with bikes can cycle all the way around.

→ Park at Penrose House off B3304, outside Porthleven.
30 mins, 50.0859, -5.3005 🏖🚴

5

5 ST ANTHONY-IN-MENEAGE

Sleepy, lost-in-time hamlet with beach and picturesque church set close to the creek. Good cockling beach.
→ Signed 3 miles E of Helford.
5 mins, 50.0888, -5.1000 🚻🏖

WOODS AND GARDENS

6 TREMAYNE WOODS, MAWGAN

Beautiful ancient oak forest leads down to meadow by estuary with beach, rope swings, old quay and boathouse.
→ From Mawgan heading to St Martin, turn on to steep narrow lane by Gear Farm. At bottom by stream find path L down through the woods.
10 mins, 50.0883, -5.1739 🏖⛰

7 GLENDURGAN GARDEN AND BEACH

With giant gunnera, an ancient tulip tree, spring magnolias and drifts of bluebells, these sub-tropical gardens are a little bit of heaven on earth. Lots of activities, including a maze and a brilliant swing; or skim stones and build sandcastles on Durgan beach.
→ Signed S of Mawnan Smith. NT property.
5 mins, 50.1061, -5.1169 🏖🌿🍴

NATURAL WONDERS

18 GODOLPHIN HILL: STARGAZING

This conical hill offers 360-degree views with no artificial lights close by. Perfect for stargazing on a clear night.
→ 1 mile W of Godolphin Cross, on R.
10 mins, 50.1326, -5.3705 📷

19 THE MANACLES: DIVING, SNORKELLING

These offshore reefs are among the best places in the UK to see marine wildlife. You might even swim with a basking shark, and there are wrecks, too.
→ Visit the Dive Centre at Porthkerris (TR12 6QJ, 01326 280620), 2 miles NE of St Keverne
10 mins, 50.0674, -5.0708 🐕🚗

20 COCKLE TRIGGING, HELFORD

On Good Friday, it's traditional for families to harvest cockles on the mudflats at low tide. Bring your buckets and wellies and head for St Anthony Beach, Tremayne Quay, Bar Beach or Gillan Creek. Only collect cockles bigger than a 20 pence piece.
50.0870, -5.1033 🏖🌿

4

20

LOST RUINS

21 WHEAL TREWAVAS, RINSEY

Epic, cliff-edge engine houses with tunnels that once stretched far out under the sea.

→ Rinsey is signed 1 mile S of A394 at Ashton. Then continue along coast path S for 15 mins. 15 mins, 50.0906, -5.3574 🖼

22 HALLIGGYE FOGOU, MAWGAN

Murky and mysterious subterranean chamber beneath an Iron Age fort, best explored by candlelight.

→ Turn off B3293 at Garras (E, direction Mawgan). Bear R after 200m into the Trelowarren Estate and find layby on R after less than a mile. Closed October–March due to hibernating bats.

5 mins, 50.0715,-5.1867 ✝

23 PORTHOUSTOCK, ST KEVERNE

Huge loading ramps and quays, relics from this heavily mined area, dominate the beach. Also an abandoned harbour and jetty.

→ 1 mile S at Polcries (50.0412, -5.0668). For refreshments, stop off at nearby Roskilly's farm (see 30).

50.0560, -5.0641 🍴

LOCAL FOOD PRODUCE

24 POTAGER CAFÉ & GARDEN

Relax in this working, organic garden with artist's studios. Enjoy lunches made from fresh produce, or tea and cake in a renovated glasshouse. Books, newspapers, hammocks to laze in, boules and badminton.

→ High Cross, Constantine, TR11 5RF, 01326 341258, 10am-5pm 50.1182, -5.1541

25 HALZEPHRON INN, GUNWALLOE

500-year-old inn with local ciders, ales and good food overlooking the stunning beach.

→ Helston, TR12 7QB, 01326 240406 50.0550, -5.2746 🏖🍺🍴

26 BAREFOOT KITCHEN, GUNWALLOE

Perfect place to watch the sun go down over Mount's Bay whilst sipping a Barefoot cocktail. Two safari tents offer luxurious facilities for overnight stays. 1 mile S of Gunwalloe on the way to Church Cove

→ Halzephron House, Gunwalloe, TR12 7QD 07768 094686 50.0527, -5.2731 🏕🌅

27 DOWN BY THE RIVER CAFÉ, HELFORD

Wonderful cream teas by the Helford River, near the car park.

→ Treath Helford, TR12 6LB, 01326 231893 50.0940, -5.1300

28 HELSTON FARMER'S MARKET

Great place for picnic supplies, and Vicky's Bread; first Saturday of month 9.30–1.30pm

→ Helston Community College, Church Hill, Helston, TR13 8NR. 01326 231146 50.1066, -5.2737

29 POLPEOR CAFÉ, LIZARD POINT

Looking deceptively like a greasy spoon, this café serves delicious, local, home-made fish pie, crab sandwiches and cream teas – all with the most amazing cliff-top views.

→ Lizard Point, TR12 7NU, 01326 290939 49.9588, -5.2064

30 ROSKILLYS ICE-CREAM PARLOUR

Visit the farm and watch the dairy cows, then taste the freshest, organic ice cream. Sit inside by a roaring fire in winter or out in the old farmyard in summer.

→ Tregellast Barton, St. Keverne, TR12 6NX, 01326 280479 50.0457, -5.0824

31 NEW INN, MANACCAN

Unspoilt, authentic Cornish pub in a pretty village near the Helford.

→ Manaccan, TR12 6HA, 01326 231323 50.0820, -5.1270 🍺

32 ANN'S PASTIES, LIZARD

Ann's mum wrote a book on the subject and her pasties are legendary. If you ask nicely, she might show you how to make them.

→ Beacon Terrace, Lizard, TR12 7PB 01326 290889, 9am–3pm 49.9691, -5.2014

33 NEW YARD RESTAURANT

Eat excellent, locally sourced food in this beautifully converted carriage house on the historic Trelowarren Estate.

→ Trelowarren, Mawgan, Helston, TR12 6AF, 01326 221595 50.0713, -5.1865

34 FERRY BOAT INN, HELFORD PASSAGE

300-year-old inn on N side of river. Sunny terrace in summer, a roaring fire in winter. Farm-to-plate food philosophy, with local oysters and shellfish when in season and

lovely walks up and down the estuary.
→ Durgan, TR11 5LB, 01326 250625
50.1003, -5.1287 ▢

CAMP AND GLAMP

35 HIGHER PENROSE FARM, PORTHLEVEN

Simple campsite in large field, open July and August. Beautifully sited with views W over Mounts Bay and Loe Pool. Camp fires and dogs welcome. Good value.
→ Off B3304 coming down into Porthleven, TR13 0RB, 01326 572714
50.0818, -5.2998 ▲🔥

36 TREMERLIN, HELFORD

Sensational views of the Helford in this 1920s riverside retreat with its own mooring. Eclectically decorated with tongue and groove boarding, old pine doors, fabulous Victorian loos (in working order!). Bookish and beautiful.
→ Sawdays.co.uk, 01275 395430
50.0950, -5.1464

37 NAMPARRA CAMPSITE, KUGGAR

Family-run site with a 6-acre meadow and stunning sea views at the end of a track.
→ Kuggar, TR12 7LY, 01326 290040
50.0054, -5.1777 ▲🔥

38 GEAR FARM, MAWGAN

Lovely campsite and farm shop stocked with home-grown organic vegetables, salads and herbs. Small café and bakery, with wood-fired pizza oven, local apple juice and shellfish supplied by George and Roly Kirby's boats moored on the nearby Helford River.
→ From Mawgan, E towards St Martin, TR12 6DE, 01326 221150
50.0806, -5.1852 ▲🍴

39 HENRY'S CAMPSITE, LIZARD

Deservedly popular village-edge campsite with ocean views. If full, try Penmarth Farm, in nearby Coverack.
→ TR12 7NX, 01326 290596
49.9690, -5.2055 ▲🔥

40 LOVELANE CARAVANS, ST KEVERNE

A quirky and select collection of vintage caravans and buses, each perfectly fitted out in 1950s style. Near Roskilly's farm (see 30).
→ Tregellast Barton, St. Keverne, TR12 6NX, 01326 340406
50.0398, -5.0819

41 DRIFTSHANE'S PLACE, PORT NAVAS

Quiet camping with sea views near the Helford River. Farm-cooked suppers on request and tennis on the grass court.
→ Tel 01326 340442, 07824 814146
50.1167, -5.1397 ▲🍴

42 FRENCHMAN'S CREEK, HELFORD

Remote and atmospheric waterside cottage on the creek celebrated in Daphne Du Maurier's romantic novel. No car access.
→ Landmarktrust.org.uk, 01628 825925
50.0851, -5.1467 ▲

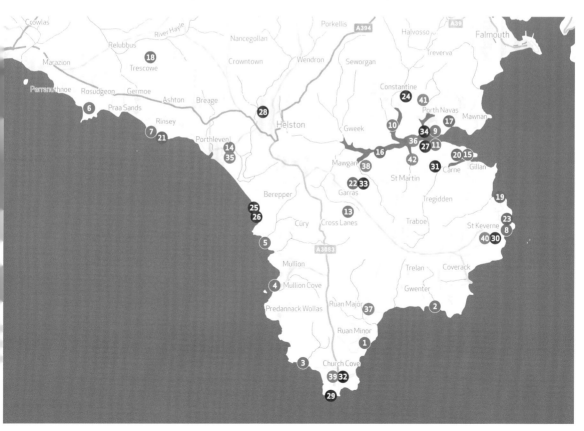

ROSELAND & VERYAN

Our perfect weekend

→ **Discover** secret coves on beautiful St Anthony's Head.

→ **Canoe** the upper creeks of the Fal-Ruan nature reserve. Go with the tide and stop for lunch at Ruan Lanihorne.

→ **Explore** old gunpowder mills deep in the forest at Kennall Vale, and swim in the spring-fed quarry pool.

→ **Climb** huge trees at Trelissick gardens.

→ **Build** dens in Devichoys woods.

→ **Wild camp** on Vault beach after watching the sunset from Dodman Point hillfort.

→ **Swim** beneath verdant woodland at St Just in Roseland and visit the waterside church.

→ **Watch** crab being landed at pretty Portloe harbour then eat them at the Lugger Inn.

→ **Descend** by rope ladder to Portholland's secret beach, then refuel with tea at Journey's End, the pop-up seashore café.

Carrick Roads, the vast tidal estuary of the river Fal, is an oasis of tranquillity. Fringed by mature woodland and sub-tropical gardens, the deep river narrows into secluded creeks that are perfect for exploring by canoe. On the wilder coast, there are tucked-away coves for swimming and no shortage of places to eat delicous, fresh food.

Cross the river from the west on the King Harry ferry (always a treat) to visit Trelissick, a wonderful garden with magnificent maritime views. The staff will happily point you to the best tree for climbing. Lose yourself among giant tree ferns in Penjerrick's jungly depths, or gaze out over carpets of spring bluebells in the parkland at Enys. At Kennall Vale, the wooded slopes are studded with the ruins of gunpowder mills that blew up in successive explosions on a devastating night in 1838. There is a silent quarry lake for swimming, and at night the sky is filled with pipistrelle bats.

To the east is Roseland, a long, thin pensinsula with secret creeks and waterside churches. At St Just-in-Roseland, a path winds down through ivy-clad tombs and luxuriant rhododendrons to the tidal creek with its charming Edwardian boathouse. The coastline around Portscatho is indented with pretty coves for swimming and wholesome local food abounds. Eat al fresco at the Hidden Hut beach shack, buy provisions for a picnic from the local produce market at Veryan, or take a canoe along the remote Ruan river creeks and lunch at the Kings Head in tiny Ruan Lanihorne.

In the countryside beyond sandy Veryan Bay, there is a network of lanes so deep, narrow and twisted, they seem to swallow cars and cycles whole. Caerhays Castle, spectacularly sited overlooking the beach at Porthluney, holds one of the finest collections of rare and exotic trees and shrubs in Britain and is well worth a visit, especially in spring. Stop off at a smaller garden café for cream tea then catch glimpses of tiny coves through hedgerows as you head on to dramatic Nare Head . Beyond Hemmick is a favourite family cove, and there's a great secret beach at Portholland, accessible via a hidden path and ropes. Once round this headland you arrive at the long naturist expanse of Vault Beach, a truly wild strand that seems to invite you to collect driftwood for a fire and camp out under the stars.

SECRET COVES

1 MOLUNAN COVES, ST ANTHONY
Three tiny sheltered coves with views out W across beautiful Carrick Roads estuary.

→ From St Anthony's Head car park bear R (N) and descend 500m to the coast path.
10 mins, 50.1450, -5.0150

2 PORTHBEOR BEACH, ST ANTHONY
Long, sandy beach with steep descent.

→ Heading N from St Anthony's Head, find footpath on R just before turn-off to Bohortha. There are good (but steep) steps down to beach from coast path. Parking tricky.
5 mins, 50.1494, -4.9919

3 ST JUST IN ROSELAND
Shingle, estuary beach by waterside church. Set in lush tropical gardens with plants brought back from Australia in 1897.

→ Heading N from St Mawes turn L off A3078 after 2 miles to find church. Walk down through gardens to water, turn L through gate and continue 200m through woods to find shingle beach on R.
5 mins, 50.1819, -5.0165

4 VAULT BEACH, GORRAN HAVEN
Wonderful long, unspoilt beach and good for wild camping. If you have a campervan, the narrow lane on the headland above is a good place to park and watch the sunset.

→ Access to beach is on NE side. Kayak or walk around from Gorran Haven, 20 mins. On the way, look out for the beautiful rock pools and lagoons beneath Cadythew Rocks.
20 mins, 50.2347, -4.7869

5 CELLAR COVE, PORTHOLLAND
A truly secret surfers' beach with a hidden path and ropes.

→ Follow coast path W from West Portholland, up hill (500m) then L downhill at junction. After 100m path bears R. Find hidden path on L which cuts back and down, becoming clear with ropes after 50m. Refuel at the Journey's End kitchen café in the village.
15 mins, 50.2316, -4.8718

6 HEMMICK BEACH, DODMAN POINT
Lovely W-facing sandy cove. Parking is back up the hill, so it's never too crowded.

→ Between Boswinger and Penare.
5 mins, 50.2299, -4.8144

7 TRELOAN BEACH
Lovely tucked-away cove, 10 mins south of Portscatho on the coast path.
10 mins, 50.1750, -4.9723

8 TOWAN BEACH ROCK POOLS
The whole stretch is scattered with tiny rock pools that are home to an amazing array of fish, anemones and seaweed.

→ NT car park/toilets at Porth Farm, a mile N of Porthbeor.
10 mins, 50.1579, -4.9823

CREEKS AND POOLS

9 BOSUN'S LOCKER KAYAK HIRE
Explore the deepest natural harbour in Europe in a kayak.

→ Upton Slip (next to Church Street Car Park), Falmouth, TR11 3DQ, 01326 312212. Reasonable daily rates for a double kayak, with room for two adults plus a bit extra. If you have a toddler or a terrier, bring them along.
30 mins, 50.1542, -5.0677

10 SEA KAYAK CAMPING SAFARI
Wild camp on a secret beach, forage for shellfish and seaweed, or fish from your

kayak. You might see dolphins, seals and basking sharks along the way.

→ Falmouth, two-day excursion.
50.1534, -5.0951 ⛺🚶

11 CARNSEW POOL, MABE BURNTHOUSE
Spring-fed lake in old quarry workings.

→ Heading W out of Mabe Burnthouse (direction Longdowns) follow a bridleway R off Antron Road (next to Antron Manor). Also see Trenoweth Common rock pools, Carnebo Barn camping (see 40).
5 mins, 50.1659, -5.1376 ⛺

LOST RUINS

12 KENNALL VALE GUNPOWDER MILLS
Steep-sided, picturesque woodland valley with streams and leats. There is a water-filled quarry and ruined mills, where gunpowder was manufactured. The gunpowder supplied many of the mines of west Cornwall until 1910, when it was largely replaced by high explosives.

→ Head north from Falmouth towards Ponsanooth (A393), turn L at Post Office up Park Road to find reserve on R.
5 mins, 50.1930, -5.1546 ⛺👣🚶

13 MINERAL TRAMWAY, POLDICE VALLEY
Cycle along one of Cornwall's old mining tramways, and experience the wild beauty of one of the best-preserved, post-industrial landscapes in Britain. Pass the derelict copper mines of the Poldice Valley and see the arsenic works along the river Carnon, south of Bissoe.

→ 2 miles N of Devoran (A39). The Bike Chain café at Bissoe hires bikes. Old Conns Works, Bissoe, TR4 8QZ, 01872 870341
30 mins, 50.2313, -5.1283 👣🚶🚲

FOREST AND MEADOW

14 DEVICHOYS WOODS & DENS
Ancient, coppiced, sessile oaks in weird and wonderful shapes in this small wood, popular with den builders. Find a small lake near the entrance and look out for the stinkhorn fungus in season.

→ Turn R off the A39, 3 miles N of Penryn, signed Mylor, Flushing and Restronguet, to find entrance immediately on L.
10 mins, 50.2000, -5.1206 🌳

15 TRELISSICK GARDENS TREE CLIMBING
Great trees to climb, including the giant spreading *Cryptomeria* on the main lawn.

There are ancient oaks in the parkland, a small, secluded beach and some of the best maritime views in Cornwall.

→ Right next to the King Harry ferry. Make the short crossing and walk up to the Smuggler's, (see 28) for tea.
10 mins, 50.2173, -5.0324,

16 CAERHAYS CASTLE GARDENS
Wonderful parkland setting by Porthluney Cove. One of the best collections in the UK of tree-sized magnolias, camellias and rhododendrons. Spectacular spring colour.

→ Signed Polmassick Vineyard/Caerhays from B3287.
10 mins, 50.2378, -4.8431 🌳

17 ENYS AND PARC LYE BLUEBELLS
Visit in spring to enjoy magical carpets of bluebells set in parkland under ancient trees, particularly in the Parc Lye meadow area.

→ Signed from Mylor Bridge near Penryn (entrance fee). St Gluvias, Penryn, TR10 9LB
15 mins, 50.1852, -5.0922 🌳

18 PENJERRICK GARDENS
Walk under giant tree ferns in this enchanting and little-known garden with

its special, secret atmosphere. One of the oldest woodland gardens in the UK. Open Sunday, Wednesday, Friday, 1.30–4.30pm. Admission fee in honesty box by gate.

→ From Penryn/A39 follow signs for Trebah / Glendurgan gardens. After 3 miles see signs for Penjerrick. Park on the grass verge along the drive.

10 mins, 50.1349, -5.1095 ⊞

SUNSET HILLFORTS

19 DODMAN POINT

Headland Iron Age fort with huge stone cross and ruined watchtower, reached by path from Penare. Visit in spring and walk between hedgerows banked with bluebells and primroses. The name Dodman or 'dead man' is attributed to the numbers of shipwrecks, and the existence of gallows here.

→ Up Lamledra hill, S of Gorran Haven
20 mins, 50.2208, -4.8022 ⊞

20 CARNE BEACON, NARE HEAD

Ancient Bronze Age burial mound, one of the largest in Britain. Wind-blown gorse and a gnarled old lilac tree. Magnificent views over Gerrans Bay at sunset.

→ 300m N of Carne on lanes find large mound

in field with footpath sign. Also, continue a mile E to Penare Farm and head out to Nare Head to watch the sunset over the ocean. Or, 15 mins down to the R is a ruined fisherman's cottage overlooking a remote pebble cove with small rock arch (Tregagle's Hole, 50.2009, -4.9243).

20 mins, 50.2109, -4.9265 ⊞⊞⊞

LOCAL FOOD AND DRINK

21 HERON INN, MALPAS TRURO

Family-run pub with good food on the River Fal just S of Truro. Walk up along the river to pretty waterside St Clement (the church does cream teas in summer), then return inland via Park Farm.

→ Trenhaile Terrace, Malpas, Truro, TR1 1SL, 01872 272773

50.2449, -5.0248 ⊞⊞

22 BAKER TOM, FALMOUTH

Beautifully fresh artisan bread for your picnic. Also in Lemon Street market, Truro.

→ 10b Church Street, Falmouth, TR11 3DR, 01872 277496

50.1542, -5.0684

23 CURGURRELL FARM, PORTSCATHO

Crabs, lobsters and fresh fish, all caught by local fishermen, plus home-grown garden produce and free-range eggs. Also self-catering accommodation.

→ Portscatho, Truro, Cornwall, TR2 5EN, 01872 580243

50.1965, -4.9680

24 HALWYN'S TEA GARDEN

On the NW bank with views over the Fal, this quaint tea garden serves ginger beer, cream teas and locally sourced lunches.

→ Halwyn, Old Kea, Truro, TR3 6AW, 01872 272152. From A39 pass through Port Kea and continue on past Higher Trelease to Halwyn.

50.2287, -5.0278 ⊞

25 ST MAWES QUAY FISHMONGER

Family-run business with a trailer stall selling super-fresh fish direct from their trawler, the *Celestial Dawn*.

→ St Mawes Quay, 07792 220821. Tuesday, Thursday and Friday, 9.30am-12.30pm.
50.1584, -5.0138

26 ROSLEAND INN, PHILLEIGH

Try the award-winning, home-brewed Gull-able in the garden or beside the log fire. Good local food. From Philleigh, a path runs down through the fields to the remote wooded shores of the Fal (about 20mins).

→ Off the A3078 on the E side of the estuary, signed Philleigh-in-Roseland, TR2 5NB, 01872 580254
50.2165, -4.9848

27 THE KINGS HEAD, RUAN LANIHORNE

Cosy winter fires and a flower-filled garden in summer. Traditional pub on the quiet upper reaches of the Fal-Ruan tributary at Ruan quay. Down the hill is the remote Sett bridge with a pretty woodland riverside walk.

→ Ruan Lanihorne, TR2 5NX, 01872 501263. Off the A3078 on the E side of the estuary.
50.2406, -4.9531

28 SMUGGLERS, TOLVERNE COTTAGE

Classic cream teas on the riverside by this historic thatched cottage. Jam from local plums, Rodda's clotted cream and a pot of fragrant Tregothnan tea – the only tea grown in the UK. Kayak hire (07970 926409).

→ Turn hard L coming up the hill from the King Harry Ferry (E side) by car, or walk from Trelissick (free ferry, then 10 mins).
50.2225, -5.0220

29 THE HIDDEN HUT, PORTSCATHO

A World War II shack now converted into a café, perched above Porthcurnick Beach. Open daily 10am–5pm with special evening feasts that are not to be missed.

→ Just above Porthcurnick Beach, 15 min walk N from Portscatho. Rosevine, Portscatho, TR2 5EW
50.1870, -4.972

30 PANDORA INN, MYLOR BRIDGE

Situated right by the waterside, with pontoon seating, beamed and flagstoned rooms and good food all day.

→ Restronguet Hill, Nr Falmouth, TR11 5ST, 01326 372678
50.1950, -5.0661

31 MELINSEY MILL, VERYAN

A restored 16th-century water mill, tucked away in a lush stream valley, now a café and art gallery. Home-made pizzas from a wood-fired oven in high season.

→ On lane W of Veryan towards A3078. TR2 5PX, 01872 501049
50.2160, -4.9373

32 BARLEY SHEAF, GORRAN

Built in 1837 by local farmer William Kendall, and recently restored and reopened by his great-great-great grandson. Produce supplied by Cotna Barton organic farm.

→ Gorran Churchtown, PL26 6HN, 01726 843330
50.2466, -4.8083

33 VERYAN COUNTRY MARKET

Home-cooking, meat, plants, handicrafts, vegetables and crabs in season. A great social occasion for residents and visitors.

→ Veryan parish hall. Every Friday, 10.30am-11.30am (except Jan.) Refreshments available.
50.2183, -4.9231

34 HUMFREYS FARM SHOP, TREGONY

Good selection of local fruit and veg, meats, jams, preserves and fish.

→ Barwick Farm, TR2 5SG, 01872 530110
50.2748, -4.8841

35 THE LUGGER RESTAURANT, PORTLOE

Watch Portloe crab being hauled up, and eat it a few hours later, right on the harbour front. This cosy 17th-century smuggler's inn is a delight on stormy nights as well as summer days. Good rooms and a spa, too.

→ Harbourside, TR2 5RD, 01872 501322
50.2189, -4.8915

CAMP AND STAY

36 KING HARRY GLAMPING

Sheltered woodland site with panoramic views and riverside walks. Tepee with camp-beds or a cosy one-room cottage with woodburning stove. Pick your own veg, herbs and fruit in teh small veg garden. Free use of a boat and kayaks. Dogs welcome.

→ 2 Ferry Cottages, Feock, Nr Truro, TR3 6QJ, 01872 861911
50.2168, -5.0281

37 TRELOAN FARM, PORTSCATHO

Chickens, a small cricket pitch and access to three secluded beaches. Children can help ollect eggs and feed the rabbits. Busy in eason and with some caravans, but family-riendly and a great location.

Treloan Lane, Portscatho, TR2 5EF, 01872 80989

0.1653, -4.9778

8 TREWINCE, PORTSCATHO

ow-key farm camping with sea views.

Trewince Farm, Portscatho, 01872 580430

0.1652, -4.9880

9 CORNISH YURT, ALBION FARM

et in its own meadow, the yurt has a voodburner for chilly nights. Look up at the ight sky through the roof light or peel back he sides to let the fresh air blow in.

Albion House, Bells Hill, Mylor Bridge, TR11 SQ, 01326 373607

0.1927, -5.0789

0 CARNEBO BARN

ive-acre smallholding, up a very rough rack, Campfires and rolling hills (sloping). ar-free and off-grid (wind power only). ecret quarry rock pool on Trenoweth ommon for a dip. *Reported closed 2016.*

→ Trenoweth, Mabe Burnthouse, Penryn TR10 9JJ, 01326 377454. Trenoweth is signed off Antrim Hill (Mabe – Longdowns road). After 400m turn sharp R at the post box, park at the end by the telephone box (100m) and continue up the road, which becomes a track, over the hill. Continue on to find common land and quarry pool on L (50.1563, -5.1511)

50.1577, -5.1463

41 TREVEAGUE, GORRAN HAVEN

Good family campsite with pigs, a wildlife lookout, playground, and storytime every evening for the kids. Can be busy, but there are secluded pitches at the far end up the hill and pretty walks to three different beaches (Gorran, Hemmick and Vault).

→ Gorran Haven, PL26 6NY, 01726 842295

50.2364, -4.8010

42 COTNA BARTON YURTS & STRAW BARN

Stay in two new yurts or a beautifully converted straw-bale barn. Located on an inspiring 14-acre organic farm with composting loos and a wind turbine. Sara and Dave can lend you bikes or take you foraging. Delicious home-grown salads with leaves and flowers in season; home-made artisan foods including preserves, dressings and honey.

→ Gorran Churchtown, PL26 6LG, 01726 84486. Follow bumpy track around back of church, signed Galowras Mill.

50.2508, -4.8071

43 BETHEL COTTAGES, COWLANDS

Two lovely creekside cottages. Watch wild birds on the incoming tide from your bedroom window, wander along the creekside path through plum orchards, or relax beside the cosy woodburning stove. Pencreek cottage is equally secluded.

→ 01872 520000

50.2274, -5.0420

44 SALLY PORT LIGHTHOUSE, ST MAWES

Stay in a former lighthouse right at the end of the Roseland peninsula. The observation room has a vast picture window giving spectacular views out to sea. Completely private, down a 300m footpath and its just a 10-minute stroll from the cottage to where you can watch peregrine falcons.

→ 01386 701177

50.1417, -5.0145

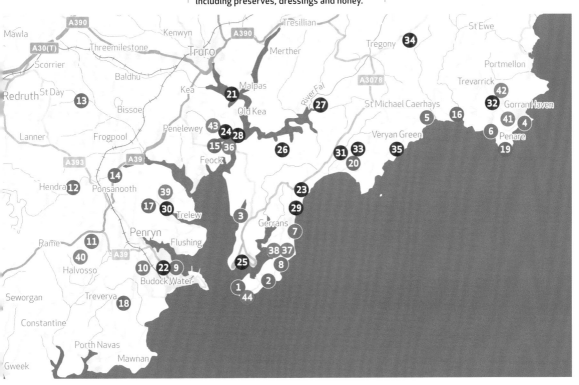

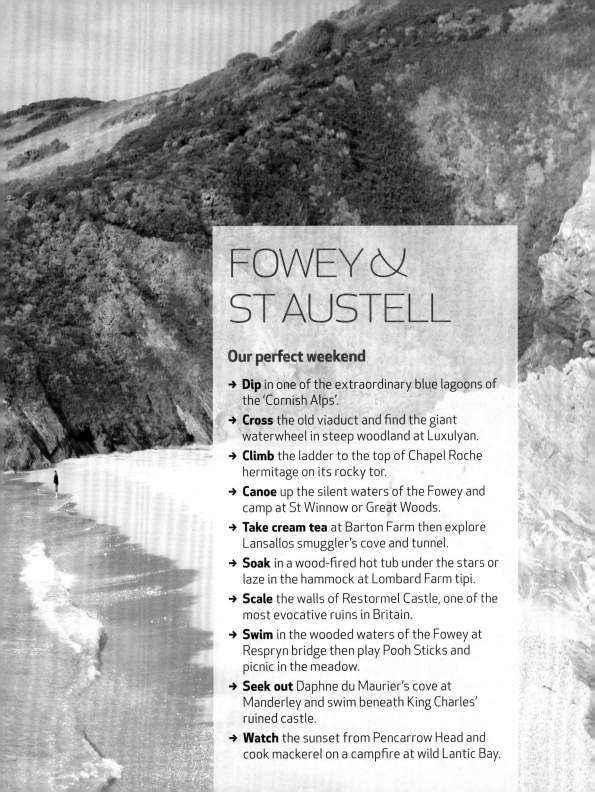

FOWEY &
ST AUSTELL

Our perfect weekend

→ **Dip** in one of the extraordinary blue lagoons of the 'Cornish Alps'.

→ **Cross** the old viaduct and find the giant waterwheel in steep woodland at Luxulyan.

→ **Climb** the ladder to the top of Chapel Roche hermitage on its rocky tor.

→ **Canoe** up the silent waters of the Fowey and camp at St Winnow or Great Woods.

→ **Take cream tea** at Barton Farm then explore Lansallos smuggler's cove and tunnel.

→ **Soak** in a wood-fired hot tub under the stars or laze in the hammock at Lombard Farm tipi.

→ **Scale** the walls of Restormel Castle, one of the most evocative ruins in Britain.

→ **Swim** in the wooded waters of the Fowey at Respryn bridge then play Pooh Sticks and picnic in the meadow.

→ **Seek out** Daphne du Maurier's cove at Manderley and swim beneath King Charles' ruined castle.

→ **Watch** the sunset from Pencarrow Head and cook mackerel on a campfire at wild Lantic Bay.

On this stretch of Cornwall's south coast, there are hidden smugglers' coves and the beautiful river Fowey weaves its way through secluded and forested creeks. Further inland, the lunar landscape near St Austell – the 'Cornish Alps' – features dramatic white peaks and turquoise lakes.

China clay brought wealth and prosperity to this area in the 19th century, when deposits of white silica enabled porcelain to be manufactured in the UK, rather than imported from China. While a few pits remain active, most are now abandoned and the extraordinary man-made landscape, punctuated by volcano-shaped peaks and hundreds of lakes of iridescent blue, has been returned to nature. The craters, with water the colour of alpine lakes, are deep and steep-sided though since 2018, they are mainly fenced off with swimming banned. However, they are widely visible, surrounded by wild heathland, filled with spring bird song and summer butterflies, and connected by miles of cycle trails called the Clay Trails.

More relics of the past can be found around St Austell. The old mining valleys of Luxulyan and Tregarsus, with their overgrown ruins and rusted machinery, are richly atmospheric. Or the adventurous might like to climb up the iron ladder to the top of Roche rock with its the ruined chapel, perched precipitously on a high granite outcrop in open moorland.

Just to the east, the valley of the river Fowey offers a gentler experience. Holidays spent around the wooded tidal creeks here are said to have inspired Kenneth Grahame when he was writing *The Wind in the Willows*. For a magical experience, explore the creeks by canoe, or stroll along quiet woodland footpaths between St Winnow and Lerryn, and around Pont Pill.

West of Fowey are the coves where writer Daphne du Maurier loved to swim, and which inspired her great romatic novel *Rebecca*. Heading east, the coast is wilder and has a long association with smuggling. From beautiful Lansallos, a wooded glade leads to a tiny beach with a smugglers' passage, complete with cart tracks worn into the stone. Or you can swim from adjacent Palace Cove and admire its old 'quay' hewn straight from the rocks.

SECRET COVES

1 HALLANE COVE, BLACK HEAD
A wooded path leads down from the headland to a little cove with mill, stream and rock pools. Not sandy.

→ Follow the lanes behind Pentewan through to Trenarren. Park and go down through hamlet on foot, following signs to the coast path.
20 mins, 50.2998, -4.7565

2 LANSALLOS COVE
Perfect family cove with smugglers' passage hewn from rocks, waterfall and snorkelling. A short walk down a pretty coombe from a charming NT hamlet. Continue 500m W on the coast path to find tiny Palace Cove where steps have been carved from the rocks to create a mini-quay. Or walk 200m E to find Parson's Cove.

→ Take path by church down through woods 15 mins to cove. Lansallos is signed 2 miles W of Polperro on lanes from Crumplehorn Inn.
15 mins, 50.3319, -4.5785

3 KILMARTH COVE, POLKERRIS
Polkerris is fun to visit but for more seclusion follow the coast path 15 mins N to find Kilmarth cove, on way to Par Sands.

→ Off A3082 between St Austell and Fowey. The Rashleigh Inn is by the beach (PL24 2TL, 01726 813991) and there is a sailing school and rocks for snorkelling to the S beyond the quay.
15 mins, 50.3410, -4.6868

4 POLRIDMOUTH, MENABILLY
Daphne du Maurier's favourite swimming cove, near her house, Menabilly (Manderley in *Rebecca*). Sometimes weedy. Concrete breakwater.

→ Continue past Polkerris to park at road end. Take path beyond farm down to cove.
15 mins, 50.3230, -4.6656

5 READYMONEY COVE & CASTLE
A pretty cove with an offshore bathing platform in season. A wooded walk leads up to St Catherine's Castle ruins on the rocky outcrop above.

→ 30 mins E of Polridmouth on coast path, or well signed 1 mile S of Fowey.
15 mins, 50.3291, -4.6445

6 LANTIC BAY, POLRUAN
Two stunning beaches (Great Lantic and Little Lantic) set beneath high cliffs, just to W of beautiful, wild Pencarrow Head. It's a steep walk down across fields from the lane and NT car park above.

→ E from Polruan on Polperro/Looe road, to find car park on L after 1½ miles. Watch out for rip currents in rough conditions.
20 mins, 50.3283, -4.6036

CORNISH ALPS

7 RESUGGA / TRESKILLING, TRETHURGY
This Clay Trail cycle/walking route has a great picnic spot with views out over the old china clay lake. No swimming.

→ For an online map search Clay Trail Eden Project to Bugle. Or pick up the trail just W of the Innis Inn access (campsite and fishing lakes, PL26 8YH) and follow trail N for 500m. Or park at Treskilling Down PL30 5EL and head S instead.
10 mins, 50.3814, -4.7674

8 CARCLAZE, TRETHURGY
This Clay Trail passes through a wild heathland area with many blue lakes and peaks, including the remains of the Great Carclaze china clay mine. Lookout for the granite tors of Carn Grey rocks and the waters of Baal Pit, whose surreal landscape

has featured in Dr Who. You may also spot the remains of old chimneys and clay driers. No swimming.

→ For an online map search Clay Trail Eden Project to Wheal Martyn. The first part, E of Trethurgy, passes through a wooded area with a lake (50.3655, -4.7552) also accessible from Chapel Lane. The second half, W of Trethurgy, enters the Carclaze area, also accessible just S of Penwithick, turn L off B3374, roundabout signed Eden Project/Innis Inn. Find wide track to Carclaze pit on R at bend (300m).

10 mins, 50.3657, -4.7703 ♿🅥

9 TRELAVOUR DOWNS, ST DENNIS

Two classic pointy clay peaks with views onto a deep, steep-side blue pool. No swimming!

→ There is pedestrian access from either Gother's Rd or Brewer's Hill (near to PL26 8DJ), E of St Dennis. Look out for double peaks and wooden double gates in the otherwise wire fence. The lake is below the S peak.

10 mins, 50.3818, -4.8685 🅥

RIVERS AND CREEKS

10 PONT PILL CREEK

Ancient woods line the shore of this isloated tributary opposite Fowey harbour. Best explored by canoe or kayak. At the creek head is a small quay, warehouse and boathouse.

30 mins, 50.3375, -4.6098 ♿🍴

11 GREAT WOOD, ST WINNOW

Mature woodland leads down to a remote, large, low-tide beach where the Fowey and Lerryn rivers meet.

→ Walk 1 mile downstream from St Winnow, a delightful riverside hamlet with 14th-century church and small farming museum (cream teas, cakes and camping at the adjacent orchard in season 50.3822, -4.6519). You can complete a long loop back via Lerryn Creek, a very atmospheric, densely wooded tidal creek said to be a source of inspiration for *The Wind In The Willows*.

25 mins, 50.3737, -4.6374 ♿⛺🍴🚶

12 FOWEY KAYAK HIRE

→ The Alcove, 47 Fore Street, Fowey PL23 1 AH, 01726 833627,
50.3348, -4.6186 🛶

13 ENCOUNTER CORNWALL KAYAK HIRE

→ Golant, Fowey, PL23 1LD, 01726 832842
50.3633, -4.6407 🛶

21

14 RESPRYN BRIDGE, FOWEY

Magical place on a sunny day, with dappled light reflecting on the river as it flows briskly through the woods. Wooden, bankside decks (for fishing) and a beachy shingle area by the lower footbridge (also good for Pooh Sticks). Up to 2m deep in sections and fun to swim against the current.

→ E on lanes from Lanhydrock House entrance. There is also a secluded, heavily wooded area with shingle beaches about 1 mile upstream, perfect for a skinny dip and accessible through white gates at end of Bodmin Station car park (50.4461, -4.6668).
10 mins, 50.4391, -4.6795

ANCIENT FOREST

15 ETHY PARK, LERRYN

One of the best locations in the county to see ancient trees with a wealth of mature oak, ash and beech.

→ 3 miles SE of Lostwithiel.
20 mins, 50.3849, -4.6181

16 LANHYDROCK HOUSE NT

Fine ancient oak and beech trees, some good for climbing, in beautiful 17th-century parkland. Swimming and paddling in the River Fowey. Also a good adventure playground with scramble nets.

→ B3269 between Lostwithiel and Bodmin.
15 mins, 50.4418, -4.6938

RUINS AND CASTLES

17 RESTORMEL CASTLE, LOSTWITHIEL

One of the finest round-keep castles in the UK, by banks of River Fowey, N of Lostwithiel. Massive 13th-century circular walls enclose the rooms of the castle, which is still in remarkably good condition. Superb views and swathes of daffodils and bluebells in season. Surprisingly peaceful location with a small car park (entrance fee).

→ Follow Restormel Road out of Lostwithiel, PL22 0EE,
5 mins, 50.4216, -4.6702

18 TIVOLI PARK, LERRYN

Pleasure garden constructed by a local industrialist in woodland next to Ethy Park in 1911. The park featured fountains, a pond, a cascade, obelisks, plunge pool and bandstand. Now dilapidated and overgrown with vegetation, the ruined structures are wonderfully evocative.

→ Follow the lane along the shore from Lerryn River Stores. Cross bridge and find ruins in woods to L after 200m.
10 mins, 50.3816, -4.6222

19 LUXULYAN WATERWHEEL

Remains of huge waterwheel, 34 feet in diameter. Fed by a waterfall and leat, which crossed the Luxulyan Valley under the now disused Treffrey Viaduct. The wheel drew wagons up the Carmears Wood incline on to the upper tramway and also operated mills. The drive gears and remains of the grinding pits can still be seen. Several other ruined buildings in woods to S.

→ Car park on lane ½ mile S of Luxulyan village. Climb to top of viaduct then follow leat path S through the wood.
20 mins, 50.3790, -4.7230

20 TREGARSUS VALLEY RUINS

Overgrown, ivy-clad remains of several ruined buildings including waterwheel in secluded valley.

→ 500m N of Stepaside between St Stephen (A3058) and Nanpean find track to R (gate and kissing gate) and continue ½ mile to ruins.
20 mins, 50.3563, -4.8860

SACRED AND ANCIENT

21 ROCHE ROCK CHAPEL

Dramatic, ruined 15th-century chapel and hermitage, built on an isolated outcrop of hard granite and only reached by climbing a ladder attached to the rock face. The Omen film *The Final Conflict* was made here.

→ Turn at L off roundabout (B3274) at Roche Inn and war memorial, just S of Roche, and find signed footpath 150m on R.

5 mins, 50.4022, -4.8286

22 MENACUDDLE HOLY WELL

Well house and ancient, carved-stone Druid's Chair in mossy glade by waterfall.

→ In unlikely position below B3274 Stenalees road on outskirts of St Austell. Turn L down narrow lane just after passing beneath viaduct and find on R.

3 mins, 50.3452, -4.7965

LOCAL FOOD

23 SAM'S, POLKERRIS

The old Fowey lifeboat house on the water's edge overlooking Polkerris harbour serves great wood-fired pizzas and delicious sea food to eat in or take away. Also offers a very cool vintage VW van for hire, which can provide outside catering and a pop-up cocktail bar!

→ Polkerris, PL24 2TL, 01726 812255
50.3384, -4.6810

24 RASHLEIGH ARMS, POLKERRIS

Authentic pub serving good local food. Sit on the terrace and watch the tall ships in the bay while the sun sets over the ocean.

→ Polkerris, PL24 2TL, 01726 813991
50.3388, -4.6801

25 THE LIFEBUOY CAFÉ, FOWEY

Quirky café with delicious breakfasts, perfect sausages and tempting cakes, all made with produce sourced locally.

→ Lostwithiel St, PL23 1BD, 01726834858
50.3349, -4.6352

26 LOSTWITHIEL FARMERS' MARKET

Exclusively seasonal food from within a 35-mile radius of the town, and sold by the producers themselves. Fortnightly market on Fridays, 10am–2pm.

→ Lostwithiel Community Centre, Pleyber Christ Way, Lostwithiel, PL22 0HA
50.4088, -4.6690

27 THE CROWN INN, LANLIVERY

Historic cosy inn with a tranquil garden and a constantly changing menu of great Cornish pub food.

→ Lanlivery, PL30 5BT, 01208 872707
50.4002, -4.7033

28 FISHERMAN'S ARMS, GOLANT

Relax on the terrace and watch Fowey river life go by. Local produce and pub grub.

→ Fore Street, PL23 1LN, 01726 832453
50.3626, -4.6413

29 THE SHIP INN, LERRYN

Historic pub with local ales by picturesque Lerryn creek.

→ Fore St, Lerryn, PL22 0PT, 01208 872374
50.3828, -4.6178

30 BARTON FARM, LANSALLOS

Delicous, farmhouse cream teas in the garden. Award-winning, home-reared organic beef and lamb to take home.

→ Lansallos, PL13 2PU, 01503 272293
50.3360, -4.5672

CAMP AND SLEEP

31 RAMBLING ROSE GYPSY CARAVAN

Authentic 'bow-top' gypsy caravan, lovingly restored with wonderful features: wood-burning stove, pull-out bed, colourful curtains, hand-painted woodwork and original paraffin lamps.

→ Delancey House, Lostwithiel, PL22 0HU
01208 871600 (off Bodmin Hill, B3268)
50.4160, -4.6781

32 ST. WINNOW BARTON

Orchard campsite right on the river Fowey by remote St Winnow church. Small and basic with just a cold-water tap and portaloo, but campfires are permitted and you can watch the sun go down over the estuary. No booking, but call ahead to check the field is open. £10 per pitch.

→ St Winnow Barton, PL22 0LF, 01208 872327
50.3822, -4.6519

33 HIGHERTOWN FARM, LANSALLOS

Tiny, rural NT campsite above Lantivet Bay with pretty coves. Solar-powered hot water, compost toilets and lovely views.

→ Highertown Farm Campsite, Lansallos, PL13 2PX, 01208 265211
50.3359, -4.5688

34 TREETOPS, LANTEGLOS

Large holiday house with Canadian log-cabin room complete with moose head and recumbent bear. From the deck there are views of dense woodland and the peaceful creek below.

→ PL23 1NQ, 01892 512800. Sawdays.co.uk
50.3405, -4.6091

35 GAZZERY'S, TYWARDREATH

Very secluded campsite on a farm, in a tiny hamlet. There is a small pond and the field is bounded by a stream and trees. Campfires and well-behaved dogs are allowed. 15mins walk from local village (shop, local pub and fish & chips).

→ campinmygarden.com/campsites/549
50.3677, -4.6881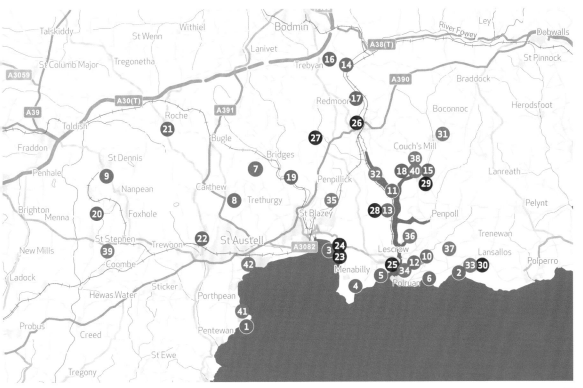

36 LOMBARD FARM, LANTEGLOS

Tiptoe through the meadows to Lombard Farm's tipi or sleep in a traditional yurt in the orchard. Enjoy a wood-fired hot tub under the stars or laze in the hammock.

→ Nr Lerryn, PL23 1NA, 01726 870844
50.3502, -4.6212

37 TREMEER YURTS, LANTEGLOS

Four yurts set in secluded positions on family-run Tremeer Farm. Log burners and campfires, pigs to feed and eggs to collect for breakfast, all close to the beach and the river Fowey.

→ Tremeer Farm, Lanteglos-by-Fowey, PL23 1NN, 01726-870545
50.3442, -4.5871

38 COLLON BARTON, LERRYN

Beautiful period B&B bedrooms in 18th-century farmhouse with superb views on the shores of the Lerryn river.

→ Lerryn, PL22 0NX, 01208 872908
50.3907, -4.6180

39 COURT FARM

With a 9.5" Newtonion reflector telescope on site and low light pollution, some serious star gazing can be done here. This is a large site with caravans, but there is a four-acre field set aside for tents.

→ Court Farm, Saint Stephen, St Austell PL26 7LE, 01726 823684
50.3368, -4.8757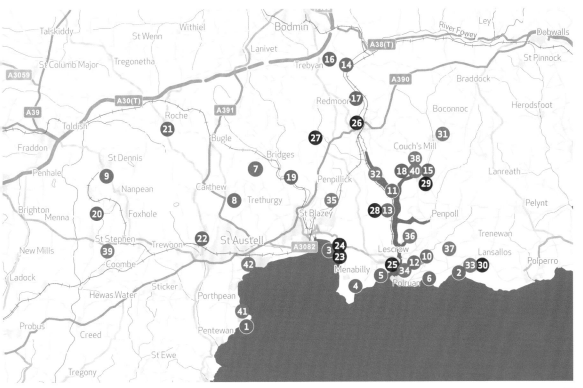

40 TANSY COTTAGE, LERRYN

Canoe or swim from your private waterfront garden with beautiful views. Sleeps four in two bedrooms.

→ PL22 0PT, 01208 872 375, Sawdays.co.uk
50.3849, -4.6181

41 THE SEA ROOM, BLACK HEAD

A beautifully converted boathouse with sunken garden, accessible only by footpath or boat. Below the cliffs of Black Head with views out across St Austell Bay and good swimming from the cove.

→ Ropehaven, Trenarren, Black Head, 01872 553 491, Boutique-retreats.co.uk
50.30771, -4.76026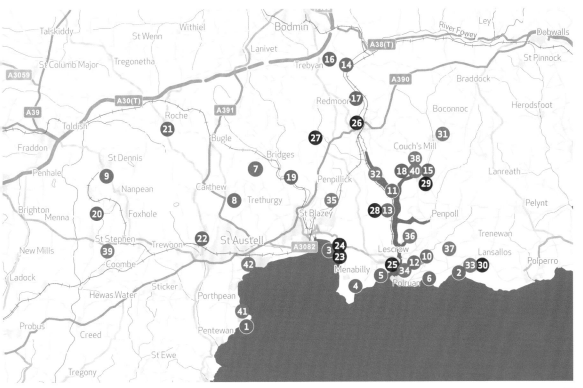

42 BROAD MEADOW HOUSE

Small campsite set in fields just above the harbour at Charlestown. Enjoy fabulous sea views and a scrumptious breakfast brought to your tent door. Bring your own tent or there are three deluxe tents available.

→ Quay Road, Charlestown, St Austell, PL25 3NX, 01726 76636
50.3325, -4.7566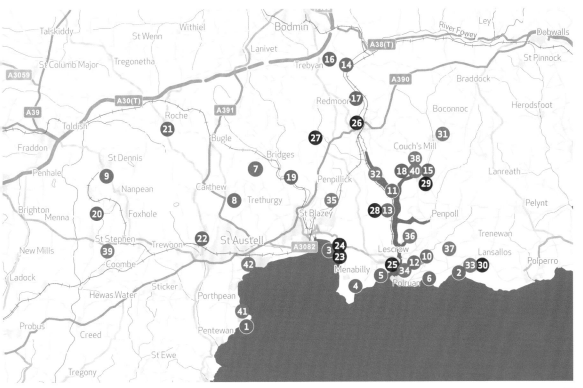

TAMAR & LOOE

Our perfect weekend

→ **Discover** the ghostly ruins of Clitter's Wood, deep in the valley of the Tamar.

→ **Watch** the sun go down from Cadson Bury hill fort and take a dip in the clear glade pool that runs below it.

→ **Enjoy** Sarah's legendary pasties in the pretty working port of Looe.

→ **Sleep** out in a tipi and soak up the peace of uninhabited St George's Island.

→ **Anoint** yourself with holy water from Dupath's sacred well.

→ **Canoe** up the Tamar with the tide at dawn. Or set out at lunchtime for Rumleigh Farm, a campsite with its own river quay.

→ **Explore** the grotto on the cliffs at Rame or hold a candlelit vigil in St Michael's chapel to the sound of crashing waves.

→ **Cycle** along the Giant's Hedge, a massive forest earthwork built by a Celtic warlord.

→ **Launch** yourself off a 30 metre cliff at Adrenaline Quarry, or take a more sedate dip at the quarry pool high on Kit Hill.

Often called Cornwall's forgotten corner, the Rame peninsula encompasses a world of cosy villages sheltered by tidal creeks, with views of tall ships sailing into harbour. Its undeveloped coastline is wild and beautiful with panoramic views from the Head, out over the ocean.

Two craggy structures on Rame Head, the picturesque grotto built into the rock, and tiny St Michael's chapel on the highest point, are wonderful places to watch the sunset. For a truly wild experience, huddle inside on a stormy night, bringing candles to light the interiors, while the sea crashes below.

There are good views west from the chapel to one of the longest stretches of sand in Cornwall, Whitsand Bay. The numerous sheltered coves along its length are very peaceful. Uninhabited St George's Island in Looe Bay, once the private home of two sisters, is well worth a visit and if you seek solitude, stay overnight in the island's tipi. Wild flowers bloom early in the gentle microclimate here, and it is a haven for sea and woodland birds.

Undoubtedly the wildest part of this region is around the River Tamar, the natural divide between Devon and Cornwall. Steep gorges and tidal flows are interspersed with ruined quays, and evocative ruins from an industrial age that is long gone. It's a surprisingly difficult river to access, bounded by stretches of private land, so one of the best options is to go by canoe or kayak.

The exquisite Cotehele Quay, where the Shamrock, a fully restored Tamar barge is moored, is the best launch point and you can eat lunch, take tea or enjoy organic ice cream before you set off. As you approach the banks of Morwellham, look out for Newquay, once a thriving centre for the copper trade but now abandoned and overgrown (also accessible by foot if you don't have a canoe).

Upstream is the quietest and most beautiful stretch of the river, especially beneath Morwell Rocks, an impressive mini-gorge and home to a noisy pair of breeding peregrines. There are herons and kingfishers, too, and many deer browsing in the woods.

Beyond Gunnislake, the Tamar becomes even wilder, with rapids and pools that are good for swimming but often far from the road. Clitter's Woods, with its derelict mill workings and ancient trees is a wonderful place to walk. Or jump on your mountain bike and cycle through Blanchdown Wood along miles of deserted trackway down to a remote swimming hole.

13

BEACHES AND ISLANDS

1 POLPERRO TIDAL PLUNGE POOL

Steps carved from the cliff lead down to a small plunge pool among rocks on the W side of the harbour mouth.

→ From the harbour docks climb the steps by the Blue Peter Inn to join the coast path. At bench drop down off the path to L, then find steps on R, before white hut shelter (not L to fishing shed).

15 mins, 50.3294, -4.5157

2 BATTERN CLIFF BEACH, DOWNDERRY

A long, wild, sandy beach under high cliffs, only accessible at low tide. You can continue for over a mile E, but take very great care not to get cut off by the incoming tide.

→ Cut down to the beach from the school and then head E.

20 mins, 50.3614, -4.3536

3 ST GEORGE'S ISLAND, LOOE BAY

Sisters Babs and Evelyn Atkins, who bought the island in 1965, lived there until they died at a ripe old age. Now a nature reserve run by the Cornwall Wildlife Trust, the island has magnificent sea views, a ruined Benedictine chapel, and wild daffodils are often in bloom

at Christmas. For the full Robinson Crusoe experience, you can rent the island's tipi (01872 273939, 3 nights minimum).

→ 'The Islander' summer ferry service from Looe quay, close to Lifeboat Station in East Looe.

30 mins, 50.3371, -4.4514

4 PORTNADLER BAY

Remote E-facing (morning sun) stretch of beach with low-tide sands. Views out to St George's Island.

→ 2 miles E of Talland on the coast path, or descend from the parking area at Hendersick Farm on the lane from Talland.

30 mins, 50.3367, -4.4719

5 POLHAWN COVE, RAME HEAD

Perfect low-tide sand cove, facing W. Just below Polhawn Fort.

→ From Rame Head car park follow coast path past Queener Point for 10 mins, then just after Monk Rock Cottages, bear L and take path down to the cove. Also look for the remains of the old fish cellars and landing steps hewn from rock on Crane Cove inlet, 300m to L along the shore (SW) at 50.3209, -4.2238.

15 mins, 50.3227, -4.2201

6 LONG SANDS, PORT WRINKLE

A beautiful, lengthy stretch of sands.

→ Head E along the coast path from Port Wrinkle and descend to the beach after Whitsand Bay Golf Course. For a loop walk (90 mins) continue along the sand 2 miles to reach the lifeguard station below Tregantle Fort and cliff, from where you can climb back up to the coast path and head back.

10 mins, 50.3604, -4.3036

7 THE GROTTO, FREATHY

A series of sandy coves, rocky inlets and sheltered grottos, connected by a wide beach. Good for snorkelling.

→ On the outskirts of Freathy (W side) find a car park on R and a path straight down to the coves by Sharrow Point.

5 mins, 50.3476, -4.2613

RIVERS AND POOLS

8 TAMAR CANOEING, COTEHELE

Launch your canoe from the historic quay at Cotehele and explore upstream with the tide as far as the weir at Gunnislake. Pass below steep woodlands and beneath the famous Calstock viaduct, to view old quays and ruined wharfs, relics of a once-thriving

copper industry. The quiet stretch above Morwhellam, beneath the crags of Morwell Rocks is stunning. Watch out for deer, kingfishers and peregrine falcons.

→ Aim to leave Cotehele quay 2–3 hours before high tide, ideally a spring tide. The whole return trip can take 3–6 hours. Organised trips are offered by Canoe Tamar, Woodlands, Gulworthy,Tavistock, PL18 8JE, 01822 833409, 07970 119510.
240 mins, 50.4913, -4.2234

9 SHEVIOCK WOOD, LYNHER CREEK
Much of the land bordering the Tamar and Lynher is private, but this path through ancient forest is one of the few giving access to the remote Lynher creek.

→ From Sheviock church, on A374, follow footpath from behind the church down to river 1 mile.
20 mins, 50.3790, -4.2830

10 ADRENALIN QUARRY, LISKEARD
Huge flooded quarry with sheer, rock walls. Try one of the longest zip wires in the UK and a giant pendulum swing. Many other atractions including climbing, swimming and scrambling (freshwater coasteering).

→ Lower Clicker Road, Menheniot, Near Liskeard, PL14 3PJ, 01579 308204. Just off A38, next to Menheniot train station.
2 mins, 50.4257, -4.4098

11 KIT HILL QUARRY
You can drive right up to the top of this hill for truly impressive views. Tower and various ruins on the hillside plus a disused quarry lake for a sunset dip. Blocks of quarried stone surround the lake, including many pieces once destined for London bridges.

→ Signed off A390, 2 miles E of Callington. Walk 300m N from monument.
15 mins, 50.5220, -4.2950

RUINS AND CASTLES

12 NEW QUAY, MORWELLHAM
Newquay began life as a stone shed by the Tamar in the 17th century. In 1860, it was handling all the surplus copper ore from Devon's Great Consols and Gawton Mines and was a bustling community, with its own inn and quay master. By 1914, the quay had been completely abandoned and the site was buried beneath dense vegetation. Its location has only recently been discovered.

→ Just 1 mile donwstream from well-known Morwellham (setting for the *Victorian Farm* TV series). Footpath follows the track of a narrow-gauge railway past the entrance to the George and Charlotte copper mine. It's also possible to walk down through Maddacleave Wood from Lower Sheepridge Farm (no through road signed at top of hill above Morwellham), or access the quay on the mountain bike trails.
20 mins, 50.5050, -4.1811

13 CLITTERS WOOD RUINS, CALSTOCK
Atmopsheric, ancient woodland, dotted with overgrown ruins and chimney stacks. At the bottom is a wild and remote stretch of the Tamar, flowing between large boulders beneath a weir. Good for a dip, only if you are a confident swimmer – the current is strong.

→ Follow dirt track then footpath, upstream from next to Gunnislake road bridge, 1 mile.
20 mins, 50.5300, -4.2255

14 BLANCHDOWN WOOD, WHEAL JOSIAH
The new Tamar Trails (bike, horse, walking) have opened up large areas of woodland and tin-mining ruins. There are many relics, several small lakes, and the S path leads close to a beautiful, remote weir pool on the Tamar for swimming.

→ 1 mile E of Horsebridge find forest car park

18

n R. Also via Bedford Mills car park (see 22,
reesurfers) but longer walk in. Bring your
ike.

0 mins, 50.5478, -4.2393

5 HOLMBUSH MINE, CALLINGTON

lmost 43,000 tons of copper ore were
nined here between 1822 and 1892. At
he peak of production, 100 men and boys
vorked underground with the same number
t work on the surface. Several ivy-clad, old
ngine houses are all that is left.

→ 300m N of Kelly Bray, signed Stoke
limsland, find gravel car park on L
mins, 50.5254, -4.3192

SACRED AND ANCIENT

6 DUPATH HOLY WELL, CALLINGTON

mall, granite well house, nicely restored, on
he edge of Dupath Farm. Stream, thought to
ave cleansing and healing properties, runs
hrough it. Pretty views.

→ Signed L off the A388 1 mile S of
allington. Park in Dupath farm yard and
valk down the track to find the well house
mmediately on R.
mins, 50.4998, -4.2930

17 RAME HEAD CHAPEL

St Michael's chapel was built in 1397, initially
as a simple hermitage, lighthouse and lookout point. Sometimes, from its stunning
location on the highest point of Rame Head,
you can see as far as the Lizard.

→ Bear R at Rame church and continue up to
the parking place, from where you can see the
chapel on the hillock. Continue on to Polhawn
Cove for a circular walk (see 5).

10 mins, 50.3138, -4.2233

SUNSET HILLTOPS

18 CADSON BURY, CALLINGTON

Walk up through drifts of spring bluebells in
these steep, ancient woods to arrive on the
grassy hill fort plateau. There are stunning
views out over the Lynher valley. Back
down in the valley there is a pretty shelving
section of stream for a woodland dip.

→ Take A390 W of Callington. After 2 miles
turn L just after the old bridge (unsigned lane).
Park immediately on the L and the path up to
the hill is a little further along on R. Pool is 5
min walk downstream, or look for kissing gate
further along the lane at (50.4840, -4.3336).
Continue 2 miles down narrow lane, turn L over
clapper bridge, then R towards Pillaton, to find

pretty paddling/swimming area, above and
below the old weir (50.4618, -4.3187).

15 mins, 50.4839, -4.3340

19 QUEEN ADELAIDE'S SEAT, PENLEE

Built in 1827 as an 'eye catcher' to
commemorate the visit of William IV (the
'Sailing King') to Mount Edgcumbe, this
wonderful grotto is named after the king's
wife. Partly cut out of the solid rock, there
is a tunnel entrance to the left and a three-
sided chamber to right. It is a spectacular
place to watch the sun set over Rame Head.

→ Turn L before the church in Rame (signed
Penlee Point) and continue down to headland.

10 mins, 50.3186, -4.1901

FOREST AND MEADOWS

20 COTEHELE DAFFODIL MEADOWS

In March, hundreds of daffodil varieties
once grown in the Tamar Valley herald the
spring at NT Cotehele. You can also explore
the perfectly preserved quay and wharves,
admire *Shamrock,* the wooden barge, have
tea at the Edgcumbe (see 26) or wander
upstream to find the working watermill
(grinds corn Tuesday and Thursdays) and
paddle in the stream.

→ Well signed from St Dominick, SE of Callington PL12 6TA, 01579 351346
10 mins, 50.4949, -4.2243

21 GIANT'S HEDGE, KILMINORTH

In mature oak woods alive with birdsong, look out for the remains of the Giant's Hedge. This prehistoric earthwork, one of the largest in the UK, runs for 9 miles through the woods at a height of 5 metres, and is stone faced in places. 'Jack the Giant having nothing to do built a hedge from Lerryn to Looe' goes one rhyme, although the structure is more likely to have marked the boundary of a Celtic chief's territory. There is a cycle path/bridleway through the wood.

→ Park at Millpool car park in West Looe by the waterside. Entrance to Kilminorth Woods is at the far W end. Alternatively, there is very limited parking on the lane by the waterside picnic spot at Watergate, at the far NW end of the wood (50.3640, -4.4852).
20 mins, 50.3604, -4.4714

22 TREESURFERS, GULWORTHY

Weave through the tree tops on swings, bridges, wooden walkways and zip wires.

→ Bedford Woodlands, Gulworthy, Tavistock, PL19 8JE, 01822 833409
5 mins, 50.5332, -4.2031

23 WARLEIGH POINT WOOD, PLYMOUTH

One of the finest examples of coastal oak woodland in Devon with stands of sweet chestnut, spindle and silver birch. Bluebells in spring. Close to Plymouth.

→ Take Station Road (signed Nature Reserve) from Tamerton Foliot on the NW side of Plymouth. Park at road end and follow path past red/white bollard.
10 mins, 50.4284, -4.1859

LOCAL FOOD

24 PORT ELIOT, ST GERMANS

The literary festival is famous for its muddy wild swim at high tide. At other times, you can stop for lunch or tea and home-made cake in the excellent tea room.

→ St. Germans, Saltash, PL12 5ND, 01503 230211. 12.30pm - 5.30pm. No house/garden ticket required for tea room.
50.3963, -4.3015

25 THE ROD & LINE, TIDEFORD

Unpretentious and unassuming local with log fire and real ales. Really good, fresh fish dishes are the speciality.

→ Church Rd, PL12 5HW, 01752 851323
50.4142, -4.3267

26 THE EDGCUMBE, COTEHELE

With an idyllic position overlooking the river Tamar, and set in a lovely garden, this old pub is the perfect spot to enjoy lunch made from local produce or a cream tea. On the NT Cotehele estate, at the Tudor mansion, you can sample rare varieties of cider apple in season.

→ Cotehele House, St Dominick, Saltash, PL12 6TA, 01579 352717
50.4913, -4.2234

27 THE PLOUGH, DULOE

imaginatively served, locally sourced food, including catch of the day from Looe and a good variety of local ales and wines.

→ Duloe, Liskeard, PL14 4PN, 01503 262556
50.3991, -4.4857

28 THE VIEW, FREATHY

Enjoy good, seasonal fare from local producers along with breathtaking views of Rame Head in this airy, modern restaurant showcasing local artists' work.

→ Treninnow Cliff Road, Millbrook, nr Plymouth, PL10 1JY, 01752 822345
50.3383, -4.2320

29 CORNISH ORCHARDS, TREDINNICK

Taste rare varieties of Cornish apples and sample the juices and ciders at the farm shop. If they're not busy, however, they might show you the orchards.

→ Westnorth Manor Farm, Liskeard, Cornwall PL14 4PW, 01503 269007
50.3962, -4.4741

30 SARAH'S PASTY SHOP, LOOE

Considered one of the best 'oggies' in Cornwall, and a great place to enjoy a traditional pasty. If it's a Friday, try the deliciously unorthodox fish special, with local mackerel, horseradish and peas.

→ 2 Buller Street, PL13 1DF, 01503 263973
50.3532, -4.4540

CAMP AND SLEEP

31 RUMLEIGH FARM, BERE ALSTON

Orchard camping field with lovely Tamar valley views and its own quay. Also offers self catering and B&B.

→ Bere Alston, PL20 7HN, 01822 840749
50.4950, -4.1933

2 DANESCOMBE MINE, CALSTOCK

This old arsenic-mine engine house has been sympathetically converted. Set in a lovely wooded valley leading down to the Tamar, just a walk away from delightful Cotehele.

→ Landmark Trust, PL12 6TA, 01628 825925
50.5028, -4.2255

3 HIDEAWAY HUTS, DULOE

A beautifully kitted out shepherd's hut set in a secluded field in Treworgey Farm. Peaceful location with Looe valley views. Gallop round on the farm's horses, walk to the beach or just gaze at the glow of your firepit. Home-made suppers and cream teas.

→ Canopyandstars.co.uk, Treworgey, Duloe, PL14 4PP, 07725 489979, 07968 791640
50.3837, -4.4751

34 KEVERAL FARM, LOOE

Organic community farm offering a small, eco-friendly campsite with a wild feel, spread over three fields. Enjoy campfires in the evening while roasting veg straight from the farm. The beach is just 15 minutes through the woods. Yurts and tipis available.

→ PL13 1PA, oak@keveral.org, 07772 155967
50.3697, -4.4057

35 OLD SOLOMON'S FARM, LATCHLEY

Stay in an apple loft or 15th- century farmhouse on the banks of the Tamar. Breakfasts with home cured own pork. Wild daffodils in spring and if you're really lucky, you might see an otter.

→ Gunnislake, PL18 9AX, 01822 833242
50.5393, -4.24555

36 TAMAR VALLEY TIPIS, CALLINGTON

Traditional tipi set in a quiet field overlooking the Tamar valley with regular visits from wild deer. Cosy inside with rugs and a wood-fired stove to keep you warm.

→ Deer Park Farm Luckett, Callington PL17 8NW, 01579 370292
50.5366, -4.2805

37 SOUTH HOOE COUNT HOUSE

Pretty cottage to rent with its own jetty on the Tamar, a cosy Aga inside and a beautiful woodland garden outside. Home-made bread and eggs from the garden's hens await you on arrival.

→ South Hooe Mine, Hole's Hole, Bere Alston, PL20 7BW, 01822 840329
50.4688, -4.2216

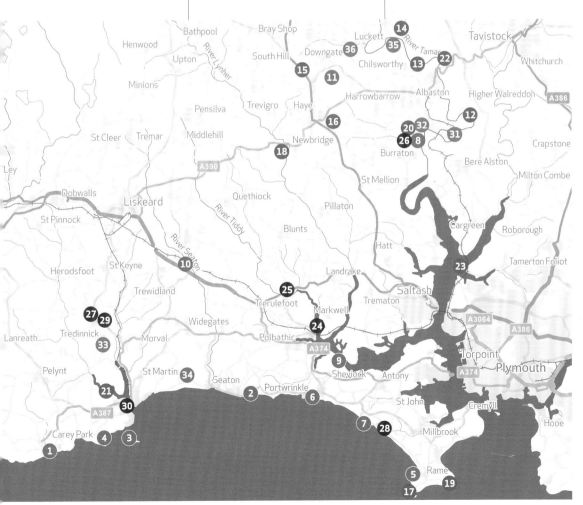

ST AGNES

Our perfect weekend

→ **Plunge** into Porthtowan's secret tidal pool, or catch an early morning surf wave, followed by breakfast at Blue Bar.

→ **Enjoy** a dip in the hilltop lake at Carn Marth, then cycle on to the lost ruins of South Wheal Francis.

→ **Explore** secret caverns along the cliff bottom beneath Wheal Coates mine and on Holywell Beach.

→ **Swim** or kayak out to the great stacks in St Agnes' bay and gather fat mussels at low tide.

→ **Cook** supper on the beach at Trevellas Cove, or retire for a sundowner at the Driftwood Spars bar.

→ **Soak** under the stars in a wood-fired hot tub at Little White Alice.

→ **Go** by sea kayak to the secret beach and find extraordinary rocks and caves beneath Cligga Head.

→ **Picnic** on the grass among wild poppies and enjoy the sea breezes on Pentire Head.

→ **Discover** St Piran's Oratory buried under the sand dunes.

Soaring cliffs, mine tunnels and gaping sea caves offer a harsh yet exhilarating backdrop to Cornwall's wild, northern coastline.

Once the centre of the county's 19th-century mining boom, this area is rich in industrial relics that stand sentinel among the gorse and heather.

For keen explorers of tumbledown places, the new Mineral Tramway cycle route connects north and south coasts (Portreath to Devoran) with extensions off to a number of ruins: Carn Brea, South Wheal Francis and the lovely swimming lake hidden on top of Carn Marth.

The ruined engine house at Wheal Coates, near St Agnes, is perched above a superb low-tide beach. A vertiginous shaft plummets down to a sea cave in the cliff below, which the brave can explore at low tide. The mines were 70 fathoms deep with tunnels that extended almost a mile out under the sea.

Heading south to Gwithian, there is a long sandy beach with funky cafés and at its north end, Virginia Woolf's lighthouse rises up from Godrevy Island. Near Godrevy Point you will find Fishing Cove, set deep beneath the rock face and so well hidden that even some local people don't know it exists. This is also a great place to see basking sharks and dolphins.

To the north, the coast is one of the most inaccessible in Cornwall. On a calm day the intrepid might like to take a sea kayak out beneath Cligga Head, to explore the soaring, 30 metre sea arch that leads into an inner cavern. An adjacent cove, with icing-sugar white sand, is perfect for a summer night's camping.

At Trevellas Cove, a more rugged neighbour of nearby Trevaunance, you can join local lads and jump into the water from the sea stacks on sunny days. If the tide is low, try skin-diving for the delicious mussels growing on the jagged rocks and cook them on an open fire for supper.

Further north, cross Perranporth's dunes to discover the remains of the medieval oratory of St Piran, where the patron saint of tin-miners was said to preach. At the end of stunning Holywell Beach, a deep sea cave leads to a sacred spring and waterfall. Above, on Pentire Point West, you will find one of the best wildflower meadows on the Cornish coast – a wonderful place for a picnic. Drop down to Porth Joke for swimming and surfing before retiring for the night at the popular campsite there.

WILD BEACHES

FISHING COVE, NAVAX POINT

Secluded, part-naturist beach, tucked away down a dramatic path to the E of Navax Point. You can also swim round into a second cove 50m to the W. Beach is N-facing and under steep cliffs, so come in the morning or at midday. Seals may be seen here.

→ Follow B3301 coast road from Hayle 5 miles to find parking at top of hill (1½ miles after Gwithian). Follow coast path 300m L (W) towards headland, then find path on R winding down through gorse down to cove (200m).
15 mins, 50.2379, -5.3726

TREVELLAS COVE, ST AGNES

Unspoilt shingle beach set at the bottom of a wild coombe with dramatic mine ruins and giant sea stacks.

→ From St Agnes Church (B3277) head towards Perranporth and take immediate L up narrow, steep, one-way hill (Wheal Kitty Lane). Continue 1 mile and turn L down track at bottom of hill. Shingle cove is to L, or continue along cliff to the stacks. Blue Hills artisanal tin works is further up the valley (TR5 0YW, 01872 553341).
5 mins, 50.3251, -5.1957

3 PORTH-CADJACK COVE, PORTREATH

Accessible only by rope, a hidden pebble cove and a super-wild, low-tide foreshore beneath cliffs. Explore the base of Samphire Island or the adventurous could swim 300m W into the chasm of Ralph's Cupboard.

→ From Navax Point continue on coast road (B3301) 2 miles E towards Portreath. Turn L down road track to cliff-top car park above Basset Cove. Walk 400m E on coast path, then drop down into obvious gully L (before the descent into Carvannel Downs). A steep scramble with ropes leads down to the cove.
20 mins, 50.2550, -5.3094

4 VUGGA COVE, CRANTOCK

Wild southwest end of the extensive white sands of Crantock.

→ Park at West Pentire (Goose Rock Hotel, 01637 830755) and follow the coast path down to the R and onto the rocks.
10 mins, 50.4065, -5.1312

5 HANOVER COVE BY SEA KAYAK

Amazing, inaccessible sandy cove beneath Cligga Head, about 2 miles E of Trevellas. There's also a dramatic collapsed yellow-rock sea cave and arch (viewable from the coast path above). If you don't have your own kayak, why not join a trip with Koru Kayaking (07794 321 827).
120 mins, 50.3327, -5.1851

6 CHAPEL PORTH, ST AGNES

Popular and dramatic NT cove. Low tide reveals a huge stretches of sand, with access to a large, part-flooded sea cave (Towanroath Vugga) beneath Wheal Coates. A chasm in the rocks above lets light penetrate into the cavern, and the cave once connected to the tunnels beneath the sea.

→ 500m E of Chapel Porth beach along the sands at low tide. Choose a spring LT to allow plenty of time. The little NT Café serves tasty toasted croques, or 'Hedgehog' ice cream, through a hole in the wall (outside seating).
10 mins, 50.3010, -5.2357

LAKES & POOLS

7 PORTHTOWAN TIDAL POOL

Wonderful, secluded tidal pool set among the cliffs, 300m to NE of main beach.

→ Follow coast path N, past Blue Bar (see 24), climb hill 300m to find eroded steps down to L. At low tide it is possible to walk all the way to Chapel Porth on the sands (1 mile).
15 mins, 50.2902, -5.2435

St Agnes, Cornwall

CARN MARTH POOL

Old granite quarry amid heather, with
smooth flat rocks and deep spring water,
near summit of Carn Marth. Outdoor theatre.
Great Flat Lode cycle route passes close by.

→ Near top of Lanner Hill (A393 between
Lanner and Redruth) take Carn Marth lane
(No Through Road) by the bus stop. Continue
up, bearing R then L and park outside the old
quarry/theatre.

10 mins, 50.2233, -5.2030

SUNSET HILLTOPS

ST AGNES BEACON

Ancient cairns, amazing views and one of
Cornwall's finest heathlands.

→ Park in layby 500m N of Beacon Cottage
Farm/Wheal Coates mine, and find path to top
of beacon on R.

15 mins, 50.3083, -5.2176 🔓

10 CARN BREA AND RUINS

Up on these blustery heights are rock tors,
a giant memorial cross, the remains of a
Bronze Age settlement and a folly castle
restuarnt. Mine ruins, Wheal Basset Stamps,
are to R on the way up.

→ Take Carn Lane up from Carnkie village,
which soon becomes a bumpy track. Parking at
top. (Restaurant 01209 218358).

3 min, 50.2217, -5.2465 🖼️🍴

RUINS AND FOLLIES

11 WHEAL COATES, ST AGNES

Famous and dramatic cliff-top mine
buildings, with processing rooms and old
engine houses, close to beautiful Chapel
Porth cove with its low-tide sands and caves.

→ 500m NE of Chapel Porth beach on coast
path, or park on Beacon Drive by Beacon
Cottage Farm campsite and take the path
down through the gorse.

10 mins, 50.3050, -5.2326 🔓

12 SOUTH WHEAL FRANCIS, CARNKIE

Remains of a large processing or 'vanner'
house, just below the Great Flat Lode cycling
trail, opposite Carn Brea. The engine house
once contained two 30-inch engines to
power the machinery here.

→ 200m E of the telephone box in Carnkie,
follow 'no through road' to the Basset Count
House to find ruins on slopes above. Or access
via Great Flat Lode trail that encirles Carn
Brea (connects to coast-to-coast trail via

Redruth and Chacewater).

3 mins, 50.2134, -5.2372 🔓

13 MINERAL TRAMWAY, CAMBROSE

Portreath (formerly Bassett's Cove) was
once one of the county's premier coal-
importing harbours. Today you can follow
the old tramway 11 miles on the Coast-to-
Coast cycle way. Connects to Carnon and
Poldice Valleys (see Fal & Roseland). From
Scorrier, you'll pass through woodlands
and dingley dells before scarred, industrial
landscape.

→ Hire bikes from the Bike Barn, Elm Farm
Cycle Centre, Cambrose, Portreath, TR16 5UF.
Farm shop here sells snacks and treats, and
real ale on tap, too.

60 mins, 50.2659, -5.2385 🔓🍴

14 CLIGGA HEAD RUINS

Dramatic cliff-top location with remains of
World War II look out and radar stations,
also amazing views down into Cligga cave
blowhole. Cavers and enthusiasts explore
the vast mines system underground and
there are openings at sea level below (kayak
access only).

→ 2 mile walk NE from Trevellas Cove along
coast path or access from behind Cligga Head

Industrial Estate, 1 mile SW of Perranporth on the B3285.

15 mins, 50.3365, -5.1778

CAVES AND CAVERNS

15 HOLYWELL CAVE AND WELL

A large cavern at the remote end of beautiful Holywell Beach, with a calcite flowstone in the corner. Holy springwater cascades down via natural pools. Until recently Christian ceremonies were held here. Find another holy well in the shallow valley leading inland from the beach.

→ Located on far NE end of Hollywell Beach. Cave has a slanting, triangular entrance, slightly higher than sea level, with boulders on the floor. Accessible only at low tide.

20 mins, 50.3985, -5.1459 ✝

SACRED PLACES

16 ST PIRAN'S ORATORY, PERRANPORTH

Buried beneath Penhale, Cornwall's largest and most diverse sand-dune system, the 6th century oratory, marked by a simple plaque, is considered one of the the oldest and most important Christian sites in the UK. A campaign is underway to have the structure uncovered. Further on through the dunes, see the remains of a 10th-century church and an 8-foot Celtic cross.

→ From Perranporth walk up the white-sand beach for 1 mile and, where the MOD land begins, follow the path through the dunes on the R, walk 800m to the oratory site and 300m further to the church ruins.

40 mins, 50.3654, -5.1405

WILDLIFE AND WILDFOOD

17 TREVAUNANCE AND TREVELLAS

The W side of popular Trevaunance Cove is good for snorkelling, or collect mussels at Trevellas. Yum!

→ If you come away empty-handed there is always the Driftwood Spars Inn.

10 mins, 50.3204, -5.2021

18 GODREVY POINT

From May to September the seas around Cornwall are home to hundreds of basking sharks as they gorge on plankton on their migration route north. Best seen from a boat but good cliff-top vantage points include Godrevy Point. Popular place to see seals hauled out on the rocks.

→ Signed Godrevy, on L 1 mile N of Gwithian (B3301).

20 mins, 50.2401, -5.3939

19 WEST PENTIRE & PORTH JOKE

On the downland above Porth Joke beach, there are wild poppies and corn marigolds in June and July. Below is a long finger of sand with a stream, caves and a small campsite set well behind the beach.

→ Park at West Pentire and continue on the road, then take track over the headland, turning L after 300m.

15 mins, 50.4029, -5.1335

20 HORSE RIDING, LANNER

Enjoy a moorland hack around the mines and Carn Brea, or a gallop on the beach.

→ Wheel Buller Riding School, TR16 6SS, 01209 211852.

50.2141, -5.2291

LOCAL FOOD

21 CALLESTICK FARM ICE CREAM

Visit the animals on this working farm and enjoy the café.

→ Inland, between St Agnes and Perranporth. Callestick, Truro, TR4 9LL, 01872 573126

50.3110, -5.1268

22 DRIFTWOOD SPARS, ST AGNES

Home-brewed beers and local bar food in a lively old inn near the beach. Also B&B.

→ Trevaunance Cove, TR5 0RT, 01872552428

50.3179, -5.2023

23 BLUE BAR, PORTHTOWAN

Modern beach bar serving local, seasonal produce. Great place to watch the sunset.

→ Beach Road, TR4 8AW, 01209 890329

50.2875, -5.2410

24 JAM POT CAFÉ, GWITHIAN

Historic, distinctive round building. Lynn has a no-fast-food policy and makes the best cakes in the county. Great value for money. Fabulously situated overlooking St Ives Bay and Godrevy.

→ Walk straight from car park to end of tarmac lane. Café is a stone's throw from the beach. Hayle, TR27 5BT
50.2246, -5.3945

25 SANDSIFTER CAFÉ, GWITHIAN
Enjoy post-surf local food or a warming hot chocolate at this funky café in the dunes behind above Gwithian beach. Good range of surfwear, great sunsets.
→ Hayle, TR27 5ED, 01736 757809
50.2294, -5.3869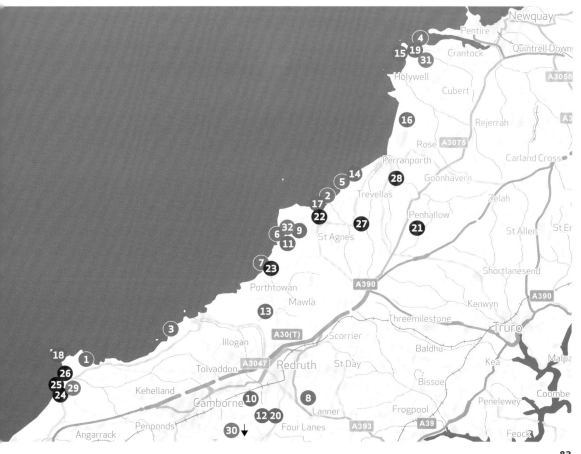

26 GODREVY CAFÉ, GWITHIAN
Delicious home-made brunches at this delightfully laid-back beach café.
→ Gwithian, TR27 5ED, 01736 757999
50.2305, -5.3882

27 MINERS ARMS, MITHIAN
Cosy, traditional 16th-century pub with real ale and food.

→ St Agnes, TR5 0QF, 01872 552375
50.3119, -5.1692

28 BOLINGEY INN, PERRANPORTH
Excellent food using the the pub's home-grown vegetables. Good ales, too.
→ Penwartha Road, TR6 0DH, 01872 571626
50.3356, -5.1441

CAMP AND SLEEP

29 GWITHIAN FARM CAMPSITE
Great sea views and a wonderful place to enjoy the sunset. 10 min walk to the beach.
→ Churchtown Rd, TR27 5BX, 01736 753127
50.2217, -5.3873

30 LITTLE WHITE ALICE
Sip Camel Valley champagne in a wood-fired hot tub beneath the stars. Six stone and cedar-clad cottages: two for romantics, four for families. Boasts hand-made kitchens,

woven-willow headboards, wood-burning stoves, heated floors, hampers with local honey and bread. Natural swimming pool.
→ Carnmenellis, Redruth, TR16 6PL, 01209 861000, Sawdays.co.uk
50.1708, -5.2251

31 TREAGO FARM CAMPSITE
Set in a little coombe 500m from the beach. Great location but very busy at peak holiday times. Worth a visit during quieter months.
→ Newquay, TR8 5QS, 01637 830277
50.3981, -5.1298

32 BEACON COTTAGE FARM
Set on the lower slopes of St Agnes Beacon, just above Wheal Coates engine house. Well-managed campsite with 70 numbered pitches in six small, landscaped paddocks.
→ St Agnes, TR5 0NU, 01872 552347
50.3087, -5.2247

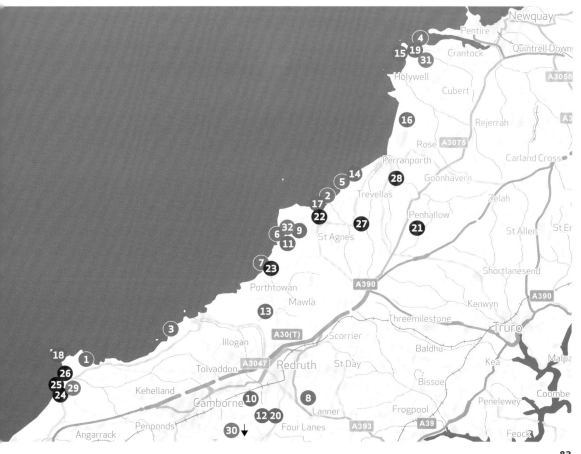

3

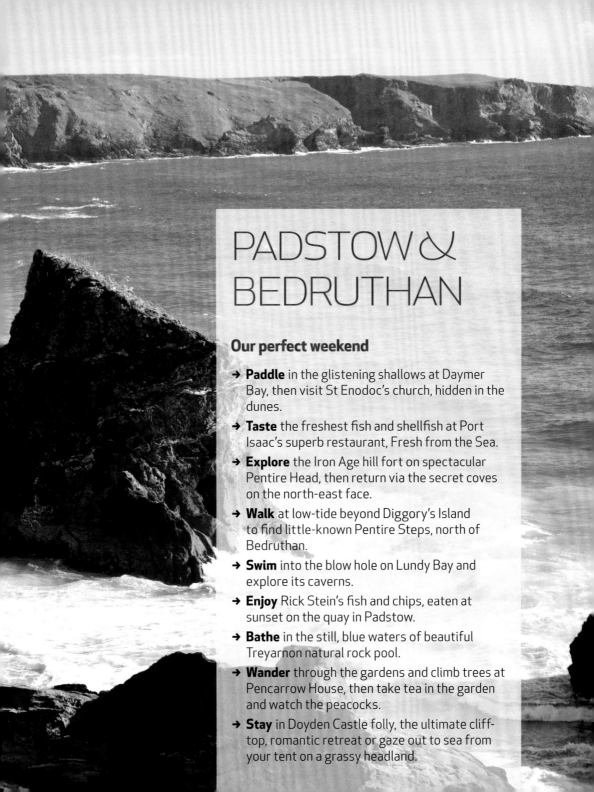

PADSTOW & BEDRUTHAN

Our perfect weekend

- → **Paddle** in the glistening shallows at Daymer Bay, then visit St Enodoc's church, hidden in the dunes.
- → **Taste** the freshest fish and shellfish at Port Isaac's superb restaurant, Fresh from the Sea.
- → **Explore** the Iron Age hill fort on spectacular Pentire Head, then return via the secret coves on the north-east face.
- → **Walk** at low-tide beyond Diggory's Island to find little-known Pentire Steps, north of Bedruthan.
- → **Swim** into the blow hole on Lundy Bay and explore its caverns.
- → **Enjoy** Rick Stein's fish and chips, eaten at sunset on the quay in Padstow.
- → **Bathe** in the still, blue waters of beautiful Treyarnon natural rock pool.
- → **Wander** through the gardens and climb trees at Pencarrow House, then take tea in the garden and watch the peacocks.
- → **Stay** in Doyden Castle folly, the ultimate cliff-top, romantic retreat or gaze out to sea from your tent on a grassy headland.

From Newquay to Port Isaac, the north Cornish coast bears the full brunt of westerly storms and swells. Great caves have been pummelled into the cliffs and dramatic blow holes have been forced up through the ground. On hot days, wander down grassy headland tracks to find secluded coves.

One of the best places to experience the drama of this wild stretch of coast is at Bedruthan Steps, its long, sandy beach packed with extraordinary rock stacks and pinnacles. Precarious steps were hewn out of the cliff-face in the late-18th century, when Bedruthan was a stopping point for poets and artists of the Romantic school. The Victorians also built steps down to the beach at Pentire, a continuation of Bedruthan to the north, and far fewer people know of this route down to the beach. The old Victorian switchback track now ends where the cliff has collapsed, but there is still faint footpath for the intrepid to scramble down.

If sea caves fascinate you then seek out the the Round Holes, sea caves that have collapsed in on themselves, at Trevone, Trevose, Lundy and Porthcothan. Those at Trevose and Lundy make a great destination for an adventure swim, but make sure the sea is calm or the tide is low.

While other Cornish estuaries, especially along the south coast, can be muddy, the river Camel winds its way to the sea leaving a trail of golden sand. Sand bars glow against the blue ocean horizon and there are long beaches, such as the famous Doom Bar, where you can splash out in the shallows. After a swim at Daymer Bay, explore the dunes to find the remains of beautiful St Enodoc's church. You can hire kayaks at Rock or cycle the length of the river on the Camel trail, a flat cycleway on the path of the disused railway (built to carry the famous sand inland for the farms). There are a couple of good spots for a river swim along the way, and you might even see an otter if you are around at dawn or dusk.

Thanks to the influence of local chef Rick Stein, you are never too far from good local food, although his establishments get very crowded in summer. A safer bet might be Stein's fish and chips on Padstow quay, but don't forget to explore lesser-known villages inland, such as quirky St Mawgan (Falcon Inn and bonsai gardens), St Kew (good pub and farm shop) and timeless Pencarrow House. When we visited, the lady of the house herself was taking a break from gardening to serve tea on the café's lawn. There are some wonderful trees to climb in the parkland, too.

SECRET BEACHES

1. FOX HOLE, WATERGATE BAY

You are unlikely to meet anyone at the far N end of Watergate Bay and this access route avoids walking a mile up the beach.

➜ Find the grassy track from the main junction in the centre of Trevarrian (opposite Kernow Trek B&B, by Shrub Cottage). This leads out to the coast and after about 700m, beyond a stile, bear L along the field boundary to reach coast path, then down to Watergate Bay.

5 mins, 50.4547, -5.0397

2. BEACON COVE

Sublime, almost inaccessible cove. Follow the surfers' route and, if you don't mind a scramble and ropes, it can be all yours. To the S is Griffin's Point Iron Age cliff castle with three ramparts and fabulous W views.

➜ As for Fox Hole, but bear R after stile and go up the hill to the coast path. Descend on very steep grass on N side of cove, traversing L at bottom to find steel rope that leads down into a cave. If swimming, be careful of rip currents around the edges of cove in high swell.

20 mins, 50.4605, -5.0378

3. PENTIRE STEPS, BEDRUTHAN

Many people visit the spectacularly wild Bedruthan Steps with its amazing sands, pools and rock spires. Yet few know about the old route down at the north end of the bay, near Park Head, where another set of Victorian steps have mostly been washed away. At low tide you can walk through Diggory's Island to Bedruthan main beach.

➜ ½ mile N of the Bedruthan Steps car park and campsite, turn L off B3276 signed Pentire Farm/Park Head. Park at track end then bear L through gate. On reaching the coast path look L and you'll see a path down the slope which ends in a rocky scramble above the beach. Turn R at the coast path to visit High Cove inlet with sea arch and caves.

10 mins, 50.4944, -5.0346

4. HARBOUR COVE, DOOM BAR

Large area of sands at the estuary mouth, reached by a pretty walk down through fields.

➜ Off B3276 N of Padstow, signed Hawker's Cove. After 2 miles turn R down track into field. Also accessible a mile N of Padstow on coast path, past war memorial. Explore the coast a mile N to find Pepper Hole, a collapsed sea cave.

10 mins, 50.5565, -4.9485

5. LONG COVE, TREVOSE HEAD

Tiny, narrow cove with great rocks for jumping at high tide.

➜ 300m S of the new lifeboat station. Walk 1 mile NW from Harlyn Bay along the coast path, or 1 mile S from Trevose Head (private toll road to lighthouse).

25 mins, 50.5471, -5.0217

6. TREYARNON ROCK POOL

Lovely, large natural rock pool above beach.

➜ Just below the YHA café (0845 371 9664) and a short walk from the car park. Trevose round hole is 1 mile N if you want more of an adventure (see 16).

5 mins, 50.5291, -5.0255

7. TREVONE TIDAL POOL

Large tidal pool (part natural rock pool, part dammed) on the rocky stretch SW of Trevone beach. A great spot for those who love rock-pooling and sea creatures.

10 mins, 50.5446, -4.9809

8. DAYMER BAY & ST ENODOC

Idyllic sands with warm tidal waters and safe swimming. 15th century St Enodoc church, much loved by poet laureate John Betjeman, is in the dunes behind.

→ From Daymer Bay car park (small lane from Trebetherick) head S across beach, then around Brea Hill (either L via St Enodoc church or R via coast path) to reach beach. NB you can hire kayaks from Rock Pontoon, Rock Road, PL27 6LD, 07791 533569.

20 mins, 50.5550, -4.9281

9 PENTIRE POINT COVE

A lovely walk across the headland leads to secluded, sandy, low-tide double coves on NE side of Pentire Point.

→ Park at Pentire Farm (1mile N of New Polzeath). Bear L of farm into field and, after 300m, turn R down to coast path. Turn L and immediately on R find rough path leading down to cliff edge. Go through a hedge tunnel and you will emerge above the rocks and sands.

15 mins, 50.5888, -4.9159

10 PORT QUIN, DOYDEN COVE

Port Quin is a beautiful natural harbour with a few NT cottages and Doyden Point folly (in which you can stay). A rocky inlet provides access to the water for swimming and some jumps. Lundy Bay caves are nearby.

→ 300m on W side of harbour. Drop down to rocky inlet and stream beneath folly. You can also join an organised coasteering (or kayaking) trip with local boys Sam and Mark, who run Cornish Coast Adventures: Scarrabine Farm, Port Quin, PL29 3ST, 01208 880280.

5 mins, 50.5898, -4.8717

11 GREENAWAY PLUNGE POOLS

Low-tide rock pools on a small beach.

→ From Daymer Bay car park head 500m N to the Greenaway (large houses) and drop down beneath second house to find the pools at low tide.

5 mins, 50.5659, -4.9297

12 PORT GAVERNE

Safe swimming cove in village, but with plenty of rocks from which older local kids like to jump, particularly to the R of the rocky promontory.

→ There are also steps down to a rocky inlet on L for swimming at low tide. If you are experienced, you could try swimming through the channel around the headland, then into the huge sea cave beneath the cliff.

2 mins, 50.5945, -4.8249

RIVER SWIMMING

13 POLBROOK BRIDGE, CYCLE PATH

If you make it this far on the cycle path, stop for a dip in this deep swimming hole. Lovely woods and tiny narrow lanes all around.

→ 3km S of Wadebridge, at the car park by the entrance to Bishops Wood, on the oppsoite side of the river from the cycle path. NB Hire bikes at Bridge Bike Hire, The Camel Trail, Wadebridge, PL27 7AL, 01208 813050 or Eddystone Road, Wadebridge, PL27 7AL, 01208 814104.

60 mins, 50.4918, -4.8015

14 DUNMERE WEIR AND OTTERS

Further along the Camel trail, Dunmere Weir has a salmon leap and makes a shady, dappled place for a swim. This is also the perfect territory for the secretive but clever otter. Watch for them at dawn and dusk and if you get a sighting, do log it with the Cornwall Wildlife Trust to be added to their research.

→ ½ mile N of Bodmin off the A389. Also try Crabb's pool 15 mins upstream (50.4850, -4.7458).

20 mins, 50.4817, -4.7470

CAVERNS AND SEA CAVES

15 PORTHCOTHAN BLOW HOLE

Large blow-hole cave in cliffs to the S side of Porthcothan. The little Trescore islands, with tiny cove, are just opposite.

→ Accessible by foot from the beach at low tide, kayak around if there is no swell, or peer down from the cliffs above. Continue on coast path further S from above blowhole to reach High Cove caves near Pentire Steps (50.49914, -5.04081).

20 mins, 50.5083, -5.0329

16 TREVOSE ROUND HOLE

Dramatic collapsed sea cave by cliff-edge path. The adventurous can swim round and into the mouth, calm seas only. 200m S from car park above. Launch from rocks 200m S of hole.

→ Trevose Head is at the end of a toll road from Harlyn. Bear S from car park, 200m.

5 mins, 50.5454, -5.0347

17 LUNDY HOLE, PORT QUIN

You can peer down the blow hole from right beside the coast path, or swim around into it at low tide or in calm seas. There is also a extraordinary 50m-long cave passage

from the R side of Lundy beach through the headland to Epphaven Cove (to the E). This area is also good for mussel gathering.

→ Lundy beach is 1 mile W along the coast path from Port Quin (see 10 Port Quin coasteering).

20 mins, 50.5825, -4.8861

18 TREVONE ROUND HOLE

Another large, collapsed sea cave on headland. Steep scramble leads down into its crater and an archway leads out to the ocean.

→ 500m on coast path NE from Trevone beach.

10 mins, 50.5480, -4.9794

SACRED AND ANCIENT

19 RUMPS POINT FORT, POLZEATH

Iron Age fort on the very tip of Pentire headland, with remains of huge ditches and earthworks clearly visible. Spectacular sunset views. Look out for the increasingly rare harebell, with its nodding, delicate blue flower in the grassland here.

→ Follow directions as for Pentire Point cove but continue on until you reach the fort.

30 mins, 50.5935, -4.9199

20 TREVELGUE HEAD & CAVERNS

The ramparts and barrows of Trevelgue Head (Porth Island) Iron Age fort can be accessed via walking over the wooden bridge . On the beach below are several large caverns.

→ Park in Porth/ Whipsiderry on the B3276 N out of Newquay.

10 mins, 50.4274, -5.0575

WILDLIFE AND WOODS

21 EXTREME ROCK-POOLING, POLZEATH

Also called 'e-coasteering', this activity offers the challenge of jumps, climbs and caves, combined with finding weird and wonderful marine life. In partnership with Polzeath Marine Centre.

→ Cornish Rock Tors, The Gazebo, Polzeath Beach, PL27 6SS, 07791 534884.

50.5755, -4.9162

22 BIRDS OF PREY CENTRE

Peregrine falcons are not uncommon on the cliffs of north Cornwall, but if you don't get lucky, see owls, eagles, falcons and hawks here. Displays at 12pm, 2pm and 4pm. There are ornamental pheasants too.

→ Meadowside Farm Winnard's Perch, St Columb, TR9 6DH, 01637 880544.

2 mins, 50.4584, -4.9249

23 PENCARROW HOUSE WOODS

The long drive through ancient woodland is a wonderful introduction to charming Pencarrow House. Also Iron Age hill fort.

→ Off A389 between Bodmin and Wadebridge

10 mins, 50.5067, -4.7663

LOCAL FOOD AND PRODUCE

24 ST KEW INN AND FARM SHOP

Nestling in the beautiful village of St Kew, this charming 15th-century inn offers excellent local food. Also a good farm shop with pork and bacon from the free-range Gloucestershire Old Spots snuffling around in the farm behind (on main A39 road at St Kew Highway, PL30 3EF, 01208 841818).

→ Bodmin, PL30 3HB, 01208 841259

50.5589, -4.7933

25 CAMEL VALLEY VINEYARD

Try the award-winning Cornish sparkling wines and buy a bottle, perfect with some freshly caught Camel trout.

→ Nanstallon, Bodmin, PL30 5LG, 01208 77959

50.4757, -4.7808

26 STEIN'S FISH & CHIPS, PADSTOW

Fried fish from the specials board, perfectly cooked chips and a bottle of Chalky's Bite is a meal well worth queueing for. Enjoy it with your legs dangling over the harbour side as the sun goes down. Stein also runs a good but busy pub, the Cornish Arms, at nearby St Merryn (PL28 8ND, 01841 520288).

→ South Quay, Padstow, PL28 8BL, 01841 532700

50.5393, -4.9361

27 PEACOCK CAFÉ, PENCARROW

Delightful café serving local produce in the garden of this lesser-known country house. Watch the peacocks strut and visit the charming outdoor play area for children, like something from a bygone age.

→ Off A389 between Wadebridge and Bodmin, PL30 3AG, 01208 841369

50.5072, -4.7709

28 FRESH FROM THE SEA, PORT ISAAC

Enjoy the taste of line-caught fish and the freshest crab and lobster, straight from Calum's boat. Or try Tregida Smokehouse's delicious smoked mackerel. Eat in or take-away. The Harbour, an excellent seafood restaurant (PL29 3RH, 01208 880237) is also recommended.

→ 18 New Road, PL29 3SB, 01208 880849

50.5941, -4.8297

29 BRE PEN FARM SHOP & BISTRO

Enjoy a full English breakfast made with local produce, or stock up on lamb-and-mint burgers, from home-reared cliff-top flocks, for your campfire feast.

→ Bre Pen Farm, B3276 S of Mawgan Porth, TR8 4AL, 01637 860420

50.4610, -5.0325

30 FALCON INN, ST MAWGAN

Superb, wisteria-clad, 16th-century inn, with lovely garden and good food. The picturesque village of St Mawgan, nestled in the Vale of Lanherne, has a celebrated Japanese bonsai garden.

→ St Mawgan, TR8 4EP, 01637 860225

50.4541, -4.9973

CAMP AND GLAMP

31 POLGREEN, MAWGAN PORTH

A handful of beautifully kitted-out bell tents in a meadow on a working farm within walking distance of the beach. One of the tents is set up as a honesty shop, with fresh

read and local produce. You can also pick
our own salad from the garden.
→ Trevarrian, Mawgan Porth, Newquay
0.4574, -5.0187 🏄

2 BEDRUTHAN STEPS CAMPING

onderfully simple campsite in a huge field
ght above Bedruthan Steps. Awesome
unsets.
→ On B3276 300m N of the NT car park
ntrance. Open July and August only.
0.4853, -5.0325 🏕🔥

3 GYPSY CARAVAN, ST WENN

wo gypsy caravans in a field with views out
o Bodmin Moor; one with a stove. Simple,
omantic accommodation.
→ St Wenn, Padstow, 0844 5005101
0.4819, -4.8744

4 DENNIS COVE CAMPING

Vell looked after, secluded site for families,
et in a pretty valley overlooking the Camel
stuary. Take the small ferry across the
stuary to enjoy the wide sands and shallow
aters of Daymer Bay.

→ Dennis Lane, Padstow, PL28 8DR, 01841
532349
50.5323, -4.9357 🏕

35 THE SHEPHERD'S HUT, POLZEATH

Snuggle up cosy in a hut for two and cook on
the fire pit.
→ Moyles Farm, St Minver, PL27 6QT,
01208 862331
50.5674, -4.8976

36 MILL VALLEY YURTS

Shepherd's huts and colourfully decorated
yurts set in meadows with pigs, goats and
chickens. Outdoor hot tubs heated by a
woodburner and a stream with weir and pool
for paddling.
→ Hingham Mill Farm, Egloshayle, Wadebridge
PL27 6JQ, 01208 841163
50.5189, -4.7939

37 CORNISH TIPI HOLIDAYS

The original tipi and wild-swimming
campsite. 16 acres of woodland and
meadows, 16 tipis of varying sizes and
its own beautiful, spring-fed quarry lake.

Borrow a canoe, catch your own fish and cook
it on your campfire.
→ Tregeare, Pendoggett, St Kew, PL30 3LW,
01208 880781
50.5813, -4.7705 🏄🛶🏊

38 DOYDEN CASTLE, PORT QUIN

Live out your fantasy in this miniature, cliff-
top castle with fantastic coastal views. Built
as a pleasure house in 1830 by an infamous
and wealthy bon-viveur for nights of feasting
and drinking. A reputation to live up to!
→ Nationaltrustcottages.co.uk,
0844 800 20 70
50.5895, -4.8731 🏰

39 MIGHTY OAK TREE CAMPING

Camp in a tree using especially designed four-
cornered hammocks suspended very safely up
in the tree. You are tied in at all times by rope
and harness and an early morning breakfast
is sent up to you as you swing serenely to the
sound of the Cornish dawn chorus. Includes a
short tree climbing induction.
→ Mighty-oak.co.uk, 07890 698651
50.4337, -4.9410 🌳🏕

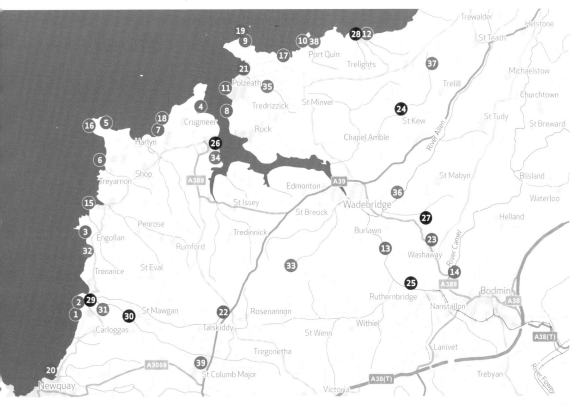

TINTAGEL & BUDE

Our perfect weekend

→ **Swim** at secluded Bossiney Haven, then head off to Tintagel to refuel with a sensational Pengenna pasty.

→ **Follow** the stream down through Rocky Valley, looking out for the ruined mill and Bronze Age labyrinth carvings.

→ **Marvel at** the twisted shapes of ancient oaks on the high cliffs of Dizzard, or the spectacular folded rocks at Millook Haven.

→ **Bathe** in the holy pool, St Nectan's Kieve, fed by a spectacular double waterfall, and climb up to the hermitage for tea.

→ **Sea kayak** from Boscastle to Pentargon looking for peregrine falcons and a spooky, bat-filled sea cave.

→ **Enjoy** Helsett's home-made, organic ice cream in Boscastle then set off to watch grey seals at Seals' Hole.

→ **Explore** the great mineral stacks in the old quarries on Treknow Cliff.

→ **Surf** with the sunset at Crackington Haven and jump in the deep Mermaid Pool.

→ **Camp wild** at Strangles Beach before the light fades, and admire the huge rock arch hidden under Cornwall's highest cliff.

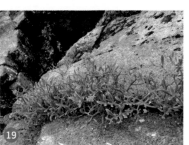

This stunning and dramatic coast is steeped in myth. Here lie the ruins of 13th-century Tintagel castle, the legendary birthplace of King Arthur, who was protected and tutored in the ways of magic by the wizard, Merlin, in the spectacular sea caverns beneath the headland.

You can still explore the caves under Tintagel castle. Clambering through with torches, feeling and touching your way over slippery dark rocks and exiting via a narrow chamber into the opposite cove, feels like you've just emerged from the underworld.

The sloping rocks of Tintagel Haven make great platforms for a swim in the crystal-clear sea. From here, a dramatic mile-long coast walk leads eastwards towards narrow Bossiney Haven, hidden among the cliffs and featuring a rock arch shaped like an elephant's trunk. It offers a great sweep of low-tide sand and secluded rocks for sunbathing. Another mile, and you're at Rocky Valley where waterfalls and giant plunge pools drop down into the sea. In this atmospheric valley, you can explore the 200-year-old ruins of a mill, or go back even further in time and gaze in wonder at the sacred labyrinths on the rock face, carved about 3,500 years ago.

Further upstream, King Arthur is said to have baptised his knights at St Nectan's Kieve before they embarked on their quest for the Holy Grail. This sacred pool, part of an extraordinary double waterfall, was the home of one of the holiest Cornish saints, St Nectan, who lived in the hermitage around AD 480. The flow of the water has sculpted a deep cylindrical well and a perfect man-sized hole through which the water spills.

At Millook Haven, the cliffs are contorted with dramatic zig-zag fault lines and as you head further south along the cliffs, you might find some tasty rock samphire near the appropriately named Samphire Rock. This stretch of coast is a haven for wildlife and at Beeny Cliff, beyond Boscastle, there is a good chance of spotting the world's fastest creature, the peregrine falcon, as it dives for prey. A little further on, and you are at Buckator, home to a huge colony of grey seals, which hauled themselves out on the rocks.

SECRET BEACHES

1 TREGARDOCK BEACH, TREBARWITH
Truly wild beach, with long stretch of sand,
but some rocks and rip currents in swells.
→ 2 miles S of Trebarwith on coast path.
Or turn R off B3314, 2 miles S of Delabole,
signed Treligga, then 15 mins walk (difficult
parking). Good cafés, surfing and sea caves at
Trebarwith.
20 mins, 50.6239, -4.7722

2 BOSSINEY HAVEN, TINTAGEL
Beautiful cove under dramatic cliffs with
small rock arch (Elephant Rock). When the
tide recedes, a long arc of sand is revealed,
linking to adjoining Benoath Cove. Good
snorkelling to the far left of the beach, but
the whole beach is N facing.
→ 1 mile E of Tintagel on B3263, park on L by
campsite and transmitter. Cross field 400m
to find coast path and steep steps to cove. Or
continue 700m down road, park by junction on
R and start with Rocky Valley stream walk.
20 mins, 50.6722, -4.7380

3 STRANGLES BEACH, CRACKINGTON
Ultimate wild beach under high cliffs, 30
mins S of Crackington Haven on coast path.

There are zig-zag rock formations and the
Northern Door, a huge rock arch. Strong rip
currents in high swell. Also High Cliff (see 9).
→ Park in small layby and find footpath 50m
S of Trevigue Farm, on coast lane S out of
Crackington. Explore at low tide only.
30 mins, 50.7287, -4.6520

4 MERMAID POOL, CRACKINGTON HAVEN
Crackington is a popular beach cove with
pub (Coombe Barton Inn, 01840 230345),
lifeguards and surfing. It has great sunsets.
At low tide follow rocks on R of bay 300m to
the deep inlets of Mermaid Pool for jumping.
→ Off A39, 8 miles S of Bude.
10 mins, 50.7416, -4.6340

5 MILLOOK HAVEN, WIDEMOUTH
Extraordinary fault lines in cliffs at this
pebble cove.
→ Small hamlet in valley bottom, on narrow
steep lanes 1½ miles S of Widemouth Bay,
signed Millook.
5 mins, 50.7726, -4.5766

WATERFALLS

6 PENTARGON WATERFALL, CAVES, SEALS
Dramatic waterfall tumbles 120 feet off
cliff into black chert (silica) rock inlet. Only
accessible by boat/kayak, from Boscastle
harbour (see 15). Head 500M N for Seals'
Hole and Beeny Cliff, with one of the largest
colonies of seals in Cornwall.
→ Follow coast path 1½ miles E of Boscastle,
or from B3263 hill 500m E of Boscastle (small
layby parking just beyond footpath sign).
15 mins, 50.6967, -4.6798

7 ROCKY VALLEY LABYRINTHS, TINTAGEL
Pretty stream path leading down to the sea.
Waterfall pools at the bottom are good for a
dip. Look out for the ruins of Trewethett Mill
with old millstones in the undergrowth. On
rock face behind are two beautiful carvings
of labyrinths, possibly 3,500 years old.
→ Park on B3263, just E of Bossiney, at layby by
turn off to Halgabron. Find footpath opposite.
20 mins, 50.6740, -4.7299

8 ST NECTAN'S KIEVE, TINTAGEL
At the head of a wild glen a tall, slender
waterfall falls into a high basin, flows
through a circular hole and drops into a

plunge pool (the kieve). This is a holy place with prayer flags, a shrine room above and lots of steps. Small tea room in hermitage. Entrance fee. The stream flows down into the Rocky Valley.

→ Find track with postbox, opposite telephone box, off B3263, in Trethevey, 2 miles E of Tintagel. Bear R and follow it for 1 mile, past St Piran's Well, down into the woods, and up along the pretty stream, finally climbing the steps up to the shrine entrance.
20 mins, 50.6644, -4.7168 🖼️🚶🏠🛏️🚻☕

SUNSET HILLTOPS

9 HIGH CLIFF, CRACKINGTON

This is the highest point on the Cornish coast, with unobstructed views W. A great place to see the famous 'green flash' before sunset; also look out for peregrine falcons.

→ 1 mile further S along coast path from Crackington find Strangles beach (see 3). Or take short cut across field from lane, opposite hamlet of Pengold.
20 mins, 50.7193, -4.6490 🖼️➡️🚶

10 LADIES WINDOW, TREVALGA

Natural rock arch creating a W-facing window. Also a good place to see puffins.

→ Just off the coast path beneath the pretty village of Trevalga, between Tintagel and Boscastle.
10 mins, 50.6850, -4.7214 🖼️

11 WARBSTOW BURY HILLFORT

At the second largest, and best preserved, Iron Age hill fort in Cornwall, you're unlikely to meet a soul. There is a barrow with several earth fortification rings, and the grave of the Warbstow Giant. Far reaching views W across open countryside to the sea.

→ Parking just outside Warbstow Cross, 3 miles E of A39, on lane via Otterham and Trelash.
10 mins, 50.6886, -4.5477 🖼️🏔️

RUINS AND CAVERNS

12 TREKNOW CLIFF & HOLE BEACH

Between Tintagel and Trebarwith, around Penhallic Point, huge sections of cliff have been quarried for slate. The most impressive section is behind Hole Beach at Treknow cliff, particularly Lanterdan quarry where a 60-foot pinnacle was left standing by miners. Many smaller stacks further towards Trebarwith and you might find the old adit (horizontal shaft) with stalactites. In places

you can follow a precarious goat track down into the quarries, and to Hole Beach below. A safer access route is from Trebarwth at low tide. If you make it to Hole Beach there is good snorkelling on the N side, and line fishing for sea bass . For a more relaxed mine visit, try Prince of Wales quarry with waterfall and beam engine, signed from the B3314 at Delabole (50.6435, -4.7298).

→ 1 mile S of Tintagel, via Treknow, or from Trebarwith at low tide.
20 mins, 50.6525, -4.7596 🖼️🚲🚻🔲🔽

13 MERLIN'S CAVERN, TINTAGEL CASTLE

Huge double-ended sea cavern runs right under the saddle of land that connects to Tintagel Castle. Take a torch and go at low tide. There are also caves opposite and good swimming from the rocks in calm conditions.

→ Climb down on to Haven beach, cavern is to R as you approach the castle.

10 mins, 50.6680, -4.7591 🏊🐚📷

14 PENHALLAM MANOR, WEEK ST MARY

Grass-covered foundations of a moated 13th- century manor house, in a delightful and remote woodland setting.

→ From A39 at Treskinnick Cross (between Bude and Camelford) follow lanes to Week St Mary, and then signs to Penhallam on R.

20 mins, 50.7485, -4.5190 📖🚶

15 SEA CAVES BY KAYAK

Between Boscastle and Pentargon there are fantastic caves, including a 50m-long sea-cave tunnel, about 800m before the falls on the tip of an inlet (50.6954, -4.6908). There is also a huge sea cavern under Glebe Cliff between Tintagel and Penhallic Point (50.6618, -4.7637) and good sea stacks beneath Trevalga (50.6834, -4.7274).

→ You can hire kayaks at Camel Canoe and Kayak (Rock, 07791 533569), Crooklets Beach (Bude, EX23 8NE, 01288 354039, 0780 5288689) and Atlantic Pursuits (Bude, 01288 321765, 07974 718145).

50.8325, -4.5550 🏊🐚▽⛰

FOREST AND WILDLIFE

16 TAMAR OTTER & WILDLIFE SANCTUARY

Otters are very cute, but nocturnal and shy in the wild, so this might be your only option to get up close. They are fed from 12pm–3pm and you can see them playing in-between times. There are wallabies and muntjac deer too, plus owls and peacocks.

→ North Petherwin, Launceston, PL15 8GW, 01566 785646, 4 miles NW of Launceston off the B3254 to Bude.

3 mins, 50.6789, -4.4251 🚗

17 PEREGRINE FALCONS & SEALS, BEENY

There are more than 20 breeding pairs of peregrine falcons along the coast from Bude to Padstow. Reaching speeds of more than 200 mph during their 'hunting stoop' (high-speed dive), these are the fastest creatures on the planet. Beeny Cliff is a good place to start looking. Buckator cove at Beeny has

the largest grey-seal colony on the North Cornish coast and is one of the four key sea "haul out" sites in the Southwest (alongside Lundy, Godrevy and the Scilly Isles). One of the world's rarest seal species, the grey seal is the biggest land-breeding mammal in the UK. Most seal pups are born from autumn to early winter, when numbers swell.

→ 1 mile N of Beeny on coast path, off B326?, E of Boscastle.

20 mins, 50.7102, -4.6665 🐾

18 DIZZARD ANCIENT WOODS

Enchanting area of wind-sculpted, oak woodland on steep cliffside.

→ 1 mile S of Millook Haven on coast path, or 2 miles N of Crackington Haven.

20 mins, 50.7626, -4.6005 🌳

19 SAMPHIRE ROCK, STRANGLES

Rock samphire, a popular wild food since Celtic times. In Elizabethan times, children were apparently dangled over the cliffs, with ropes tied around their ankles, to pick the rock samphire that grew in crevices and clefts. It was either eaten fresh or pickled in vinegar. You might be lucky and find some growing on the rock at ground level but only break off as much as you need and always leave the roots intact.

→ At the N end of Strangles beach (see 3).

50.7287, -4.6520 🏖📷

LOCAL FOOD

20 BANGORS ORGANIC

Small, homely restaurant on an organic small holding. Seasonal menu based on garden produce and food from local suppliers.

→ Bangors House, Poundstock, Bude, EX23 0DP, 01288 361297

50.7672, -4.5417

21 CABIN CAFÉ, CRACKINGTON HAVEN

Family-run café with home-made cakes, and pasties made with Cornish beef from the next-door farm's cattle.

→ St Gennys, EX23 0JG, 01840 230238

50.7408, -4.6327

22 ANDREA'S FARM SHOP, DIZZARD

Andrea is the head baker for the Cabin Café down in the Haven. Up at Dizzard, she sells their Red Ruby beef and Zwartble lamb.

→ On the coast road between Crackington and Widemouth Bay. Dizzard Farm, Bude, EX23 0NX, 01840 230238.

50.7569, -4.5984

23 TREVIGUE FARM, CRACKINGTON
Farm restaurant serving home-reared meat and garden produce in season. Open Thursdays, Fridays and Saturdays. Near Strangles beach and High Cliff.
→ Trevigue, EX23 0LQ, 01840 230418
50.7264, -4.6418

24 HELSETT ICE CREAM, BOSCASTLE
Try this delicious, award-winning organic ice cream from the wooden hut at Boscastle Harbour. You can also stay in the converted barn on the farm.
→ Helsett Farm, Lesnewth, Boscastle, PL35 0HP, 01840 261207
50.6834, -4.6336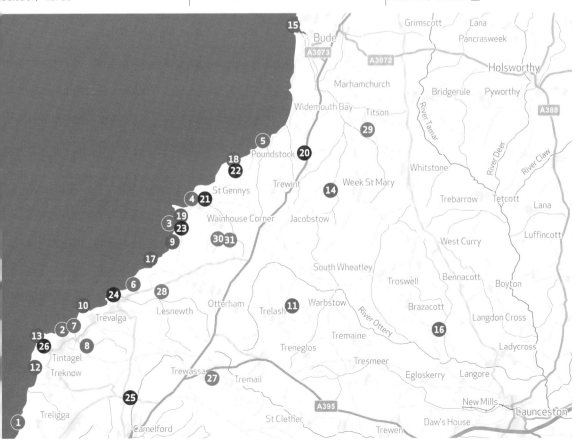

25 HILLTOP FARM, SLAUGHTERBRIDGE
Handpicked, locally sourced groceries and a lovely tea shop. Light lunches cooked by the owner using local produce.
→ Camelford, PL32 9TT, 01840 211518
50.6387, -4.6793

26 PENGENNA PASTIES, TINTAGEL
Watch the pasties being made then get take-aways, fresh from the oven, for your picnic.
→ Tintagel, PL34 0DD, 01840 770223
50.6643, -4.7534

CAMP AND STAY

27 BELLE TENTS, DAVIDSTOW
Beautiful collection of hand-made circus and bell tents on the side of a shallow valley surrounded by open farmland and Bodmin Moor. Ponies, chickens and rare-breed cattle.
→ Owls Gate, Davidstow, Camelford, PL32 9XY, 01840 261556
50.6500, -4.6122

28 THE OLD RECTORY, BOSCASTLE
Lovely B&B with walled kitchen garden offering fruit, vegetables and eggs for sale all year round. Pigs, sheep and bees.
→ PL35 0BT, 01840 250225
50.6936, -4.6562

29 ANNIE'S WAGON, MARHAMCHURCH
An original 1940s wagon, full of mahogany charm, sitting in rolling pastures just a few miles from the coast.
→ Canopyandstars.co.uk. Lower Bakesdown Farm, Nr Bude, EX23 0HJ, 01275 395447
50.7802, -4.4901

30 WOODA FARM, CRACKINGTON HAVEN
Artist's retreat cottage hidden in 20 acres of south-facing organic meadow, with woods full of bluebells in spring. Pick your own vegetables from Wooda's kitchen garden.
→ Bude, EX23 0LF, 01840 230140
50.7217, -4.6089

31 PENCUKE FARM, CRACKINGTON HAVEN
Self-catering farm cottages and upmarket yurts with a lovely farm shop selling an array of local breads, home-baked treats and meats from the farm.
→ St Gennys, EX23 0BH, 01840 230360
50.7212, -4.6021

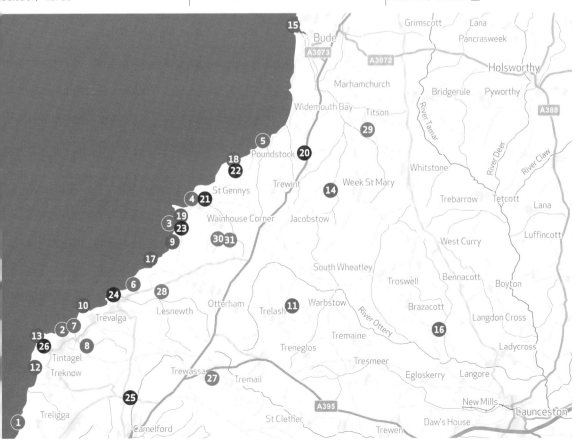

BODMIN MOOR

Our perfect weekend

→ **Explore** stone circles high on the moor around Minions, and take a dip in one of the crystal-clear swimming lakes.

→ **Go on horseback** across the moor to discover some of its most remote places.

→ **Spook** yourself by imagining the macabre scenes that took place in the galleries and execution pit at Bodmin jail.

→ **Search** for the Jubilee Rock, then sample local ales at the lovely Blisland Inn.

→ **Climb** Roughtor and watch the sun go down over one of the few really wild landscapes left in England.

→ **Wild camp** near King Arthur's Hall, an ancient ceremonial enclosure deep in the heart of Bodmin Moor.

→ **Discover** St Clether's lovely chapel and holy well and stop for lunch at the nearby Rising Sun.

→ **Treat yourself** to home-made scones at Woods Café, after a walk in the forest.

→ **Watch for** otters and kingfishers in Golitha woods, then take a plunge in the magical lower pool.

→ **Camp** on South Penquite Farm and grill some home-reared moorland lamb for supper.

Bodmin Moor, first farmed by Bronze Age settlers over 4,000 years ago, is now one of the country's last truly wild areas. Visit the mysterious standing stones or walk through its tranquil woods and leave urban life far behind.

Much of the moor's prehistoric and medieval past has remained untouched by the march of time, and the whole area is richly endowed with stone circles, burial chambers and mysterious ceremonial structures. While the Hurlers and Cheesewring are fairly well known, there are other impressive but rarely-visited stones, such as those near Roughtor and Carbilly.

Arthurian legends shroud many of these sites. The large, rectangular King Arthur's Hall, in the wildest part of the moor, has steep earthen banks that were once topped with over one hundred standing stones. Far too elaborate for a cattle shelter, the structure's true purpose is unknown. Out on Kilmar Tor, there is further evidence of the mythical king in the form of a massive stone with a coffin-sized depression, known as King Arthur's Bed.

Those who love peaceful woods and babbling streams can follow the Fowey from the edge of Bodmin Moor at Golitha Falls. Here it drops in cascades down through dense, sessile-oak woodland. There are lush, aromatic glens and the trees are draped with rare ferns, mosses and ivy. Wagtails criss-cross the stream and a small, hidden pool opens up a few hundred yards below. On a hot summer's day, the yellow sand of the stream bed throws a golden light on the rocks and creates a magical place to take a dip.

Further downstream, the trackways of Cabilla and Redrice Woods, Cornwall's largest tract of ancient woodland, remain unchanged since the 16th century. The woods support a host of wild creatures, from otters living among the underwater tree roots, to bats, which sleep in the old mine workings.

The moorland lakes, relics of Bodmin's more recent quarrying and mining history, are wonderful places to swim. At Goldiggins, St Breward and Carbilly you can take a dip in these dramatic, freshwater hollows. Once the source of stone for great structures such as London's Tower Bridge, these deep quarries, set in stunning landscapes, now lie silent.

Fans of caves may enjoy Carnglaze caverns but those who climb the various wind-sculpted tors – Roughtor, the Cheesewring and Kilmar are three of the best – will be rewarded with breathtaking views over the lofty expanse of moorland, the perfect place to camp wild and watch the sun set.

1 DELFORD BRIDGE, DE LANK

Pretty moorland stream and bridge with a nice shallow, sandy pool for children. Not far off the A30.

→ On lanes 2 miles N of Blisland (follow cycle route signs and pass South Penquite Farm). Or turn R off A30 3 miles SW of Jamaica Inn just as dual carriageway ends, opp turning for Temple), continue past Bradford and turn next R.

2 mins, 50.5524, -4.6632

2 CARBILLY POOLS & STONE CIRCLE

Three deep, spring-fed quarry pools among tors and ruins. The impressive but rarely-visited Trippet Stones circle is 500m to the SE, on track to Hawk's Tor farm (50.5448, -4.6395).

→ From A30, as for Delford Bridge but after 1 ½ miles find gate on R with track onto access land. You'll see the tors and chimney up on the R, 300m.

5 mins, 50.5492, -4.6460

3 TOR DOWN QUARRY, ST BREWARD

This quarry once employed 80 people and supplied the building blocks for the notorious Bodmin jail (see 16) as well as the major Thames bridges in London. The pits have long since filled up with pure spring water and you can swim below their sheer cliff walls. REPORTED CLOSED / PRIVATE.

→ Follow footpath from main street in St Breward, 50 m before /S of the school on L.

3 mins, 50.5590, -4.6920

4 COLLIFORD LAKE

A huge moorland reservoir, the highest and largest in Cornwall. Open access on the W side with chalky, shelving beaches. Lots of bird life: dippers, wagtails and sand martins. Sunny, but windy. NO SWIMMING SIGNS.

→ Signed Colliford Lake Park/Warleggan, off A30, 2 miles SW of Jamaica Inn. Then continue ½ mile beyond the Lake Park.

2 mins, 50.5202, -4.5918

5 GOLITHA FALLS, REDGATE

Here, the young river Fowey flows through ancient oak and beech woodland. Small beaches before the river cascades down over boulders and several falls to form a small plunge pool with golden sand. Good bluebells in spring. King Doniert's inscribed stone is in an enclosure just off the roadside ½ mile back towards St Cleer (50.49283, -4.49128).

→ 2 ½ miles W of Minions, then R at Redgate (signed Draynes/Golitha). Follow the path for 10 mins to top of cascades. Find a rough track which continues 200m down, beyond the mine ruins, to the shady secret pool at bottom. Slippery rocks!

15 mins, 50.4907, -4.5071

6 GOLDIGGINS QUARRY, MINIONS

A secret, spring-fed quarry lake, out on the open moors but hidden in a small grassy amphitheatre. Flat rock ledges for jumping.

→ From the Hurlers car park follow the vehicle track which heads N onto the moor, past the stone circle. After 15 mins bear L at the junction and continue another ½ mile to find the quarry.

25 mins, 50.5248, -4.4711

7 THE PONY POOL, MINIONS

Beachy areas and gently shelving shallows make this small, sheltered lake perfect for kids. There's even a waterfall.

→ Follow as for Goldiggins but bear R at the junction. After the stream (about 300m) turn R off the track to find the lake and dam on the stream valley above.

20 mins, 50.5223, -4.4629

8 LAVETHAN WOOD, BLISLAND

Small, deciduous wood with stream on the edge of this pretty village with a fine church. Mosses and ferns convey a primeval feel.

➜ 300m SE of Blisland. Follow the lane past the church.

5 mins, 50.5255, -4.6759

9 CABILLA AND REDRICE WOODS

One of the largest ancient woodlands in the county, along secluded banks of the Fowey in the Glyn Valley. The network of paths has remained largely unchanged from maps dating back to 1602. Look out for the rare, nocturnal, blue ground beetle, five species of bat and the elusive dormouse.

➜ 1 mile E of Bodmin Parkway station (A38) turn L signed Cardinham. Entrance on R after 300m.

5 mins, 50.4573, -4.6375

SUNSET HILLTOPS

10 KILMAR TOR & KING ARTHUR'S BED

Wonderfully remote and evocative tor stack, set at an angle. To N is King Arthur's Bed, a man-shaped, coffin-like depression worn into the stone. It's so large you can actually lie inside it and even have a snooze! Also, a derelict quarry with crane and chambered long cairn en route.

➜ Find junction with track on L, ½ mile N of Henwood. Walk 15 mins to Bearah Tor and quarry ruins (50.5440, -4.4574). Another 15 mins leads up on to Kilmar Tor (50.5475, -4.4689). Head 20 mins NW from here to Trewortha Tor and King Arthur's Bed is on its W end (50.5545, -4.4854).

40 mins, 50.5475, -4.4689

11 CHEESEWRING, STOWE'S HILL

Spectacular columns of weathered granite seem to form into strange shapes, including a nose and face. Pony Pool, good for a dip, is immediately below. On the route up, close to quarry fence, look out for a cave shelter, home to stone-cutter and mathematician Daniel Gumb, who lived here until his death in 1776. Some of his geometric diagrams are chiselled into the top of the granite slab that forms the roof (50.5246, -4.4599).

➜ Approached along the track (old Kilmar stone tramway) from heritage centre (NE) car park in Minions village. Visible from the Hurlers stone circle.

20 mins, 50.5258, -4.4596

11

12 ROUGHTOR, CAMELFORD

One of the most satisfying tors on Bodmin and an easy climb with great views. Interesting, stacked stone formations and you can extend the walk on to Brown Willy (60 mins) via various hut circles. Impressive but rarely visited Stannon stone circle is on lanes 2 miles to the S via Highertown (50.5897, -4.6493).

→ From Camelford, A39 direction Bude, turn R 500m from town centre, signed Tregoodwell. Continue 2 miles up hill to road end.
20 mins, 50.5974, -4.6217 🏞️🏕️

13 JUBILEE ROCK, BLISLAND

Huge ornamented boulder in the middle of heathland with wonderful views W. First inscribed in 1810 by Lt. John Rogers to celebrate the golden jubilee of George III. You can see a figure of Britannia, a beehive, a ship, a plough and the Cornish Arms. Recently updated for Elizabeth II's jubilee in 2012. Tricky to find, but there are lots of ponies to keep you company on your search.

→ ½ mile N of Blisland (signed St Breward, also a marked cycle route), at the hill brow and junction, find path on to moor L. Head along hill crest 300m then bear L down the hillside 200m.
15 mins, 50.5384, -4.6776 🚴🏞️🏕️

RUINS AND CAVERNS

14 CARNGLAZE CAVERNS, ST NEOT

Three cathedral-sized caverns, hand-dug by slate miners. You can wander around by yourself and descend to the subterranean lake with its crystal-clear, aquamarine water. Regular music concerts are also held inside. Entrance fee.

→ On road to St Neot, signed off A30, 4 miles W of Liskeard. PL14 6HQ, 01579 320251.
5 mins, 50.4730, -4.5558 📷

15 PHOENIX UNITED MINE, MINIONS

Remains of the failed tin-mining venture of 1907, with the engine house over the Prince of Wales shaft taking centre stage. Adjoining are the ruins of the boiler house, winding-engine house and compressor house.

→ Park at the heritage centre car park in Minions and take the lane (signed Henwood) for 500m to find track bearing off to R.
15 mins, 50.5223, -4.4476 🏞️

16 BODMIN JAIL

Overgrown, five-storey jailhouse ruin with resident ghosts – 48 hangings took place here. The main building and galleries are roofless. Exhibits include the only working execution pit in the UK. Best visited on a misty day to increase the sense of foreboding.

→ Bodmin Jail, Berrycoombe Road, Bodmin, PL31 2NR, 01208 76292. Open 10am until dusk. All funds go to renovation. Good restaurant.
2 mins, 50.4741, -4.7268 🍴🏞️

SACRED AND ANCIENT

17 ST CLETHER'S WELL

Remote stone chapel and holy well by the side of the river Inny. Reached by walking ½ mile up valley behind the village, with gorse in bloom and carpets of wild daffodils in spring. If you like holy wells, St Breward (on the W of the moor) also has a charming and secluded structure (50.5607, -4.6972).

→ Follow the track behind St Clether church, signed off A395, W of Kennards House.
15 mins, 50.6325, -4.5433

18 KING ARTHUR'S HALL

A large Bronze Age rectangular enclosure, with steep earthen banks, lined with 56 standing stones (there may once have been up to 140). Many suggestions have been made for its origin and function, including a

Neolithic mortuary, a Bronze Age ceremonial site and a medieval animal pound. Set in the wild moorland of King Arthur's Downs.
→ 1 mile E of Churchtown (St Breward) find a R turning signed Casehill/Candra. Park at the road end and follow footpath ½ mile E.
15 mins, 50.5686, -4.6425

19 TEMPLE CHURCH
A tiny, remote 12th-century church, built by the Knights Templar as a refuge for pilgrims and travellers en route to the Holy Land.
→ Signed off A30, 2 miles SW of Jamaica Inn
3 mins, 50.5296, -4.6172

20 HURLERS STONE CIRCLE, MINIONS
Famous and impressive circle with far-reaching views. Close to the Cheesewring, Goldiggins lake, Pony Pool, Phoenix United mine ruins and Daniel Gumb's cave. There are other good circles – with far fewer visitors – near Carbilly (Trippet) and Roughtor (Stannon).
→ 300m from the Hurlers' car park in Minions, off the B3254, N of Liskeard.
5 mins, 50.5166, -4.4583

WILDLIFE WONDERS

21 MOORLAND HORSE RIDING
Bodmin Moor, with its open spaces, tors and scenic ruins, is one of the best places in the South West to explore on horseback.
→ Hallagenna Riding Stables, St. Breward, Bodmin, PL30 4NS, 01208 851500. From 1hr pony rides, suitable for children, to full-day treks far out onto the moor, including lunch.
60 mins, 50.5605, -4.6769

22 CROWDY STARLINGS, DAVIDSTOW
Watch thousands of winter starlings make amazing patterns as they roost at dusk over Crowdy reservoir.
→ From Camelford as for Rough Tor, but turn L, signed Davidstow, to find reservoir on R.
5 mins, 50.6203, -4.6319

EAT LOCAL

23 THE BLISLAND INN
Popular hostelry with real ales and no-nonsense pub food in this charming village on the edge of the moor. Good place to stop for lunch when visiting Jubilee Stone and Lavethan Wood.
→ Blisland, Bodmin, PL30 4JY, 01208 850739
50.5280, -4.6817

24 WOODS CAFE, CARDINHAM
Wood-smoke, scones and cake baked fresh every morning. Warming winter stews and sausages from Dave's pigs, reared just up the lane. Good value, daytime opening, cash only. Then walk up to Lady Vale bridge where kids can play by the stream.
→ Cardinham Woods, Bodmin, PL30 4AL, 01208 78111
50.4694, -4.6796

25 BODMIN MARKET, MOUNT FOLLY
On the first and third Thursday of every month, head to Bodmin to sample local produce – fresh and unpretentious.
→ Mount Folly, Bodmin, PL31 2DB
50.4707, -4.7184

26 COWSLIP CAFÉ, LAUNCESTON
Small traditional farm with craft workshops and a local-produce café serving light lunches, cream teas and home-made cakes. Wonderful views over stunning landscape.
→ Cowslip Workshops, Newhouse Farm, St Stephens, Launceston, PL15 8JX, 01566 772654
50.6454, -4.3858

27 RISING SUN INN, ALTARNUN
Good, locally sourced, seasonal food. Real ales brewed in Penpont Brewery down the lane. Near St Clether's well.
→ Altarnun, PL15 7SN, 01566 86636
50.6146, -4.5226

28 CROWS NEST INN, DARITE
Cosy old pub with good food, near the Hurlers and Golitha Falls.

Darite, Liskeard, PL14 5JQ, 01579 345930
).4982, -4.4495

9 THE OLD INN, ST BREWARD

rnwall's highest pub, offering real ales and
earty, home-made pies. Roaring fires in the
inter months.
→ St Breward Churchtown, Bodmin, PL30 4PP,
1208 850711
).5643, -4.6885 ⏹

0 CORNISH CHEESE COMPANY

ward-winning, delicious blue cheese, made
n the farm and suitable for vegetarians.
→ Cheesewring; Knowle Farm, Upton Cross,
_14 5BG, 01579 363660
).5278, -4.4412

SLEEP WILD

31 EKOPOD, ST CLETHER

Two large pods perched on the edge of
Bodmin Moor in secluded wildflower
meadows. Beautiful views around the Inny
valley. A hamper awaits you on arrival and
there's an honesty shop.
→ The Old Vicarage, St Clether, Launceston,
PL15 8QJ, 01275 395447
50.6297,-4.5356

32 TREGILLIS FARM, SOUTH PETHERWIN

Ditch your car and walk through the
biodynamic farm to get to this lovely
camping field by the river Inny. Bell tents and
campfires.
→ Tregillis Farm, South Petherwin,
Launceston, PL15 7LL, 01566 782418
50.6068, -4.4066 ◭◭

33 SOUTH PENQUITE FARM, BLISLAND

Small wild campsite on an organic farm
in the heart of Bodmin Moor. Buy home-
made lamb burgers or mutton sausages for
your campfire, or stay in one of four yurts,
equipped with futons and woodburners.
→ South Penquite, Blisland, PL30 4LH, 01208
850491
50.5463,-4.6764 ◭◭

34 YURT WORKS, ST BREWARD

Yurts, log fires and big open skies on the
edge of Bodmin Moor. Unspoilt natural
heathland sprinkled with blue bells and wood
anemones in spring; tormentil and rosebay
willow herb in summer.
→ Greyhayes, St Breward, Bodmin, PL30 4LP,
01208 850670
50.5597, -4.6920

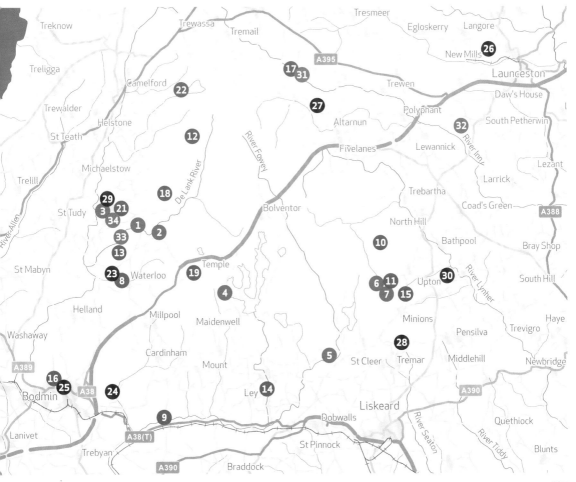

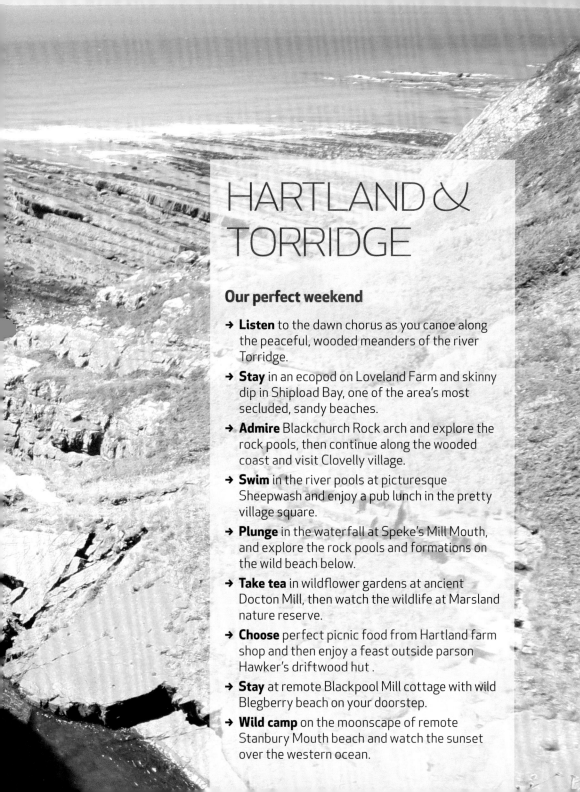

HARTLAND & TORRIDGE

Our perfect weekend

→ **Listen** to the dawn chorus as you canoe along the peaceful, wooded meanders of the river Torridge.

→ **Stay** in an ecopod on Loveland Farm and skinny dip in Shipload Bay, one of the area's most secluded, sandy beaches.

→ **Admire** Blackchurch Rock arch and explore the rock pools, then continue along the wooded coast and visit Clovelly village.

→ **Swim** in the river pools at picturesque Sheepwash and enjoy a pub lunch in the pretty village square.

→ **Plunge** in the waterfall at Speke's Mill Mouth, and explore the rock pools and formations on the wild beach below.

→ **Take tea** in wildflower gardens at ancient Docton Mill, then watch the wildlife at Marsland nature reserve.

→ **Choose** perfect picnic food from Hartland farm shop and then enjoy a feast outside parson Hawker's driftwood hut .

→ **Stay** at remote Blackpool Mill cottage with wild Blegberry beach on your doorstep.

→ **Wild camp** on the moonscape of remote Stanbury Mouth beach and watch the sunset over the western ocean.

On Hartland's dramatic shoreline, waterfalls tumble down sheer rock faces and the cliffs are contorted into remarkable folds and pinnacles. Formed when Earth's tectonic plates collided some 320 million years ago the scenery here is wild and breathtakingly beautiful.

One of the best places to view the cliffs and ocean is the lone pub and hote at Hartland Quay, once a large, busy port that was devastated by violent storms. After a pint of Wreckers ale, visit the Shipwreck Museum to read accounts of ships being lured on to the rocks.

Just over the Devon border in Cornwall's Morwenstow, the eccentric pasto Robert Hawker was the self-appointed guardian of those drowned on the Hartland coast. Celebrated for scribing the Cornish anthem *Trelawney* and for wearing a seaweed wig, Hawker built a lookout on the cliff made entire of wood salvaged from the shore. In 1842, when the *Caledonia* was wrecke on rocks at Morwenstow, Hawker buried the bodies of the dead and rescued the ship's figurehead – a Scottish girl armed with a cutlass – which now stands in the graveyard of Morwenstow church.

Remains of the Caledonia can still be seen at remote Stanbury Mouth beach, a great, grey moonscape of folded rock and silvery sand and probably the most remote beach in the area. Speke's Mill Mouth has a similar feel, but with the added attraction of the South West's highest waterfall cascading down the cliffs via plunge pools. Here, sand drifts between long fingers of rock and there are rock pools to explore at low tid – a perfect picnic spot.

Shipload Bay, just to the east of Hartland Point, is another wrecking and smuggling site, but the people along this coast also fished for a living and the tiny fishing village of Buck's Mills has a truly timeless feel. For the freshest fish, head along the coast to Clovelly and eat at the harbourside Red Lion, or buy your own for barbecuing later.

Inland, the Torridge and Taw rivers meander gently through gentle hills and woodland valleys. This is Tarka country and the otter population is almost back to its pre-1950 levels, thanks to the much-improved river wate quality. At Halsdon nature reserve you may see white-legged damselflies, kingfishers, sand martins, herons, dippers and grey wagtails. There are even freshwater pearl mussels. Bathing in the rivers and streams of Devon's rolling landscape was one of Tarka author Henry Williamson's greatest pleasures. The horrors of World War I had taken their toll and he took a long time to recuperate, but in this unique and beautiful region, Williamson could finally feel 'a part of the great stream of life'.

SECRET BEACHES

WELCOMBE MOUTH, WELCOMBE

Popular locals beach. Great rock pools and sandy strips of beach at low tide. Waterfall and pools at N end of beach.

→ After Welcombe (signed from A39) bear L then R on lanes, following course of stream. Take the rough narrow track which leads down to parking area. Also Marsland glades (see 17).
2 mins, 50.9338, -4.5444

SANDY MOUTH, STIBB

Perfect family beach at end of a little lane. NT café, rock pools and lifeguards.

→ Turn L off A39 4 miles N of Bude/Stratton (signed Stibb /Coombe). After Stibb bear L for Sandy Mouth.
2 mins, 50.8613, -4.5570

BUCK'S MILLS

Tiny, unspoilt fishing village with beach, sandy 'gut', waterfall and limekiln. Cream teas at Buck's Cross church, June to August.

→ 6 miles W of Bideford (A39) turn R 300m before Hoops Inn (01237 451222).
10 mins, 50.9895, -4.3465

4 BLEGBERRY BEACH, HARTLAND QUAY

Wonderful west-facing beach, with huge round boulders at high tide and sandy patches at low tide. Just to the S is another smaller cove in front of Blackpool Mill cottage (see 32).

→ Walk a mile N on coast path from Hartland Quay hotel, or take the pretty path along the enchanted stream valley from Stoke church.
15 mins, 51.0049, -4.5302

5 BLACKCHURCH ROCK ARCH

Dramatic triangular rock arch, ruined limekilns and lots of rock pools. Pretty walk through Brownham Woods, carpeted with wild flowers in spring.

→ From A39 turn R off B3248 (signed Hartland Point) then first R (signed Brownsham) and find car park at road end. Turn R through farm, down through the woods for 15 mins, then bear L, keeping stream to R for 15 mins, to reach Blackchurch Rock.
30 mins, 51.0142, -4.4271

6 DUCKPOOL, COOMBE

Dramatic rocky beach with low-tide sand and rock pools with giant crabs. There's also a freshwater pool and lovely stream with grassy banks. A little way upstream (via Stow Mill) is a streamside path through NT Lee Woods (50.8769, -4.5371).

→ Turn L off A39 4 miles N of Bude/Stratton), (signed Stibb/Coombe). After Stibb bear R for Coombe, then first L to Duckpool.
2 mins, 50.8761, -4.5576

7 PEPPERCOMBE & PORTLEDGE BEACH

Remote shingle and sand beach with waterfall and ancient woodland paths all around. Portledge beach stretches to E, Buck's Mills is to W.

→ 4 miles W of Bideford A39, at Horn's Corner, park by Coach and Horses (01237 451214). Walk N down lane, and bear R on footpath/ private road to beach, 1 mile.
25 mins, 50.9950, -4.3073

8 STANBURY MOUTH, MORWENSTOW

A wild, remote and rocky beach with some sand at low tide.

→ On the coast path 30 mins S of Morwenstow or N of Duckpool. Or drive 1 mile N of Duckpool and it is signed on L (No Through Road), with small car park at end of lane.
10 mins, 50.8918, -4.5612

9 SPEKE'S MILL MOUTH, HARTLAND QUAY

A dramatic waterfall, with a deep plunge pool on its lip, tips down on to a magnificent bay with strips of sand and large low-tide pools.

→ On coast path 1 mile S of Hartland Quay, or a very pretty walk from Docton Mill Tea Gardens (see 22).

20 mins, 50.9848, -4.5297

RIVERS AND POOLS

10 TORRIDGE CANOEING, HELE BRIDGE

The Torridge is a wild, wooded and very beautiful river, remote from main roads or built up areas. Mainly Grade 2 with a lively flow after rains (take care), it's an important river for fishing. Canoe access is only permitted from October to February.

→ Hele Bridge, on A386 between Hatherleigh and Meeth, is the usual access point. Park in the layby 100m beyond the bridge on the Meeth side and access river on L bank upstream, through field. 3 miles downstream is New Bridge (50.8822, -4.0649, L bank downstream). Then another 4 miles to Beaford Bridge and another 4 miles to Blinsham (see listings above).

5 mins, 50.8379, -4.0744

11 SHEEPWASH, TORRIDGE

Superb section of the young Torridge. There is a large, deep swimming hole just below the bridge. A little upstream there are many more sandy beaches and deep pools in open meadow (Sheepwash Woodland). Charming village with square and fine pub (Half Moon Inn, EX21 5NE, 01409 231376). A good place to pick up the Tarka cycle trail.

→ Sheepwash is signed off A3072. Find path from bridge on downstream, L bank. For meadows continue 300m up lane towards village and find entrance on L. For best pools and beaches bear L.

5 mins, 50.8314, -4.1498

12 CHAPELTON STATION, TAW

Open meadowland by footbridge behind small halt on Barnstaple branch line. Wide, fast-flowing, but mainly shallow (1m). Good for swimming against the current. Popular with fishermen.

→ 5 miles S of Barnstaple on A377 (dir Exeter find station on L, after the chapel. Walk through gate to L of station building, over railway line and across field to footbridge.

5 mins, 51.0173, -4.0228

3 BEAFORD BRIDGE, TORRIDGE

emote wooded stretch of river with ladder
teps down to deeper water above old weir.

➤ Between Merton (A386) and Beaford
3124). Climb lane 300m from Beaford
ridge (dir Beaford) and follow footpath on R
or 10 mins down through woods. Also a good
ace for canoe launch.

0 mins, 50.9083, -4.0699 🏊🚶🛶💧

4 BLINSHAM, GREAT TORRINGTON

small, secluded, sandy bay on the lively
orridge. Once a ford, so it is mainly shallow
ith boulders and rapids but also deeper
ections. A good place to launch a canoe.

➤ Turn R off A3124, 2 miles S of Torrington,
gned Blinsham and conifer nursery. After
00m find gates on R with parking area.
ollow middle trackway down to river 200m. If
ou fancy a dip you could also try the riverside
alk below Great Torrington (50.9486,
4.1471).

mins, 50.9295, -4.1105 🛶🚶

WOODLAND AND WILDLIFE

5 CLOVELLY PARK, CLOVELLY

lovelly, a well-preserved fishing village with
o cars, can be approached from the woods.

➤ It's best to walk in from Blackchurch Rock
30 mins) via the coast path and enjoy ancient
ak woodland and exhilarating views, with
luebells in spring. Saves on the entrance fee
o the park, too.

0 mins, 50.9985, -4.3972 🔁🍴

6 DUNSLAND ANCIENT TREES

udor Dunsland House house was destroyed
y fire, but the 900-year-old woods and
arkland survive with several fine, ancient
rees including pollarded oaks, lime and
weet chestnut; some are good for climbing.
Bluebells and primroses abound in spring
nd you may hear the rustle of doormice and
oe deer. Look out for sparrowhawks, too.

➤ Take A3072 from Holsworthy towards
Hatherleigh. Turn L at Brandis Corner, then
ollow signs for Holemoor.

20 mins, 50.8256, -4.2573 📷🔁🔀

7 MARSLAND GLADES & BUTTERFLIES

Large, varied nature reserve with steep
valleys, oak woodland, coastal heath,
grassland and meadows. Home to the rare
pearl-bordered fritillary butterfly that flits
around the woodland glades in spring.

➤ Head S from Welcombe Mouth beach along
coast path then inland at the next valley (after

1 mile). Or park at 50.9244, -4.5374 on lanes N of Morwenstow (signed Marsland). For a guided botanical tour contact Clare Gurton at Plantwalk (07790 844548).

20 mins, 50.9252, -4.5199

18 HALSDON WOOD OTTERS

Visit at dawn or dusk for the best chance of seeing the shy resident otters in the heart of Tarka country. Lovely valley of deciduous woods and pasture land along the river Torridge. Also canoeing (see 10).

→ Parking on lanes 1 miles W of Dolton (B3217, of A3124) or 1 mile N at Ashwell.

20 mins, 50.8866, -4.0479

RUINS AND FOLLIES

19 HAWKER'S HUT, MORWENSTOW

Quirky lookout hut, built from shipwrecked timber by Robert Hawker, the eccentric parson who wore fisherman's boots, wrote poetry, smoked opium and dressed as a mermaid. Great place to watch the sunset.

→ From Morwenstow church head to the cliff and turn L. To the N on the coast path is Henn Cliff, one of the highest in Cornwall.

15 mins, 50.9077, -4.5623

20 WARREN TOWER, HARTLAND QUAY

A ruined church tower stands on this wonderfully wild and rugged piece of coast. Just to the N is Blegberry Beach with its remarkable, folded rock strata. Return via the wooded banks of the Abbey River or head back to the Hartland Quay Hotel for a drink at the Wrecker's Retreat bar (01237 441218).

→ 500m N of Hartland Quay on coast path.

50.9979, -4.5283

LOCAL FOOD

21 THE BUSH INN, MORWENSTOW

Cosy 13th Century Inn, once the haunt of smugglers and wreckers. Now boasts fine local ales, game from the local shoots and home-reared beef from the farm. Enjoy magnificent sunsets on the cliff and then settle down inside by the fire.

→ Morwenstow, EX23 9SR, 01288 331242

50.9071, -4.5491

22 DOCTON MILL TEA GARDENS

Beautiful wildflower gardens and an ancient mill set in a secluded valley. Perfect cream teas, Brixham crab sandwiches and salad from the garden. March to October, 10am–

5pm. Near Speke's Mill Mouth (see 9).

→ Lymebridge, Hartland, EX39 6EA, 01237 441369

50.9767, -4.5172

23 RECTORY FARM TEA ROOM

Quaint 13th-century farmhouse serving home-made lunches, authentic pasties, scones, cakes, meat from the organic farm and vegetables from the garden. Also serve tea grown in Cornwall.

→ Rectory Farm, Morwenstow, Bude, EX23 9SR, 01288 331251

50.9088, -4.5537

24 THE OLD SMITHY INN, WELCOMBE

Archetypal 13th-century thatched exterior and a quirky, relaxed interior with a friendly atmosphere and great burgers.

→ Bideford, EX39 6HG, 01288 331305

50.9339, -4.5193

25 HARTLAND FARM SHOP

Local veg, home-made jams and cakes, free-range, rare-breed pork.

→ 16 Fore Street, EX39 6BD, 01237 441332

50.9921, -4.4799

26 THE RED LION, CLOVELLY

Harbour-side inn with real ales and fresh fish landed daily, just outside the door. Seasonal produce, game from Clovelly estate and a list of Devon's own wines to choose from.

→ The Quay, EX39 5TF, 01237 431237

50.9983, -4.3973

27 DAN THE FISH MAN, CLOVELLY FISH

Find Dan and his barrow of the freshest fish at Bideford Quay Farmer's market and other local markets. Or try his Fish Lovers' Saturday lunch club. Call him for the latest venue.

→ Starfish Cottage, Higher Clovelly, EX39 5ST 07970 932566

51.0190, -4.2043

SLEEP WILD

28 LOVELAND CAMPING AND POD

Working farm with two resident water buffalo who paddle in the stream and Lily and Agnes, the cutest pigs. 16 camping pitches and a sumptuous eco pod.

→ Canopyandstars.co.uk, Loveland Farm, Hartland, EX39 6AT, 01237 441894

51.0097, -4.4832

29 SCADGHILL FARM CAMPING

Basic small camping field at a quiet location close to Sandy Mouth. No camp fires.

→ Stibb, Bude, EX23 9HN, 01288 352373.
50.8619,-4.5234

30 SPEKE'S HOUSE, HARTLAND

Wild cliff-top self-catering above Speke's Mill Mouth. Aga and fire to retreat to after walking and exploring. Sleeps 9.

→ Speke's Mill Mouth, Hartland, EX39 6DY, 01458 850 120
50.9814,-4.5226

31 VINTAGE VARDOS, UMBERLEIGH

Trio of gorgeous Gypsy wagons set in a very secluded glade. Stylish interiors with a dash of glitz, sleeps 12 with children (or 10 adults). Climb down from the cosy pull-out beds to breakfast sizzling over the campfire, and a full day of exploration and adventure ahead. Eat together around the enormous hand-crafted dining table and try the hot outdoor shower.

→ Canopyandstars.co.uk, Higher Fisherton Farm, Atherington, Umberleigh, Devon, EX37 9JA, 01275 395447
50.9917, -3.9997

32 BLACKPOOL MILL COTTAGE, HARTLAND

Unspoilt, 15th-century self-catering cottage situated at end of long, private track in a beautiful remote valley, a stone's throw from Blegberry Cove and waterfall. Sleeps 8 but also perfect for 2!

→ Hartland Abbey, EX39 6DT. 01884 860225, 01237441234
51.0030, -4.5287

33 YARDE ORCHARD BUNKHOUSE & CAFÉ

Ancient orchards, rustic bunkhouse and a yummy organic café. Close to the river Torrington and on the Tarka cycling trail.

→ East Yarde, Petersmarland, Torrington, EX38 8QA, 01805 601778
50.909700, -4.147266

34 STOWE MILL, COOMBE

The watermill, mill house and picturesque cottages cluster in orchards around the ford on the shallow stream. Just half a mile from the sea at Duckpool. Self-catering.

→ 01628 825925 , landmarktrust.org.uk
50.8768, -4.5484

35 BEARA FARM, BUCKLAND BREWER

Delightful, olde-worlde farm in deepest Devon. The quirky barn and old cow shed have been beautifully restored. Home-made scones and fresh vegetables and eggs from Ann's garden. Self-catering.

→ Buckland Brewer, EX39 5EH, 01237 451666
50.9785,-4.2386

36 DOLLY'S PLACE, BIDEFORD

A 1930s bow-top Romany wagon with private woodland to explore. Within walking distance of coastal paths and the fishing villages of Buck's Mills and Clovelly.

→ campinmygarden.com/campsites/540
50.9758,-4.3118

37 HOLE STATION, HIGHAMPTON

No kids, tents only and camp fires allowed at this campsite set in 23 acres of native, deciduous woodland and wildflower meadow. Zero light pollution.

→ Highampton, EX21 5JH, 01409 231266
50.8137,-4.1729

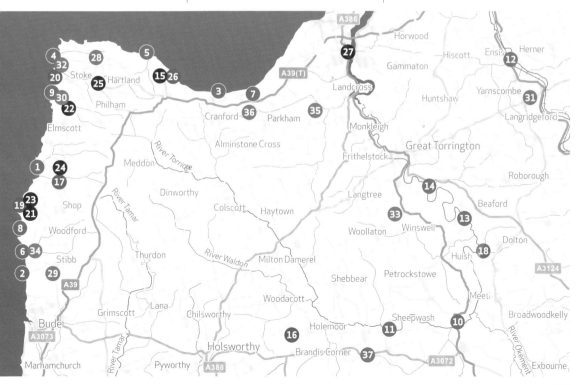

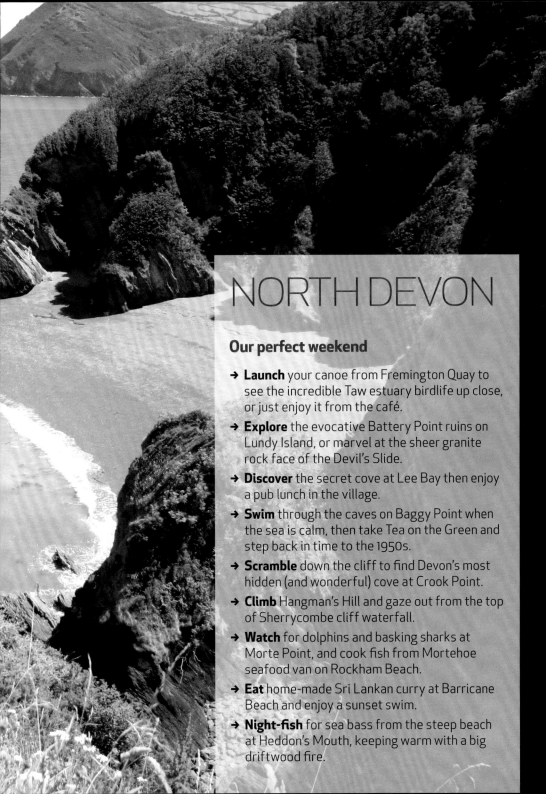

NORTH DEVON

Our perfect weekend

→ **Launch** your canoe from Fremington Quay to see the incredible Taw estuary birdlife up close, or just enjoy it from the café.

→ **Explore** the evocative Battery Point ruins on Lundy Island, or marvel at the sheer granite rock face of the Devil's Slide.

→ **Discover** the secret cove at Lee Bay then enjoy a pub lunch in the village.

→ **Swim** through the caves on Baggy Point when the sea is calm, then take Tea on the Green and step back in time to the 1950s.

→ **Scramble** down the cliff to find Devon's most hidden (and wonderful) cove at Crook Point.

→ **Climb** Hangman's Hill and gaze out from the top of Sherrycombe cliff waterfall.

→ **Watch** for dolphins and basking sharks at Morte Point, and cook fish from Mortehoe seafood van on Rockham Beach.

→ **Eat** home-made Sri Lankan curry at Barricane Beach and enjoy a sunset swim.

→ **Night-fish** for sea bass from the steep beach at Heddon's Mouth, keeping warm with a big driftwood fire.

From the extraordinary desert-like sand dunes of Braunton Burrows, to the formidable cliffs of northern Exmoor, this wild stretch of Devon coast is a delight. You can even catch and cook your own supper – there are fish in the sea and plenty of driftwood for fires on the secluded beaches.

The rocky outcrops, mud flats and steeply shelving shingle beaches are perfect places for sea fishing, but head east along the precipitous Exmoor coast and it is difficult to see an easy way down to the dramatic foreshore lying far below. During World War II, German submariners anchored their U-boats in the deep water of this coastline and came ashore to collect much-needed fresh water supplies from the streams and waterfalls at Sherrycombe and Heddon's Mouth.

Today, walking down from remote Hunter's Inn to the stony beach, it's hard to imagine that much has changed in this landscape since the U-boats visited these wild shores. Coconut-scented gorse and purple heather grow on the hillside and native rowan, holly and sessile oak flourish along the pretty stream. After a two-mile walk to the east, the remote, rocky beach of Woody Bay opens up at the end of the valley, below the trees. There is an ancient, cobbled track winding down past a limekiln and a wonderful bathing pool. At low tide, you can see the old quay, the relic of a grandiose but doomed scheme to develop this bay into a Victorian resort.

To the west, at Combe Martin, Wild Pear Beach has long been used by naturists, but Broad Sands, a little further to the east, is a surprising discovery. This deep, double cove lies far beneath wooded cliffs with many caves, and offers a welcome refuge from the busy camping and caravan sites at Water Mouth harbour.

On the western coast, there are several tiny coves to explore that are perfect for picnics, and Barricane Beach is one of the most charming. It has a little island look-out, steep rocks from which children jump and gritty shell-sand washed in from the Caribbean. The whole scene is set aflame at sunset. After a hot day's swimming, buy a plate of delicious Sri Lankan curry from the beach shack here and it's not hard to imagine you are far away, staring out into tropical waters.

SECRET BEACHES

BARRICANE BEACH, WOOLACOMBE
mall but perfectly formed sunset sand cove
n Woolacombe. Good swimming and jumping
nd a little rock island to climb. Bring a
ug, your own beer, and eat home-made Sri
ankan curry from the shack (see 24).
→ From Woolacombe beach head N along the
splanade and the cove is on L after 300m, by
evon Beach Court.
mins, 51.1784, -4.2118 🏊🖼🍴📶🐚

ROCKHAM BAY, MORTEHOE
arge, isolated W-facing beach with remains
f a wreck. You can camp in the fields above
t North Morte Farm camping caravan park.
→ 2 miles from Woolacombe on coast path, or
ia footpath from Mortehoe (signed Rockham
each). Also reached via bottom field of
ampsite (see 38).
0 mins, 51.1934, -4.2070 ⛺🏕🐚

LEE BAY SECRET COVE, ILFRACOMBE
ilver shingle cove with soapstone rocks,
mall caves and a secret route across the
each to a second cove. Rocks for jumping.
iood pub in Lee (see 30).

→ Lee village is 3 miles W of Ilfracombe
on lanes (or a lovely walk along coast path
through Torrs Park, Ilfracombe). At low tide
follow the causeway across rocks 300m via
carved steps to second cove on L. Otherwise
take path from top of the hill heading W out
of village.
51.1994, -4.1815 🏊🚣📶🚶🐚

4 BROAD SANDS, COMBE MARTIN
Dramatic double cove with caves, shingle
beach, sheltered swimming and an island
lookout to climb.
→ Take main coast road out of Combe Martin
(A399 dir Ilfracombe) and turn R down Barton
Hill after 1 mile, signed Sandy Cove Hotel.
Turn L at end and continue on foot, past hotel,
along track through woods. After 500m, near
picnic area, drop down through woods R to
find steep, long stairway to cove.
15 mins, 51.2121, -4.0589 🏊🚣🐚

5 HEDDON'S MOUTH, MARTINHOE
Wild, stony beach with limekiln ruin, at the
end of a deep, wooded valley, with stream.
The bracken-covered hillside, sheltered
valley and flower-rich meadows provide an
ideal habitat for fritillary butterflies. The
steep beach is a good place for sea fishing.

→ Signed Trentishoe/Hunters' Inn off A399,
between Combe Martin and Parracombe. Park
at Hunters Inn (01598 763230) and take track
down valley 1 mile, crossing bridge half-way.
20 mins, 51.2304, -3.9279 🏊🍴🖼⛺🚶📶

6 WOODY BAY, MARTINHOE
This wild, rocky cove has a magical tidal
pool, a waterfall, an old lime kiln and the
fascinating remains of a grand resort
scheme, with a pier and plans for a cliff
railway. Damaged by storms, the pier was
demolished in 1902, and the rest remained
the unfulfilled fantasy of entrepreneur
solicitor Benjamin Lake who ended up
bankrupt and imprisoned for embezzlement.
→ Pass Martinhoe church, heading E, and turn
L signed Woody Bay. Find lay-by for parking
on R and walk down switchback road. Or
approach from Valley of the Rocks and Lynton
(2 miles).
25 mins, 51.2248, -3.8949 🍴🖼

7 WILD PEAR BEACH, COMBE MARTIN
A sheltered naturist shingle beach beneath
steep cliffs.
→ Accessed via partly eroded steps on W side
of Combe Martin, 700m along coast path.
15 mins, 51.2112, -4.0328 🏊🖼

8 CROOK POINT SANDS, LEE BAY

With beautiful sands and usually deserted, this is perhaps the best and most secret beach on this wild coastline. A small path leads through a hedge tunnel and there's a tricky scramble down steep slopes, with the help of ropes.

→ Find the section of coast path ½ mile W of Lee Bay that passes around the fenced edge of a field. Just 100m SW of the apex, Crook Point, there is a clear gap in the hedge/fence and a path leads on through thicket and soon descends, with ropes.

10 mins, 51.2267, -3.8833 🏊🏕🔻❄

9 DEVIL'S SLIDE POOL, LUNDY

This little pond sits near the cliff edge – a perfect place for a dip with a sea or sunset view. Just to the SW is the impressive Devil's Slide, a 400-foot rock face and the largest unbroken rock slab in the UK. Around it are crystal clear waters, and the offshore rock stacks of Matthew, Mark, Luke and John.

→ Follow the island road to the Threequarter Wall then bear NW for 300m.

40 mins, 51.1915, -4.6729 🏊🏞

CAVES AND TUNNELS

10 BAGGY POINT SEA CAVES

At low tide you can explore this long tunnel by foot. At mid-tide you can swim right through but take care if there is a swell – you could get thrown up against the roof.

→ Park in the NT car park at end of Moor Lane, signed Baggy Point/NT from Croyde. Continue through gate up track 15 mins. Pass houses and whalebone sculpture. Look out for interesting little natural harbour with carved slipway and iron rings on L (good swimming). 300m further, take faint path L to rock outcrop and find caves below to the L.

20 mins, 51.1394, -4.2550 📷🏊🔻

11 TUNNELS BEACH, ILFRACOMBE

Fun Victorian sea-bathing complex with old tunnels leading through cliff to two large tidal pools. Also some great rock-pooling. Lots of interesting history plus café. Entrance fee.

→ Bath Place, Ilfracombe, EX34 8AN, 01271 879882

5 mins, 51.2100, -4.1287 🏊🚲🚌♿🍴

SUNSET HILLTOPS

12 MORTE POINT, MORTEHOE

Jagged pinnacles and razor-sharp slates hint at the deadly offshore reef that has robbed many sailors of their lives. Watch the sunset and feel as if you are at the end of the earth.

→ From just beyond Barricane Beach (see 1) follow the coast path along the edge of Grunta Beach and for a further mile to the point.

20 mins, 51.1881, -4.2293

13 LITTLE AND GREAT HANGMAN

A steep climb leads to a craggy headland with tawny heather. Sherrycombe Water flows through the wild valley below, then tumbles over the cliff. German U-boats once anchored below to collect fresh water.

→ As for Wild Pear Beach, then another mile on

40 mins, 51.2146, -4.0042 🏞🥾🏔

14 BATTERY POINT, LUNDY

Steep steeps lead down to the cliffside ruins of the gun house and two cottages, which housed the gunner's families. Built in an attempt to prevent shipwrecks in fog on Lundy, this signal station was built low down on the western cliffs in 1862. Two cannon fired a blank shot every 10 minutes. These

were replaced by rockets in 1878 and the site was abandoned when lighthouses were constructed in 1897.

→ On the W side of the island, 20 mins from the campsite.
20 mins, 51.1724, -4.6798

15 KINEVER VALLEY, MORTEHOE
This wonderful hidden valley is full of wild flowers, butterflies and a bubbling stream leading down to the sea at Bennett's Mouth. Play Pooh Sticks on the bridges and search the higher rock pools for toad spawn.

→ Turn down North Morte Road by the Smuggler's Rest, continue to the road end, and continue 1 mile on footpath, bearing R through woods and along the stream.
30 mins, 51.1988, -4.1945

16 BRAUNTON BURROWS DUNES
This Sahara-like expanse is England's largest sand-dune system and the UK's first UNESCO biosphere reserve. With nearly 500 species of wild flower, many butterflies and seasonal ponds and pools, this is one of the country's most biodiverse places. Cycling is a great way to explore it.

→ 1 mile W of Braunton, signed Braunton Burrows off B3231. Continue to parking at road end and walk 1 mile through dunes out towards the sea. The best panorama is from Saunton Sands Hotel (EX33 1LQ, 01271 890212). You can hire bikes at Otter Cycle Hire, The Old Pottery, Station Road, Braunton, EX33 2AQ, 01271 813339.
20 mins, 51.0942, -4.1956

17 ARLINGTON COURT
NT parkland with ancient oaks, lakes and wooded valleys along the river Yeo. In the cellar of the main house you can see Devon's largest colony of lesser horseshoe bats via a special camera. Also, look out for the ancient heronry in the garden.

→ Off A39 between Barnstaple and Lynton. EX31 4LP, 01271 850296.
10 mins, 51.1474, -3.9873

18 TAW & TORRIDGE ESTUARY CANOEING
One of the most important reserves for waders in the UK, the Taw estuary is home to a huge variety of birds, including peregrine falcons and merlins. A canoe will give you access to estuary and also to the RSPB nature reserve at Yelland. Fremington Quay is the best place to launch (see 26), and

you could continue around to Instow on the Torridge estuary (4 miles).

→ Navigable +/- 2 hours of high water (tide times as for Plymouth). Kayak hire at Bideford Cycle Hire and Sales, Torrington Street East, The Water, Bideford, EX39 4DR, 01237 424123. Also river trips using a custom-built amphibious vehicle from 1 April–31 October, 4 hours before high tide to 3 after. Marine Parade, Bideford, EX39 4JL, 01271 861077.
60 mins, 51.0513, -4.1821

19 LUNDY ISLAND PUFFINS
Lundy means Puffin in Norse and this is the only place in Devon where puffins breed. Visitors can note details of their sightings in the Marisco Tavern's wildlife logbook.

→ Lundy Shore Office, The Quay, Bideford, EX39 2LY, 01271 863636
20 mins, 51.1639, -4.6581

20 SEA FISHING
Devon has some of the best fishing in the country for sea bass, mackerel, wrasse, sea trout and sea salmon. The terrain is so diverse that you can fish on mud flats, sandy beaches and rocky outcrops, all on the same day. You don't need a license for sea fishing, as long you aren't selling your catch. Fishing

off deep shelving beaches or rocks can yield exciting bounty and you don't need fancy bait or equipment, just some bread. Try and catch a mullet for your campfire supper.

→ Lee Bay stone jetty is good for catching Tope, one hour each side of low water on spring tides but watch out for lobster pots and cast straight out or to the right to avoid losing your tackle. It's also a good place to forage for some seaweed (51.2285, -3.8730). Catch a bass after dark at Heddon's Mouth (see 5), two hours each side of high water and aim for the right hand side of the beach. Or try Rockham Bay (see 2).

10 mins, 51.2285, -3.8730

SACRED AND ANCIENT

21 ST BRANNOCK'S HOLY WELL

Large enough to immerse youself in, this heart-shaped ancient well has been called the Lourdes of Devon. Tucked away on the edge of Braunton.

→ From Braunton, take lane signed Georgeham and just after St Brannock's Well Close find small car park and sign for St Brannock's.

5 mins, 51.1155, -4.1629

22 ST MICHAEL'S CHAPEL, BRAUNTON

Built in the 15th century, this votive chapel was a place to pray and keep watch for sailors and fishermen. It was a conspicuous landmark and the ruins are still clearly visible at the top of the hill.

→ Follow Silver Street, from opposite St Brannock's Church, and follow 'No Through Road' track up to R, to top of hill, to find a footpath on the R across fields.

15 mins, 51.1152, -4.1564

23 ST NICHOLAS'S CHAPEL, ILFRACOMBE

Hill-top chapel of the patron saint of seafarers and a former lighthouse. A wonderful, wild location.

→ Perched on Lantern Hill above the harbour wall.

5 mins, 51.2114, -4.1125

LOCAL FOOD

24 BARRICANE BEACH CAFÉ

Arrive early (6pm!) to put in your order for a delicious and authentic Sri Lankan curry at this tiny shack on the beach. Open your wine or have a swim while you wait, then eat curry on the beach while the sun goes down. Open May–Sept, closed in bad weather.

→ The Esplanade, Barricane Beach, Woolacombe, EX34 7DJ, 0796 918930
51.1734, -4.2123

25 CORNER BISTRO, BRAUNTON

After a long walk on the Burrows enjoy a delicious breakfast made with local produce in this much-loved bistro/restaurant.

→ 8 The Square, EX33 2JD, 01271 813897
51.1086, -4.1611

26 FREMINGTON QUAY CAFÉ

With stunning views over the Taw estuary and RSPB reserve, plus its own wildflower meadow, this former railway station on the Tarka Cycle Trail serves delicious and hearty local food. On Mondays, owner Paul leads RSPB tours from the café. A good place to launch canoes to explore the estuary and sand flats (check tide times).

→ Fremington Quay, Barnstaple, North Devon EX31 2NH, 01271 268720
51.0795, -4.1210

27 MORTEHOE SHELLFISH VAN

Eat in or choose a seafood platter from the cart. Their mobile seafood van also stops at the local campsites and villages. Buy crab for sandwiches or whole lobsters for feasts.

→ 5 Kinevor Close, Mortehoe, Woolacombe, EX34 7EE, 01271 870 633
51.1870, -4.2074

28 SANDLEIGH TEAS, CROYDE

NT community allotment project with delightful café serving a huge variety of produce from the beachside walled garden.

→ Moor Lane, Croyde, North Devon, EX33 1PA 01271 890930 (see 10).
51.1360, -4.2455

29 TERRA MADRE, BROOMHILL ART

Take the winding drive through forest to find garden sculptures, a hotel and this slow food restaurant.

→ Muddiford, Barnstaple, EX31 4EX, 01271 850262
51.1131, -4.0514

30 THE GRAMPUS INN, LEE

Charming village pub loved for its beer selection, which also serves cream teas in the garden.

→ Lee, Ilfracombe, EX34 8LR, 01271 862906
51.197338, -4.172494

GRAYLINGS, FREMINGTON

…ing fresh, local potatoes (yes, it does …ake a difference) and with a specials board …r locally-caught fish, this has the best fish …d chips in the area. Also in North Tawton.

2 Higher Road, Fremington, Barnstaple …31 3BG, 01271 346661
…0721, -4.1261

TEA ON THE GREEN, WESTWARD HO!

…tro, fun, family-run tea room with …tdoor seating and superb views out …Lundy Island. Generous portions and …outhwatering cakes. Every second Tuesday …the month there is a pudding club – a light …ain course followed by six desserts.

Golf Links Road, Westward Ho!, Bideford, …39 1LH, 01237 429406
…0414, -4.2364

THE BEAVER INN, APPLEDORE

…cally caught seafood and wonderful views …er the estuary.

Irsha Street, Appledore, North Devon, …39 1RY Tel: 01237 474822
…0528, -4.2053

34 GRASSROOTS CAFÉ, ILFRACOMBE

High-street setting with a small courtyard garden. Owner, Sarah, cooks almost all the food – vegetarian with vegan options – on site Try the elderflower cheesecake in summer, yum!

→ 97 High Street, Ilfracombe, 01271 867574
51.2073, -4.1247

SLEEP WILD

35 LITTLE MEADOW, NR ILFRACOMBE

100-acre organic farm with only 50 pitches and really stunning sea views. There's a small farm shop where you can pick up local eggs and bacon for breakfast.

→ Off A399, EX34 9SJ, 01271 866862
51.2125, -4.0712

36 CHERRY TREE FARM CAMPSITE, CROYDE

Sea views, lots of space and no caravans. A bell tent, surfboards and wetsuits can be organised ready for your arrival. No dogs or campfires.

→ Croyde, EX33 1NH, 01271 890495
51.1353, -4.2268

37 LUNDY ISLAND

The only campsite on 'Puffin Island' is a large grassy field sheltered from the W by a granite wall. Wonderful for star-gazing on clear nights. Close to the centre of the village and near the Tavern and shop. Booking essential.

→ landmarktrust.org.uk, Lundy Shore Office, The Quay, Bideford, EX39 2LY, 01271 863636
51.1647, -4.6622

38 NORTH MORTE FARM, CAMPING

A field just 200m above secluded Rockham Beach with amazing sunset views. It is a caravan park and looks unpromising as you enter, but persevere and head right down to the field at the very far left of the site. Ground is a bit slopey.

→ North Morte Road, Mortehoe, EX34 7EG, 01271 870381
51.1879, -4.2052

39

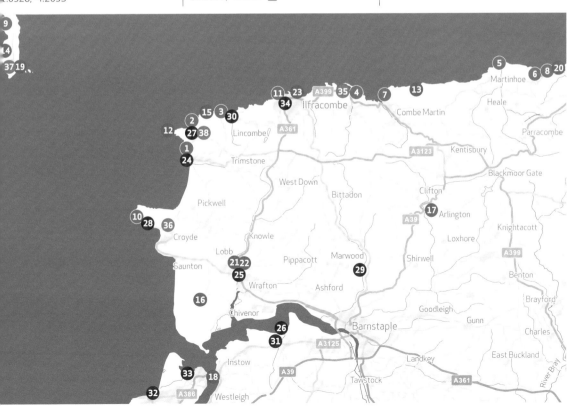

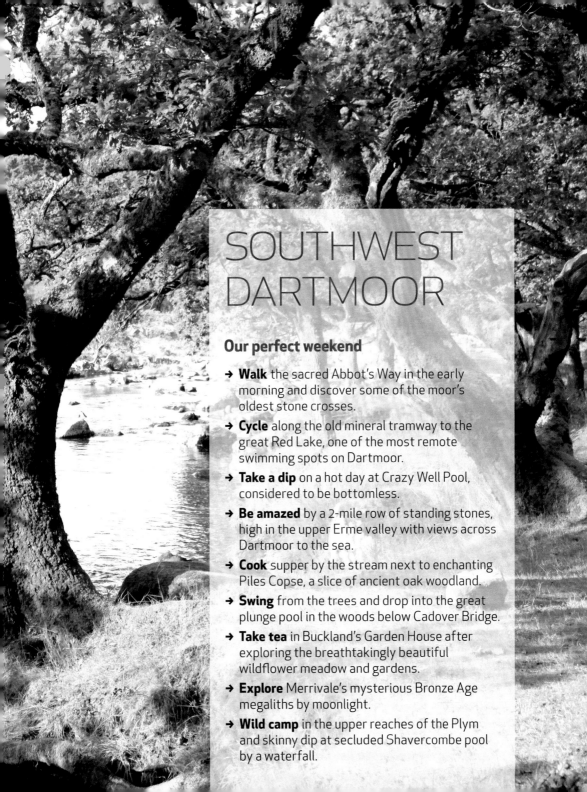

SOUTHWEST DARTMOOR

Our perfect weekend

→ **Walk** the sacred Abbot's Way in the early morning and discover some of the moor's oldest stone crosses.

→ **Cycle** along the old mineral tramway to the great Red Lake, one of the most remote swimming spots on Dartmoor.

→ **Take a dip** on a hot day at Crazy Well Pool, considered to be bottomless.

→ **Be amazed** by a 2-mile row of standing stones, high in the upper Erme valley with views across Dartmoor to the sea.

→ **Cook** supper by the stream next to enchanting Piles Copse, a slice of ancient oak woodland.

→ **Swing** from the trees and drop into the great plunge pool in the woods below Cadover Bridge.

→ **Take tea** in Buckland's Garden House after exploring the breathtakingly beautiful wildflower meadow and gardens.

→ **Explore** Merrivale's mysterious Bronze Age megaliths by moonlight.

→ **Wild camp** in the upper reaches of the Plym and skinny dip at secluded Shavercombe pool by a waterfall.

Clusters of weatherbeaten, megalithic remains – stone rows, circles and menhirs – have been standing on these high moors for at least 3,000 years. Their true function and purpose remain a mystery, and we can only imagine how people lived and worshipped on these high lands.

Merrivale is one of the best and most easily accessible of the ancient complexes on Dartmoor. There are three stone rows, two double and one single, and a wealth of other Bronze Age structures that suggest this was a place of considerable, if mysterious, activity.

If you can spare a whole day, head into the upper Erme valley. One of the longest stone rows in the world begins at the Dancer's circle, about an hour's walk from the road end. To appreciate the drama of these extraordinary structures, approach by the Cornwood Maidens, a further row of stones straddling the summit of Stalldown Barrow like watchtower

The beautiful Erme valley has more delights to offer, so make time to visit the enchanting, ancient woodland of Piles Copse, set by a beautiful pool (also a good camping spot), and consider climbing up to Leftmire Lake on the old mineral tramway. The route follows the high ridge to Red Lake, one of Dartmoor's most remote quarries. From this elevated vantage point, there are superb sunset views out across south Devon and all the way down to the sea.

Further east, the Dousland-to-Princetown railway is a spectacular walkwa and rough cycle track that winds through deciduous woodland and past hig moorland tors. There are views of Burrator Lake and the Walkham Valley, and the track passes the quarries of Sweltor and Foggintor, the source of the granite used to build many London structures, including London Bridge

The beautiful rivers Plym and Tavy are two of the best rivers on the moor for wild swimmers, with many dips around Denham Bridge, Cadover Bridge and in Walkham Woods at Double Waters, where the rivers Walkham and Tavy converge. On the upper stretches of the Plym, there is a secret, woodland waterfall, but if you yearn for a truly wild swim, try the old quarries at Leftmire and Red Lake, or the mystical Crazy Well. According to legend, this pool is not only haunted by a wicked witch, but also bottomless Local villagers tried lowering the church's bell ropes into the middle of the pool in the 19th century, but the ropes sank to a depth of between 80 and 90 fathoms (165 metres) and still didn't reach the bottom...

RIVERS AND POOLS

DENHAM BRIDGE & WEIR, TAVY

eep-section pool below Denham Bridge (40
eet deep, according to the old sign). Swim
ere or follow the river 300m through the
oods to a wide, open, pebble-beach area
ith a large, deep, secluded pool where the
ver bends. More upstream.

→ Bridge is on narrow lane between
uckland Monachorum and Bere Alston. Find
ownstream path on R bank, above bridge.
xplore upstream (20 mins) to find a lovely,
uiet stretch of river and old weir (50.4944,-
.1539). Follow lane up towards Buckland for
00m, then following track/driveway down to
past house and along river for 10 mins.
mins, 50.4899, -4.1481

BURRATOR RESERVOIR

ecluded beach areas, good for a dip, are
idden among trees on S shore.

→ From Dousland follow the lane over the dam
 Sheepstor, turning L 200m before church.
here are various routes down to the shores
om the lane.

mins, 50.5018, -4.0293

3 CRAZY WELL POOL

A spring-fed, mystical, moor-top lake
excavated by medieval tin miners and
reputedly bottomless. Look for an ancient
cross once used to mark the Monk's Path
from Buckfast Abbey to Tavistock Abbey.

→ From the small car park at the head of
Burrator reservoir (between two bridges and
the two source streams 50.5068, -4.0208)
follow the track/bridleway 1½ miles up onto
the moor, along the edge of the plantation
forest. 300m after the end of the forest find a
small stream bed which leads 200m up to the
lake. The cross is 150 m E at 50.516, -3.999.

35 mins, 50.5167, -4.0011

4 SHAVERCOMBE WATERFALL, PLYM

A very wild and remote, rowan-clad glade
with a small pool and waterfall.

→ As for Burrator but continue through
Sheepstor to the road end, 1 mile. Continue
up and past the Scout Hut following the
main track 800m. Look to your R to see
Shavercombe valley which sits below and to L
of Hen Tor. Head down into the valley towards
it, cross Drizzle Combe stone row, the Plym
stream and follow Shavercombe brook 500m
upstream to the pool.

50 mins, 50.4776, -3.9818

5 FOGGINTOR QUARRY

Impressive flooded quarry with cliffs and
ruins, and the source of the granite used
for London Bridge. Close to Merrivale stone
row (see 20) and on the cycle track from
Dousland/Burrator.

→ 2 ½ miles W of Two Bridges on B3357, and
½ mile from the telephone box at the B3357
junction (signed Princetown), find a farm track
and parking on L (Yellowmeade Farm). Follow
track 1 mile.

20 mins, 50.5444, -4.0245

6 CADOVER BRIDGE, PLYM

Open moorland stream with shallow pools
and grassy banks. There is ample parking
and safe paddling upstream for a mile.
Attracts crowds on hot August weekends,
but about 20 mins downstream there is
an excellent, large, deep pool with a high
rope swing and cliff for jumps, plus several
secluded smaller pools along the way.

→ Well-signed from Plympton (6 miles) via
Shaugh Prior. For the deep pools follow the
path downstream about a mile from the
bridge, keeping on the near side of the river,
through North Wood, to reach the waterfall
and main pool (50.4557, -4.0589).

20 mins, 50.4644, -4.0370

16

7 BIG POND, CADOVER BRIDGE

A large, shallow lake in open moorland with pebble beach. Warms up on hot days and usually deserted.

→ Turn R on road track, 10m before Cadover Bridge. Continue 1 mile to car park and stone cross at end then bear L along quarry fence to find lake, 300m. REPORTED NO SWIMMING ALLOWED 2018.

5 mins, 50.4503, -4.0090 ✝

8 RED LAKE, HUNTINGDON WARREN

Possibly the most remote swim on Dartmoor. Two large lakes with dramatic hillocks.

→ Easy 6-mile route, possible on a bicycle, along the old mineral tramway (Two Moors Way) from Harford (see Leftlake Mires 12). Shorter, harder route (3 miles) across moor is from Lud Gate road end (50.4913, -3.8567, 3 miles W of Buckfastleigh) via Huntingdon Cross and clapper bridge.

60 mins, 50.4863, -3.9107 🚴✝⛺🏊

9 PLYMBRIDGE, PLYM

A deep, long section of the river in beautiful woodland on the edge of the city.

→ From the Estover industrial estate dual carriageway roundabout (B3432) take Plymbridge Road, signed Earlswood. Park at Plymbridge car park and head downstream 200m.

5 mins, 50.4089, -4.0821 🏊💬

10 SHAUGH BRIDGE POOL, PLYM

Pretty shaded pool with small beach.

→ Shaugh Bridge is 1 mile NW of Shaugh Prior. Find path by post box and bus stop and continue downstream on R bank.

5 mins, 50.4530, -4.0721 🏊💬

11 IVYBRIDGE WATERFALLS

Series of fun jacuzzi pools, waterfalls and small weirs in pretty woods.

→ Park underneath the railway viaduct on Station Rd, Ivybridge (on rd to Cornwood), then follow track down to the river in Erme woods.

5 mins, 50.3990, -3.9170 🏊📖💬

12 LEFTLAKE MIRES POOL

High on the old tramway from the Red Lake, and with far-reaching views over Piles Copse (see 14) and the Erme Valley, this is a wonderfully deep, dark and silky lake.

→ Climb the moorland path from Harford Moor Gate (20 mins), then bear N to follow the Two Moors Way over Piles Hill until the old

5

mine works are reached (45 mins). Harford is ⅔ miles N of Ivybridge.

60 mins, 50.4555, -3.9076 🚴🏊💬⛺

ANCIENT FOREST

13 WALKHAM WOOD, DOUBLE WATERS

The River Walkham babbles through oak woodland. In early spring the banks are carpeted with wood anemones, then come bluebells and, later whortleberries. There are some deep plunge pools as the stream approaches the Tavy confluence, then the path winds up onto a rocky outcrop and down to flat rocks. There is a good pool 200m upstream or head downstream 300m to a beach, cliff and a larger, deeper pool.

→ Turn R off the A386 2 miles S of Tavistock at Grenofen, opposite the Halfway House. Take first L, cross river at Grenofen Bridge and park (50.5189, -4.1312). It's 1½ miles to the confluence and you can return S on the other bank via Buckator and Sticklepath wood or the N via West Down.

30 mins, 50.5090, -4.1511 🟦🟦🟦🟦🟦🟦

14 PILES COPSE, CORNWOOD

Remnant of ancient oak woodland with exquisite stream and waterfall, deep enough for a short swim. Popular with wild campers. Continue up the moorland valley, where masses of bluebells grow wild during May, to find a pool above a weir. Further up the Erme into the moor is the Dancers stone circle and the upper Erme stone row (see 16). Leftlake Mires pool is on the ridge to the R.

→ Quickest access is from road end NE of hamlet of Tor (via Ivybridge then Cornwood, 50.43373, -3.93769). Follow track up and around waterworks and around hillside, 1 mile, dropping down to the copse and stream.

20 mins, 50.4417, -3.9113 🟦🟦🟦

15 DENDELLS WOOD, CORNWOOD

Probably the wildest ancient woodland on Dartmoor, and officially off-limits without a permit. Lovely in May for the bluebells and in late autumn for the foliage colour. Rare barbastelle bat colonies.

→ 2 miles N of Cornwood, on the southern edge of Dartmoor. The nearest parking is in the village. Applications for permits should be sent to the Site Manager at Natural England, Yarner Wood, Bovey Tracey, TQ13 9LJ, 01626 832 330.

15 mins, 50.4392, -3.9502 🟦🟦

RUINS AND SACRED

16 UPPER ERME ROW & DANCER'S CIRCLE

At 2 miles, this is probably the longest stone row in the world. Its head is the Dancer's stone circle (also known as Kiss-in-the-Ring). A truly wild place in the upper reaches of the river Erme and a wonderful walk when combined with Piles Copse and Leftlake Mires.

→ About 45 mins beyond Piles Copse or 20mins below Leftlake Mires (see 12).

60 mins, 50.4638, -3.9245 🟦🟦

17 CORNWOOD MAIDENS & STALDON ROW

If the upper Erme is the longest row then the Staldown Row, on the next hill, is the most spectacular, with four person-sized stones crowning the summit and magnificent views.

A wonderful place to watch the sunset, especially if you are camping at Piles Copse, with the whole of Dartmoor at your feet.

→ As for Piles Copse, but bear N after the waterworks and make for the W edge of the summit. You should pick up the bottom of the row after 800m (15 mins).

30 mins, 50.4464, -3.9274 🟦🟦🟦

18 ABBOT'S WAY, NUN'S CROSS

An ancient 24-mile path, originally marked by stone crosses, running across S part of the moor. Some crosses remain, the oldest Nun's (or Siward's) cross, dating from 1050 at the junction of the Monk's Path and the Abbot's Way, which link Buckfast Abbey to Tavistock Abbey and Buckland Abbey.

→ Turn down Tor Royal Lane by church in Princetown and continue to end, 2 miles. Turn down lane. See also cross at Crazy Well Pool.

20 mins, 50.5126, -3.9698 🟦

19 DOUSLAND TO PRINCETOWN RAILWAY

The Princetown railway was a 10 mile long Great Western, single-track branch line that ran from Horrabridge. It is now a rough, off-road cycle path through woodland, high moorland tors and ruined mine buildings with spectacular views of Burrator Lake and the Walkham Valley.

→ From the public car park in Princetown, next to the Dartmoor Visitor Centre, head down Station Road and pick up the signed trail. The energetic could return via the bridleway from Burrator to Crazywell Pool.

60 mins, 50.5432, -3.9979 🟦🟦🟦

20 MERRIVALE STONE ROW

This is one of the best and most easily accessible megalithic complexes on Dartmoor. There are three rows: two doubles and a single, with both the doubles running E to W. The purpose of the complex is unclear: the stones are too low to be used for astronomical observation, and too narrow for processions. There are also a stone circle, cairns, cists and standing stones, dating back over 3,000 years.

→ There is parking on the B3357, 500m after the Dartmoor Inn heading E from Merrivale. Follow the path 200m to rows and circle.

5 mins, 50.5550, -4.0418

21 DRIZZLE COMBE STONE ROW

At the Drizzle Combe complex you'll see Dartmoor's tallest standing stone, over 4m and the impressive Giant's Basin cairn, next to it. Other remains in this once-bustling

Bronze Age site include a group of small stone circles, cairns, stone rows, standing stones, cists, hut circles and pounds.

➜ See directions for Shavercombe Waterfall (see 4).
30 mins, 50.4853, -3.9872 🏞️✝️⛰️🚶

LOCAL FOOD AND PRODUCE

22 GARDEN HOUSE, BUCKLAND

To see wild gardening at its most beautiful, visit the wildflower meadow at The Garden House from April until the end of August. Run by a charitable trust, there are more than eight acres of stunning gardens to explore and tea rooms in the old vicarage for delicious refreshments.

➜ Buckland Monachorum, Yelverton, PL20 7LQ, 01822 854769
50.4937, -4.1213 🔳

23 DRAKE MANOR INN, BUCKLAND

Cosy old pub in the centre of the village serving locally-sourced meats and good vegetarian options, or just enjoy a refreshing local ale in the sunny garden.

➜ Buckland Monachorum, Yelverton, PL20 7NA, 01822 853892
50.4952, -4.1304 🍴

24 ROBERTSON'S CAFE, TAVISTOCK

The location may not be very wild, but much of the food in this all-organic café comes from the owner's Tamar Valley garden. Serves great pizzas, smoothies and healthy, delicious food to eat in or take-away.

➜ 8 Pepper Street, Tavistock, PL19 0BD, 01822 612117
50.5508, -4.1447

25 THE ROYAL OAK, MEAVY

Set on the village green, this is a lovely traditional Devon pub owned by the parish council and serving very good local food. The pub takes its name from the giant tree in the village centre. Historical records suggest it dates back to the time of King John. Scientific studies have concluded that the tree is 950 years old. King Charles is said to have hidden in it.

➜ 2 miles E of Yelverton, A386. Meavy, Yelverton, PL20 6PP, 01822 852944
50.4864, -4.0579 📖🍴

SLEEP AND STAY

26 FOX TOR CAFÉ & BUNKHOUSE

Fill up on a hearty breakfast or home-made cake by the fire at this travellers' haven. The café also has a bunkhouse, offers cycle hire and doubles as the village off-licence.

➜ Two Bridges Road, Princetown, PL20 6QS, 01822 890238
50.5444, -3.9902

27 THE OLD MINE HOUSE, HORRABRIDGE

Large house to rent for groups, with bothy and outdoor sauna with wood burner. Good value, Grade II listed and hidden in 9 acres of woods.

➜ Sortridge, Nr. Horrabridge, PL20 7UA, 01822 855586
50.5191, -4.1094

28 WILD CAMPING

Wild camping is encouraged on Dartmoor. Piles Copse is an idyllic place to camp wild, with a pretty stream setting, or continue further up the Erme valley, or up to Leftlake Mires. Crazy Well Pool, another good site is near water, but watch out for the witch said to haunt this area!
29

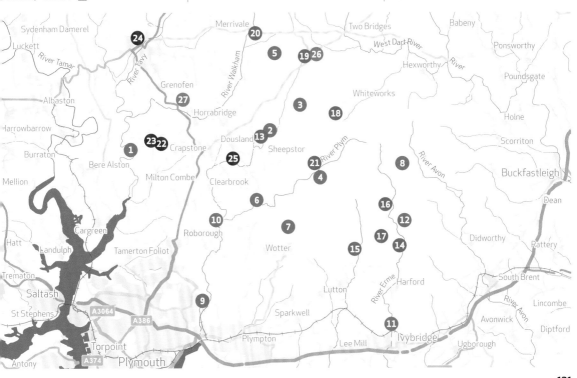

NORTHWEST DARTMOOR

Our perfect weekend

→ **Walk** the Lych Way by the full moon and arrive at tangled Wistman's Wood as dawn breaks over the moor.

→ **Enter** the heart of the thundering Lydford Gorge on the old Victorian iron gangplank, then refuel with a delicious cream tea.

→ **Find** Druidic inscriptions on the rocks along the pretty Cowsic river and enjoy a paddle in the stream.

→ **Discover** the letterbox at Cranmere, the oldest and most remote site of this intriguing and impressive pastime of 'letterboxing'.

→ **Cycle** along the Meldon viaduct, wild swim in the Meldon lakes and explore the tumbledown ruins.

→ **Watch** the sunset from Brent Tor church, then retire for a pint at the 16th-century Elephant's Nest.

→ **Wild camp** on the West Okement stream by Black-a-Tor copse at sundown after climbing Hunt Tor.

Whether you believe it to be a sacred grove planted by Druids or a remote and haunted place, Wistman's Wood is one of Dartmoor's most beautiful fragments of ancient forest. Its unique habitat and wilderness feel have inspired poets and artists through the centuries .

The wood is dominated by contorted, dwarf oaks with impenetrable, tangled branches and roots that have spread out between huge moss-carpeted boulders. Lichens festoon the aged branches and bilberries grow on the rocky floor in this feral place with green, earthy scents.

Near to the northern edge of the wood is the ancient Lych Way corpse road. The dead were wrapped in shrouds and carried along it for 12 miles for burial at Lydford, the nearest church from this remote part of the moor. Dusk on the night of a midsummer full moon is an ideal time for a spine-chilling walk. As the indigo night slowly draws in, you can easily imagine the slow creaking of an old cart and in parts the old wheel ruts are still visible. As you near the Tavy, stop at Coffin Wood where the corpses were transferred into caskets.

Lydford is also the site of an impressive wooded gorge, home of the outlaw Gubbins clan who lived in rough shelters here and terrorised travellers. In this narrow chasm, churning river stones have hollowed out smooth, rounded bowls and thundering waterfalls have carved their way deep into ancient rocks. The National Trust has repaired a Victorian viewing gangway that goes right into the heart of one of the pots, allowing you to stare down into the terrifying whirlpools of the great Devil's Cauldron. Further downstream there are paddling places and the impressive Whitelady Falls, which tips a 30-metre plume onto sightseers below, its huge, white drops as hard as hail.

There are many fine streams in this area of Dartmoor. The west-facing aspect of Tavy Cleeve makes it a wonderful place to camp wild and soak up the last rays of the sun. One of the best views is from East Okement, where the army is said to have dynamited the rock to create a small but beautiful plunge pool at Cullever Steps, for servicemen to cool off during hot summers. It can still be reached via the decaying network of moorland military roads. As you bathe here, among the grazing wild ponies, Devonshire's rolling countryside unfolds like a soft counterpane below.

8

RIVERS AND LAKES

WIDGERY CROSS, LYD

mall plunge pools in moorland glen beneath
rat Tor/Widgery Cross. Tumbling stream,
orse and heather. Secluded location, yet not
ar from Dartmoor Inn and car park.

→ Turn off A386 by Dartmoor Inn, opposite
urning for Lydford. Follow lane to car park
nd walk up onto the moor. After 800m meet
tream and follow its R bank 400m to find
ench and plaque on R up under tall rocky
utcrop. Pool directly below.

0 mins, 50.6500, -4.0772

MELDON LAKES & VIADUCT

Quarry pool with rope swing and steep rock
liffs. Limestone and aplite, a rare form
f granite, give the water its milky-green
ue. Remains of lime kilns, wheel pits,
ramways and weighbridges to explore and
lso impressive wrought-iron viaduct built
n the 1870s (now cycle route 27, the Granite
Vay between Okehampton and Lydford). No
wimming signs have recently appeared, so
e discreet or ascend to Meldon reservoir.

→ Travel SW from Okehampton on the B3260
A30 direction). Meldon Quarry is signed on L
pposite garage) and leads over the A30 to a

car park and information board. Walk ½ mile
down across stream to lake. Continue up the
stream 300m to find a small waterfall pool, or
head up to the reservoir (500m) if you want a
serious swim!

10 mins, 50.7109, -4.0350

3 TAVY CLEEVE, TAVY

Wild Dartmoor stream and plunge pools, high
in the valley of Tavy Cleeve.

→ Turn off A386 at Mary Tavy (signed
Elephant's Nest Inn) and follow signs to
Horndon, then Willsworthy, to Lanehead
and park. Follow the track, bearing L and
join the leat for 1 mile until it ends at pump
house. Good pool about 300m downstream
(50.6274, -4.0533) but the main one is further
upstream, another 15–20 mins.

40 mins, 50.6297, -4.0452

4 CULLEVER STEPS, EAST OKEMENT

Small plunge pool in a pretty, rocky valley
below Scarey Tor. Grass for picnics and large
rocks for sunbathing.

→ From Okehampton town centre follow
red army signs S to 'Camp'. After 1½ miles
arrive at T-junction on moor (army camp on R)
and turn L on old army 'ring road' with many
potholes. After 1 mile, up and over a hill, 50m

before the bridge/ford, find rough track off to
L. Park and follow track down to another ford,
800m. Follow stream L another 300m down
to pool.

15 mins, 50.7148, -3.9769

5 ROADFORD LAKE & SPRYTOWN WEIR

Pastoral reservoir lake surrounded by
meadows. Traditionally people have
discretely dipped on the E shore, but now
there are No Swimming signs. Camping on
western shore near the sailing club.

→ Follow the approach road from A30 but
turn R before the dam, onto a lane signed
'Clovelly Inn'. There's a car park picnic area
on the L after ½ mile, or continue, bearing L,
to find another after 1 more mile (50.7026,
-4.2126). Do not disturb the fishermen! Those
keen to explore might also like to swim at
remote Sprytown weir on the River Lyd, 4
miles to S (50.6430, -4.2482, 20 min walk
from the farmyard).

10 mins, 50.6932, -4.2270

ANCIENT FOREST

6 WISTMAN'S WOOD, TWO BRIDGES

The most famous of Dartmoor's original
ancient forests. Mossy boulders, twisted

trees and an otherworldly atmosphere.

→ 2 miles along good flat track from the car park opposite the Two Bridges hotel on B3357, on E side of bridges.
30 mins, 50.5779, -3.9611

7 BLACK-A-TOR COPSE, WEST OKEMENT

Trees as stunted and gnarled as Wistman's Wood, but this copse is much less visited. There's a pretty stream and an interesting tor above.

→ A beautiful walk from Sourton (A386) or from Meldon quarry (see 2 above).
60 mins, 50.6846, -4.0330

8 TUCKER'S POOL & LYDFORD GORGE

Secret plunge pool in jungly terrain just upstream of the famous NT gorge. Continue on informal path into main Lydford Gorge area (or via main car park and visitor centre) for ancient woodland walks down to Whitelady Falls.

→ Take dead-end lane opposite Lydford war memorial (EX20 4AT) to 6 50.6456, -4.1031. Follow footpath to old viaduct then downstream on perilous small path (not footpath) along gorge 200m down to Tucker's Pool for swim up into cataracts. Ford stream at pool to find small path downstream into NT

Lydford Gorge area for Devil's Cauldron and Whitelady Falls - no swimming!)
5 mins, 50.6427, -4.1053

SUNSET HILLTOPS

9 GIBBET HILL, MARY TAVY

A brooding and very wild hilltop. The stretch of the A386 passing below was once notorious for highwaymen and those captured were held in an iron cage on the summit until they were hanged on the gibbet. Enjoy the fantastic, panoramic views towards North Devon and Cornwall, but don' hang around after sunset...

→ Coming S on A386 find track and parking on R at the Mary Tavy village entry sign. On opposite side of road is a track leading to the ruins of Wheal Betsy, an old lead and copper mine, with a precarious-looking chimney, that closed in 1877.
15 mins, 50.6107, -4.1168

10 BRENT TOR, NORTH BRENTOR

An underground volcano erupted about 320 million year ago and left this impressive rocky outcrop. The little church of St Michael de la Rupe (built just 800 years ago) literally clings to its side; its silhouette

is a distinctive landmark on the Dartmoor skyline. A great place to watch the sunset and contemplate the wonders of nature.

→ Approach from Mary Tavy (A386), through North Brentor then L, signed Brent Tor church.
10 mins, 50.6035, -4.1622 ⊞

SACRED AND ANCIENT

11 THE LYCH WAY CORPSE ROAD

Visit this ancient trackway by the light of a full moon on a summer night for the full, hair-raising experience. In medieval times bodies of the dead would be carried along it from the high moor, a 12-mile treck to the nearest parish church at Lydford. At Conies Down the cart tracks and sunken holloway can still be seen, or walk the whole route from Bellever, via Longaford Tor north of Wistman's Wood, up and over Conies Down, over the Tavy and down to Lydford. At the Tavy you pass Coffin Wood (50.61107, -4.06371) where the shrouded dead would have been set down and laid in coffins.
90 mins, 50.5932, -4.0044 🚶🏔🚩

12 COWSIC VALLEY CARVINGS

Several rocks inscribed in Druid-esque language adorn the valley, etched by the eccentric Reverend Bray in the 1840s, who also created a Merlin's Cave and wished to turn the valley into a shrine. Also, a series of plunge pools with waterfalls on the river Cowsic just before it meets the West Dart.

→ Park opposite the Two Bridges Hotel, walk back across the road bridge W and find footpath on R just over the bridge. Walk through woods (Beardown Farm) and follow track along the Cowsic.
15 mins, 50.5616, -3.9768 🟦📘

13 CRANMERE LETTERBOX

Letterboxing on Dartmoor started in 1854 when James Perrott of Chagford set up a small cairn at Cranmere Pool, N Dartmoor. Inside, he put a glass jar where those who had ventured to the lonely spot could leave their visiting cards. Further letterboxes were established at Taw Marsh (1894), Ducks Pool (1938) and Crow Tor (1962).

→ To reach any of these locations was, and still is, a significant achievement. Today there are thousands of such locations on Dartmoor and you can buy a book of clues to help you find them, a little like geocaching. The Cranmere letter box still remains the wildest and most remote of them all.
200 mins, 50.6552, -3.9780 🚶🏔🔽

LOCAL FOOD

14 THE SPRINGER SPANIEL, TREBURLEY

An upmarket gastro-pub, with produce supplied by their own organic farm.

→ Nr Launceston, PL15 9NS, 01579 370424
50.5764, -4.3341

15 CASTLE INN, LYDFORD

Characterful and cosy 16th-century, oak-beamed pub with pretty gardens looking out at the castle. It also offers rooms. The ruined castle is free to enter.

→ Lydford, EX20 4BH, 01822 820241
50.6439, -4.1086 🏚

16 THE ELEPHANT'S NEST INN, HORNDON

Set in a wonderfully isolated position overlooking Dartmoor. Roaring fires and local food.

→ Off A386, Nr Mary Tavy, PL19 9NQ, 01822 810273
50.6016, -4.0929 🏠🏔

17 PETER TAVY INN

Originally built as lodgings for the stonemasons while they rebuilt the village church of St Peter, in the 14th or 15th

ntury. Lovely, secluded pub in a quiet
oorside village with good food.

→ Off A386, Langsford Rd, Peter Tavy, PL19
NN, 01822 810348

0.5809, -4.1024

8 THE DARTMOOR INN, LYDFORD

With New England-meet-Sweden styling, this
a smart pub with modern cooking using
cal produce on the edge of the moor.

→ A386, Moorside, Nr Lydford, EX20 4AY,
1822 820221

0.6478, -4.0908

9 HARRIS ARMS, PORTGATE

naginative food sourced from local farmers
nd the occasional hunter and forager.

→ Nr Lewdown/Stowford, EX20 4PZ, 01566
83331

0.6509, -4.2381

CAMP AND STAY

0 WILD CAMPING

he Dartmoor National Park encourage
ild camping - as long as you are remote
nd discrete. West Okement stream, above

Meldon Reservoir is a good spot, or head up
as far as Piles Copse. Tavy Cleeve, Widgery
Cross and Cullever Steps (see 1,3 and 4)
are also possible for one small tent, as is
anywhere along the remote Lych Way (see 11)
– if you dare spend a night on a corpse road!

30 mins, 50.6944, -4.0442

21 THE MOWHAY, TREBURLEY

Hidden in a meadow in complete privacy
this cabin/pod has a king size bed pod and a
lovely terrace kitchen. The nearby Springer
Spaniel pub does great food (see 14).

→ Trekkener Mill, PL15 9PN, 01275 395 447,
www.canopyandstars.co.uk/the-mowhay

50.5726, -4.3438

22 POND COTTAGE, ENDSLEIGH

An authentically picturesque cottage
with a rustic porch, honeysuckle-covered
tree trunks and very cosy rooms. Set on a
beautiful pond where you can fly fish. The
thatched Swiss Cottage nearby is also nice.

→ Milton Abbot, Tavistock, Devon PL19 0PQ,
01822 870000

50.5808, -4.2673

23 LITTLE WENFORK, REZARE

Small family-run site with space for five
pitches on well-kept, gently sloping grass
surrounded by fields and far-reaching views.
Also offers two bell tents with woodburners.

→ Little Wenfork, Rezare, Launceston, PL15
9NU, 01579 370755

50.5736, -4.3244

24 REZARE FARMHOUSE B&B

This is a characterful and very welcoming
B&B with very special breakfasts and home-
made biscuits and dinners by request. Cosy
and in a lovely, peaceful location.

→ Rezare, PL15 9NX, 01579 371214

50.5753, -4.3152

25 DEVON YURTS, LIFTON

Set on an organic farm on the edge of
the upper Tamar valley. Its two yurts are
situated in a pretty meadow and share a
heated bathing tent.

→ Borough Farm, Kelly, Devon PL16 0HJ,
01822 870366

50.6114, -4.2404

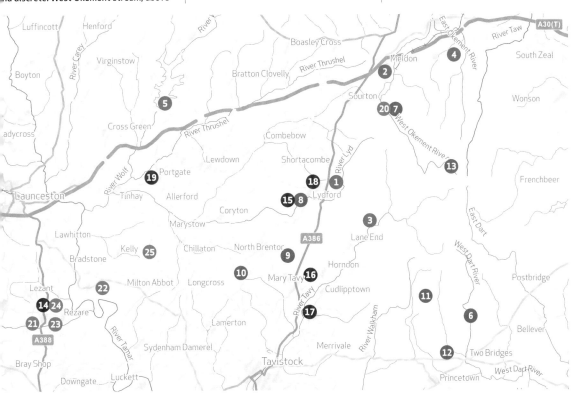

NORTHEAST DARTMOOR

Our perfect weekend

→ **Soak up** the atmosphere of Hound Tor lost village in the quiet of early morning, then enjoy a dip in nearby Becca Brook lakes.

→ **Ride on horseback** over the heather from Shillstone Rocks stables and feel energized by the moorland air.

→ **Stroll** through glades filled with wild spring daffodils at Dunsford Wood, then enjoy a drink at the Drewe Arms, Drewsteignton.

→ **Follow** the remains of the Templer Way, the old granite tramway, from the heights of Haytor Down through Yarner Wood.

→ **Climb up** inside the 2,000-year-old hollow yew at Kennford, or walk through huge, ancient trees to the top of Shaptor.

→ **Swim** in the Salmon Leaps plunge pools near Castle Drogo or wander further downstream towards Fingle Bridge.

→ **Explore** the Bronze Age hut circles of Grimspound village then visit Widecombe-in-the-Moor market for tea and cake.

→ **Wild camp** at remote Scorhill stone circle after watching the sun go down from nearby Kestor Rock.

13

4

15

Large stretches of ancient forest, especially along the upper Teign valley make this area of Dartmoor perfect for secluded river swims. Up on the high moor, abandoned villages and the rocky remains of a once-thriving mining industry dominate this extraordinary landscape.

One of the most famous iron-ore mines can be found beneath Haytor, an amphitheatre of smooth granite reflected in its clear, quarry pool. Look ou for the tramway that runs out along the hillside. Made of flanged granite rails, it is an eerie reminder of Dartmoor's industrial past.

Follow the tramway north to reach Holwell Lawn, carpeted with bluebells i spring, and then on to Hound Tor and the remains of its medieval village. A combination of population growth and favourable weather seems to have encouraged people to move higher up on to the moor and abandon it in the early 15th century. The remains of four distinctive Dartmoor long houses – family lived at one end, livestock at the other – have been identified as wel as smaller dwellings and barns.

Follow the tramway steeply down and you'll find yourself deep in Yarner Woods, passing through an avenue of ancient beech to further mine ruins. Don't miss other large tracts of ancient and often remote woodland at Shaptor and Lustleigh Cleave, but for more lost villages head further north to Grimspound, a late Bronze Age village that may date from 1300 BC.

In the far north-east corner of the moor, close to Scorhill stone circle, the river Teign rises. The most spectacular pools are the Victorian 'Salmon Leaps' in woods beneath Castle Drogo. Three rectangular square pools cascade, one into the other, like stacked glasses of champagne. The turbulence literally lifts you off your feet but you soon get the knack of bobbing about in these moorland jacuzzis.

Another mile or so downstream, you'll find a second weir and river pool before arriving at beautiful Fingle Bridge, deep in woods. This 17th-century narrow packhorse bridge was built to transport goods from local enterprises, such as corn-milling and charcoal burning. It has long been a local paddling and picnicking spot.

An important source of the Teign is Blackaton Brook, and you may like to search out the tiny and rather secret Shilley Pool. In this sheltered and sunny glen bathers and nymphs have built up a low dam to create a perfect bath. The water flows in across wide stone slabs, perfect for sunbathing and summertime picnics.

16

RIVERS AND POOLS

1 HAYTOR QUARRY

Sheltered, south-facing, sun-trap under popular Haytor Rocks. There are two pools big enough for a short swim. Both have clean, waist-high water and smooth, rounded stones on the bottom. Look for the granite tramway that runs from here: one of the only railways made entirely from stone – rails, points and all. Explore more of this old railway in Yarner Wood (see 10).

→ Park at Lower Haytor by the Vistor Centre, (B3387, 3 miles from Bovey Tracey). There's a visitor centre at this car park and usually an ice-cream van. Cross the road and walk 500m to the piles of broken rocks below the tor.
10 mins, 50.5835, -3.7529

2 FINGLE BRIDGE, TEIGN

A deep, thickly-wooded gorge, 1 mile downstream from the Salmon Leaps.

→ Walk upstream 5 mins (200m) from the bridge and pub (Fingle Bridge Inn, EX6 6PW, 01647 281287) to find a deep pool above a small weir. 1 mile E of Castle Drogo/ Drewsteignton.
5 mins, 50.6955, -3.7811

3 BECKA BROOK LAKES

Two small super secret lakes hidden in beautiful, ancient woodland on Becka Brook.

→ As for Hound Tor village (see 15) then descend to stream below (E of) Greator rocks and bushwhack upstream on far bank 300m.
30 mins, 50.5931, -3.7655

4 SHILLEY POOL, THROWLEIGH

Series of small plunge pools in brook at the edge of the moor. Paddling for children and a great place for picnics.

→ 1 mile NW of Throwleigh, park and find rough track on L, 100m before cattle grid and stream bridge, just after Clannonborough Cottage. Follow Blackaton Brook up onto moor ½ mile.
10 mins, 50.7050, -3.9093

5 FERNWORTHY RESERVOIR, CHAGFORD

Remote forested reservoir. Shores may be sandy or muddy, depending on water level. Tucked away in the forest are stone circles, ceremonial stone rows and hut circles. The area is a nature reserve where milkwort and bilberry grow. NO SWIMMING SIGNS.

→ 5 miles SW of Chagford. Continue right around the lake until you come to a large

wooden hangar. Park and head down past the bird hide to the R.
50.6387,-3.8930

6 SALMON LEAPS, RIVER TEIGN

Long river pool above weir in woods beneath Castle Drogo. Three large, square, smooth-lined plunge pools cascade down into each other. Great for a pummelling massage!

→ 150m S of Sandy Park Inn (Chagford, TQ13 8JW, 01647 433267, W of Castle Drogo/ Drewsteignton) find footpath and follow the river downstream into woods, ½ mile.
10 mins, 50.6926, -3.8097

7 TRENCHFORD, TOTTISFORD, KENNICK

Secluded reservoir lakes deep in conifer woods. Shallow, clear and warm water with shelving beach access. NO SWIMMING SIGNS and occasional fishermen, so be discreet.

→ Second R off A382, 2m N of Bovey Tracy
5 mins, 50.6333, -3.6829

ANCIENT TREES

8 LUSTLEIGH CLEAVE, BOVEY

Classic Dartmoor woodland walk through ancient oaks. Look out for deer, rare

15

butterflies, and dippers darting among mossy boulders in the stream. Bluebells and foxgloves carpet the slopes in early June.

→ 3 miles NW of Bovey Tracey. Walk from Hammerslake (Lustleigh) on the higher path up the valley to Hunter's Tor and return via the lower path and stream.

20 mins, 50.6211, -3.7333

9 SCANNICLIFT, DODDISCOMBSLEIGH

Seldom-visited woodland with ancient oaks and horned rhinoceros beetles. Find numerous manganese mining tunnels in the upper NE corner.

→ 7 miles SW of Exeter on B3193, turn L for Doddiscombsleigh and find footpath on R opposite the Sheldon Centre.

10 mins, 50.6646, -3.6370

10 YARNER WOOD, TEMPLER WAY

Large tract of ancient oak and beech woods with holly thickets and the sound of woodpeckers. The old Templer granite tramway, built in 1820 from flanged granite blocks, is visible in several places and connects up to Haytor Quarries, and down to the old Stover canal, and thence to Teignmouth. There are also remains of Yarrow copper mine.

→ Turn R off B3387 at Edgcumbe Hotel, W of Bovey Tracey. Continue 1 mile to find woods signed on L. The tramway is in the S section of the woods, about 300m S of car park/visitor centre.

10 mins, 50.5937, -3.7177

11 KENN ANCIENT YEW, KENNFORD

Massive yew in St Andrew's churchyard, estimated to be at least 2,000 years old. You can climb up into its centre.

→ First exit off the A38 travelling S from M5.
50.6611, -3.5258

12 SHAPTOR WOODLAND AND ROCK

Giant mossy boulders and large fern-clad trees lead up to the wooded top of the tor with far-reaching views. A little-visited woodland with a mixture of open clearings and big, veteran trees.

→ Situated between Henock and the A382, N of Bovey Tracey. Parking for three cars at Furzeleigh Cross (50.6055, -3.6700) then 1 mile walk up to the tor through Stonelands Waste.

20 mins, 50.6150, -3.6846

13 GRIMSPOUND VILLAGE

This is one of the best preserved Bronze Age villages on Dartmoor. It consists of 24 hut circles surrounded by a low stone wall set in a wild, sweeping location beneath Hameldown Tor.

→ Turn S off B3212 at the Challacombe signpost, signed Widecombe. Finding parking in layby R after 1½ miles.

5 mins, 50.6135, -3.8367

14 SNAILY HOUSE, BELLEVER

The ruined farmhouse of two spinsters who were said to be partial to bottled, salted slugs and snails. Also marked as Whiteslade.

→ About a mile down the East Dart river on the L bank, hidden just inside the conifer woods.

20 mins, 50.5714, -3.8922

15 HOUND TOR VILLAGE

Isolated Dartmoor hamlet, probably abandoned in the early 15th century. You can still see the remains of four 13th-century stone farmsteads. The site lies ½ mile E of popular Hound Tor, just N of Greator rocks.

Hound Tor car park is on lanes between Widecombe and Manaton. To the S is Holwell Lawn (50.5900, -3.7757), which has a fabulous display of bluebells in spring. The impressive rock stack of Bowerman's Nose is 1 mile to (50.6095, -3.7803). See also Becka Brook lakes if you fancy a dip.

5 mins, 50.5954, -3.7726

6 SCORHILL CIRCLE, TEIGNCOMBE

Set amid wild, heather-covered moorland, this is one of the most impressive stone circles on Dartmoor. There's also a clapper bridge, a holed stone and a further stone row. Kestor Rock is nearby.

Signed Teigncombe, Batsworthy and Kestor, on tiny lanes 4 miles W of Chagford. Then a short walk N of the Teign clapper bridge. NB Follow the Teign 500m downstream from the clapper bridge to find a deep, secluded pool.

10 mins, 50.6705, -3.9052

MEADOW AND MOORS

7 DUNSFORD WOODS, WILD DAFFODILS

One of the best displays of wild daffodils in the West Country, nurtured by the sheltered environment of the Teign valley. Plants are

usually in bloom in early March; in mid-spring look out for rare marsh fritillary butterflies, with striking, bright orange wings. You can also swim along here, above the weir.

→ Park on the hill down to Steps Bridge, 1 mile before (W of) Dunsford village and head upstream from the bridge. You can complete a loop via Bridford Wood on S side of road.

20 mins, 50.6845, -3.7049

18 PARKE ESTATE, BOVEY TRACEY

Bluebells and wood anemones carpet the riverside woodland walks in spring, and you can see delicate, native orchids in the estate's meadows later in the summer.

→ Parke, Bovey Tracey, TQ13 9JQ
15 mins, 50.6410, -3.8865

19 SHILLSTONE ROCKS STABLES

Recharge your batteries with a hack through the wild heather and gorse, then pick up some of the farm's grass-reared, succulent Dexter beef.

→ Chittle-Ford Farm, Widecombe-in-the-Moor, Newton Abbot, Devon TQ13 7TF, 01364 621281

60 mins, 50.5703, -3.8064

20 RUGGLESTONE INN, WIDECOMBE

Charming, wisteria-covered inn on the moor. Enjoy local ale from the barrel, farm ciders and home-cooked food, sourced from local suppliers.

→ Widecombe-in-the-Moor, TQ13 7TF, 01364 621327

50.5702, -3.8066

21 NOBODY INN, DODDISCOMBSLEIGH

Award-winning local food including their 28- day-hung Dartmoor beef speciality. Everything you want from a 17th-century inn, including inglenooks and beamed ceilings.

→ Doddiscombsleigh, EX6 7PS, 01647 252394

50.6674, -3.6208

22 POWDERMILLS POTTERY, POSTBRIDGE

Delicious cream teas served in the courtyard of the 19th-century gunpowder factory, now a studio offering pottery courses.

→ Powder Mills Farm, Princetown, PL20 6SP, 01822 880263

50.5757, -3.9391

23 DREWE ARMS, DREWSTEIGNTON

Good local food and particularly tasty pies in this rustic, thatched pub.

→ The Square, EX6 6QN, 01647 281224
50.7031, -3.7911

24 ROCK INN, HAYTOR VALE

Traditional, cosy restaurant with a string of awards for its locally sourced food. Rooms.

→ Haytor Vale, TQ13 9XP, 01364 661305
50.5814, -3.7368

25 CRIDFORD INN, TRUSHAM

Thatched old Devon longhouse with pizza oven outside. Bar or restaurant dining and particularly good game.

→ Newton Abbot, TQ13 0NR, 01626 853694
50.6293, -3.6200

26 WARREN HOUSE, POSTBRIDGE

Enjoy Warrener's Pie – the pub's famous rabbit pie – in this isolated moor-top pub where, acccording to local legend, the fire has been burning continuously for over 150 years. Welcoming and cosy, serving up traditional pub grub with glorious views.

→ Nr Two Bridges, PL20 6TA, 01822 880208
50.6133, -3.8755

27 WIDECOMBE VILLAGE MARKET

Home-grown vegetables and plants, artisan bread and cheeses, beef, lamb and pork from local farms – all are on sale in Widecombe's 16th-century Church House, traditionally used for parish festivities. Refreshments include delicious home-made cakes, with all proceeds going to local charities. Fourth Saturday of the month 10am – 4pm.

→ Church House, Widecombe-in-the-Moor, TQ13 7TB
50.5755, -3.8128

28 MANOR INN, LOWER ASHTON

Riverside pub with local food. A mile from Canonteign country park and waterfall.

→ Exeter, EX6 7QL, 01647 252304
50.6458, -3.6364

29 RING OF BELLS, NORTH BOVEY

Upmarket, thatched inn with commitment to food sourced from local suppliers.

→ North Bovey, TQ13 8RB, 01647 440375
50.6412, -3.7824

30 LOVATON FARM, SHOP/B&B

Meat from heritage breeds as well as mutton and hogget are sold at this lovely farm. Well worth a visit to learn where the meat comes

rom: watch your bacon being prepared and
hen eat it for breakfast if you stay at the
&B. Tuesday and Wednesday are cutting
ays at this small family-run farm.
→ South Tawton, Okehampton, EX20 2RA,
1647 231649
0.7341, -3.8762

SLEEP WILD

1 THE WOOD LIFE, KENN

Get a taste of the Swiss Family Robinson
festyle in this fully kitted-out safari tent
with woodburner. Set in a clearing among
acres of secluded private woodland. Wood
hopping and tree swings. Bluebells in May.
→ The Linhay, Mill Yard, EX6 7UR, 01392832509
0.6615, -3.5279

2 COCKINGFORD FARM, WIDECOMBE

Simple family camping in a stunning
Dartmoor valley. Children can play in the
Webburn stream, campires are allowed and a
welcoming, relaxed atmosphere pervades.
→ Widecombe-in-the-Moor, TQ13 7TG, 01364
521258
50.5614, -3.8129

33 LITTLE SHOTTS, HAYTOR

Lovely eclectic woodland cabin retreat with
woodburner. Pick up locally sourced supplies
from the community-run village shop or walk
through the woods to the Rock Inn.
→ Newton Abbot, TQ13 9XX, 01364 661536
50.5824, -3.7307

34 SUMMERHILL FARM, HITTISLEIGH

Yurts and belltents, each allocated a lovely
spot, on this Soil Association owned organic
farm. Collect eggs and treat yourself to a
delicious hamper, delivered to your tent
door. Campfires allowed.
→ Hittisleigh, EX6 6LP, 01647 24250
50.7581,-3.7790

35 RUNNAGE FARM CAMPING

Camping barn, bunkhouse and a riverside
meadow site for tents. A traditional working
moorland farm that's been in the family for
generations. Cook home-reared beef and
lamb on your firepit campfire.
→ Runnage Farm, Postbridge, PL20 6TN,
01822 880222
50.5909, -3.8826

36 WARCLEAVE COTTAGE, CHAGFORD

Roomy woodland lodge with amazing views
over the River Teign from the balcony.
→ National Trust 0844 8002070
50.6779, -3.8412

37 LONGHOUSE/CHAPEL, LETTAFORD

15th-century Dartmoor longhouse and
chapel, self-catering. Stream for paddling.
→ Landmark Trust 01628 825925
50.6417, -3.8374

38 YHA BELLEVER

Basic YHA accommodation with magical
views in the heart of the moor, serving
hearty locally sourced evening meals.
→ Bellever, Postbridge, Dartmoor National
Park PL20 6TU, 0845 3719622
50.580635, -3.901642

39 WILD CAMPING

Follow the Tarka Trail from Belstone and
camp in sight of the Nine Stones circle.
→ The Tors Inn provides backup in case of
poor weather (EX20 1QZ, 01837 840689)
50.7185, -3.9670

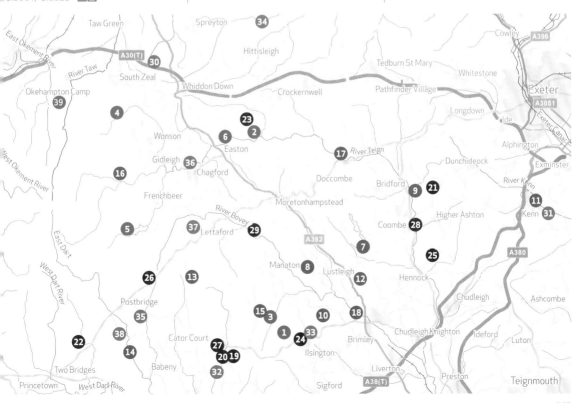

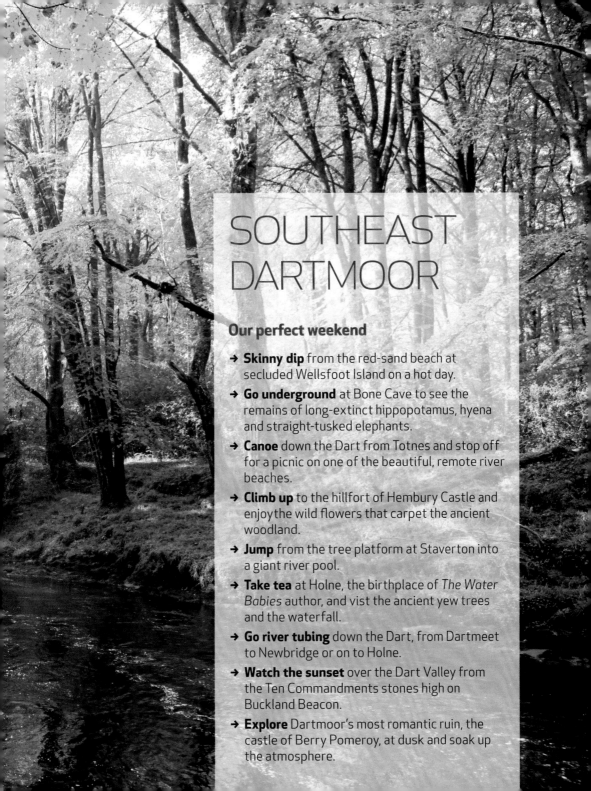

SOUTHEAST DARTMOOR

Our perfect weekend

→ **Skinny dip** from the red-sand beach at secluded Wellsfoot Island on a hot day.

→ **Go underground** at Bone Cave to see the remains of long-extinct hippopotamus, hyena and straight-tusked elephants.

→ **Canoe** down the Dart from Totnes and stop off for a picnic on one of the beautiful, remote river beaches.

→ **Climb up** to the hillfort of Hembury Castle and enjoy the wild flowers that carpet the ancient woodland.

→ **Jump** from the tree platform at Staverton into a giant river pool.

→ **Take tea** at Holne, the birthplace of *The Water Babies* author, and vist the ancient yew trees and the waterfall.

→ **Go river tubing** down the Dart, from Dartmeet to Newbridge or on to Holne.

→ **Watch the sunset** over the Dart Valley from the Ten Commandments stones high on Buckland Beacon.

→ **Explore** Dartmoor's most romantic ruin, the castle of Berry Pomeroy, at dusk and soak up the atmosphere.

In a deep, wooded gorge, far from the noise of traffic, there are pools for refreshing dips and sandy bays for picnics. Overlooked by towering tors, the ancient oak forest is alive with birdsong. Cool water gurgles over rocks, sending up a light spray that creates rainbows in the clear air.

Writer Charles Kingsley was born in the village of Holne, just south of the river, and its wild beauty must have inspired his well-loved story about a young chimney-sweep who falls into the water and is transformed into a water baby. The Dart is the iconic moorland river and one of the best for wild swimming in the whole of the UK.

A ten-minute walk from Holne, down through the fields, brings you to Horseshoe Falls, the perfect place for a picnic, but continue upstream to enter the wild woods and discover a long stretch of river with many more pools and cascades. Downstream at Wellsfoot Island, a secluded spot sheltered by Holne cliff, there is a red sandy beach and a fabulous deep pool by a birch coppice. Back at Holne, there is a fine, local pub for refreshment.

Adventurous swimmers might be tempted by the five-mile stretch from Dartmeet to New Bridge, or the shorter run down to Holne via Lover's Leap. Wear a wetsuit and take an inner tube – a great way to ride the rapids that also offers protection from rocks. A more conventional means of transport would be a canoe : the Dart is open for canoeing from October to March. You can hire canoes and kayaks and even take part in organised canoe foraging or night paddles. The stretch of river from Staverton to Totnes is perfect for trying out your flat-water canoe skills and, if you feel confident, continue on to the tidal stretches below, as far as Dittisham. There are several beaches here for discreet overnight wild camping.

This area of Dartmoor has a rich historical heritage, from the spectacular medieval fortifications of Berry Pomeroy castle to the forested hill fort in Hembury Woods, set above an enchanting stretch of river. For a taste of prehistory, visit the amazing caverns in High Kiln Quarries outside Buckfastleigh. Bone Cave was gouged out of the rock by the waters of the Dart at least 100,000 years ago and contains the ancient remains of wild beasts including bison and straight-tusked elephants.

RIVER AND BEACH

SHARRAH POOL, HOLNE FOREST
Sharrah is the largest and best pool on this wild and wonderful stretch of the river, in the forested Dart Valley nature reserve.

➤ Descend to river from Holne and bear L along a good path for 40 mins to find this long narrow pool. 500m upstream are the Mel pools (50.5346, -3.8447), a range of smaller pools, including a few good chutes if you have an inner tube.

40 mins, 50.5301, -3.8396 🏊🚶🚗🏕🧗🚻

BELLPOOL ISLAND, HOLNE FOREST
Pretty wooded island and deep secret pool with old iron ladder scaling the cliff.

➤ As for Sharrah Pool, but 300m downstream. For ladder pool cross to the far side of island (L bank branch) and swim downstream 200m. Or approach from Aish Tor (steep descent) or from New Bridge (40 mins along the L bank).

40 mins, 50.5272, -3.8363 🏊🚶🚗🔻🧗🚻

HORSESHOE FALLS, HOLNE
Small, easily accessible, horseshoe-shaped waterfall and natural jacuzzi. Large rock for sunbathing above and Salter's pool below.

➤ Follow path on the river's R bank from Newbridge (500m) or on footpath down through fields from Holne (on R as you enter Holne from Holne bridge direction).

15 mins, 50.5195, -3.8200 🏊🚗🚶🧗🚻

4 WELLSFOOT ISLAND, NEW BRIDGE
Wonderful wooded island with secluded red-sand beach shelving into deep river bend with Holne cliff towering up behind.

➤ Follow the river upstream from Newbridge car park side (river's L bank) just under 1 mile, to reach the wooded island with its small bridge.

20 mins, 50.5170, -3.8274 🚗🚶🏊

5 LOVER'S LEAP, NEW BRIDGE
One of the most enigmatic and remote of the Dartmoor pools, set beneath a 12 metre cliff deep in ancient woodland.

➤ Canoe, float or swim 1 mile downstream from Spitchwick, or swim across the river at Spitchwick and walk on the woodland track opposite.

30 mins, 50.5359, -3.7989 🏊🔻

6 SPITCHWICK COMMON, NEW BRIDGE
The most popular and accessible Dart swimming location, especially in summer,

when litter can be a problem (take some away). Flat, grassy areas lead to river with deeper section on far side and high cliffs, from which some people jump. Also known as Deeper Marsh.

➤ From Ashburton A38 follow signs to River Dart Country Park. Cross Holne bridge, then park at New bridge. Cross road and follow path downstream 300m.

5 mins, 50.5261, -3.8141 🏊🚗🚻

7 STAVERTON WEIR
Great stretch of the Dart. Deep and straight above the weir, more secluded with a tree jump downstream.

➤ Park at the charming steam-train station (50p). Continue downstream, passing several small beaches to reach water (10 mins) then another 10 mins for the tree jump above the deep pool. From here, you can loop back through village, across the field (private with access), over the rail tracks and past Staverton church and pub (Sea Trout Inn), then back along lane. NB Riverford farm shop and café (see 23) are close by.

10 mins, 50.4613, -3.7051 🏊🚗🍴

8 DUNCANNON BEACH, ASHPRINGTON
A wild, remote beach on this secluded and

seldom-visited stretch of the tidal Dart, downstream of Sharpham estate.

→ Find footpath opposite church and follow for just over a mile. At low tide you can return to Ashprington via twisted trees and rocky crags on N shore of Bow Creek. Malsters Arms (see 28) at nearby Tuckenhay.

20 mins, 50.4048, -3.6343 🚶🏻🍴🏞🛶

9 REDGATE BEACH, TORQUAY

Swim or kayak from Anstey's Cove round to isolated Redgate beach for a slice of tranquillity close to Torquay. Coastline here is indented with sea caves and grottoes – great for exploring by kayak.

→ Anstey's Cove Road, Torquay, TQ1 3YY (off A379, near Kents Cavern). Great views and kayak hire from Anstey's Cove café (07780 554603).

20 mins, 50.4739, -3.5010 🛶🍴▽

10 DART CANOEING, STAVERTON

The Dart is the perfect river for canoeing with open access between 1st October and 15th March. The best beginners (grade 1–2) stretch is from Staverton to Totnes (2 miles).

→ Launch your canoe from Staverton bridge and railway car park and portage (carry canoe over) all weirs. There are several places to get out in Totnes, including the riverside car park.

You can also continue down the tidal section as far as Tuckenhay (4 miles) or Dartmouth (10 miles). For a longer run, launch from Buckfastleigh. For 12-seat longbow canoe trips from Tuckenhay try Canoe Adventures (01803 865301) or the Kayak Academy (07799 403788) from Stoke Gabriel.

2 mins, 50.4610, -3.7132 🛶🍴

11 WILDWISE CANOEING, DARTINGTON

A whole calendar of wild and wonderful courses suitable for all ages including night paddles on the Dart, food foraging by canoe and bushcraft.

→ Dartington Space, Dartington Hall, TQ9 6EN, 01803 868269

50.4501, -3.6918 🛶🏊🛶

ANCIENT TREES

12 HEMBURY WOODS, RIVER DART

Ancient oak woodland leads down to a deep, secret stretch of the river Dart with island. There are primroses, wild daffodils, wood anemones and bluebells in spring. Above are the slopes of a prehistoric hill fort, home to Neolithic, Iron Age and Viking settlers. Excavations have revealed cobbled roadway and elaborate palisades and gateways.

17

→ Take the Buckfastleigh turning off the A38. Cross Dart bridge and turn immediately R, signed Buckfast, then take R fork after village, signed Hembury Woods. After bridge, park on L, entrance to woods on R (river is 500m). Further parking at top of hill for hillfort.
15 mins, 50.5026, -3.7912

13 HOLNE YEW & HOLNE WOODS

The churchyard of 13th-century St Mary the Virgin in Holne has several ancient yews – one is completely hollow. Charles Kingsley, author of *The Water Babies*, was born in the village. See also Sharrah Pool (1) and Holne Woods (12) for more ancient woodland.

→ Next to Church House Inn, Holne, TQ13 7SJ, 01364 631208
5 mins, 50.5111, -3.8265

14 STOKE GABRIEL YEW AND CRABS

1,000-year-old churchyard yew. Walk backwards around it three times and your wishes will come true.

→ The mill pond opposite is one of the UK's top crabbing spots. Watch the action from the River Shack café (TQ9 6RD, 01803 782520)
2 mins, 50.4033, -3.6210

CAVES AND CAVERNS

15 KILN QUARRY CAVES, BUCKFASTLEIGH

A hole in the roof of Bone (or Joint Mitnor) Cave led many prehistoric animals to fall to their deaths and over 4,000 bones were found, including hippopotamus, bison, hyena, and straight-tusked elephant. Adjacent Reed's Cave is home to Britain largest colony of horseshoe bats: watch them emerge 30 mins after sunset. You can also follow the footpath up to the eerie, roofless remains of the old Trinity church on the hilltop.

→ Caves are open August, Wed and Thurs, 11am–2pm; entrance fee. Heading S on main road (B3380) through Buckfastleigh, turn R up tiny Russets Lane, 500m S of roundabout for A38. There's some parking after 300m on R then follow footpath into old High Kiln Quarries to see the cave openings.
5 mins, 50.4842, -3.7720

16 TEN COMMANDMENTS, BUCKLAND

In 1927, Lord Buckland inscribed the Ten Commandments on these great boulders above the Dart valley. Fine views.

→ 1 mile walk SW from the parking on Buckland Common, 3 miles NW of Ashburton.
20 mins, 50.5445, -3.7863

17

17 PRIDHAMSLEIGH CAVERN

This large cavern is reached by tiny lanes and orchards, just outside Buckfastleigh. Adjacent to the noisy A38. Don't venture into the inner tunnels unless equipped.

→ From A38 Buckfastleigh exit head N on the Ashburton Rd. After a mile find a lane signed Pridhamsleigh on R. Cross A38 and park on L by orchard gate and cave sign on hut. Follow path past ancient dovecote into woods.
5 mins, 50.4976, -3.7649 V

RUINS

18 BERRY HEAD FORT & CAVES

Impressive ruins of a Napoleonic-era cliff-top fort (Old Redoubt) with canons, dramatic cliffs and crashing seas below. Abundant bird life and many sea caves in the cliffs below to explore by sea kayak.

36

27

23

31

23

→ Signed Berry Head from Brixham. Follow Berry Head road to the car park and visitor centre. (Torbay Kayak Hire, 7 Hillpark Close, TQ5 9EX, 01803 856009 or Torbay Sea School, Berry Head Road, TQ5 9BW, 01803 853843). Guardhouse café (see 27).
15 mins, 50.3998, -3.4847

19 BERRY POMEROY CASTLE

The 15th-century defences of the Pomeroy family castle enclose the dramatic (and haunted) ruins of the great, abandoned Elizabethan mansion of the Seymours, tucked away in a deep wooded valley.
→ 3 miles E of Totnes, signed off A385. TQ9 6LJ, 01803 866618.
10 mins, 50.4490, -3.6363

LOCAL FOOD

20 COUNTRY CHEESES, TOTNES

Making and selling artisan cheeses for 22 years, this wonderful shop offers over 100 different varieties, all British and mostly from the West Country. Two other shops in Tavistock and Topsham.
→ 1 Ticklemore Street, Totnes, TQ9 5EJ, 01803 865926
50.4305, -3.6837

21 THE VINEYARD CAFÉ, SHARPHAM

Outdoor café, with beautiful views over the river Dart. Rosie and her team serve delicious cooked-to-order local, organic produce. Café open in good weather.
→ Sharpham Estate, Ashprington, Totnes, TQ9 7UT, 01803 732178 (follow signs for Sharpham Vineyard)
50.4098, -3.6517

22 BRIMPTS FARM TEA ROOMS, DARTMEET

Homely, locally-sourced, farmhouse breakfasts, lunches, dinners and scones smothered in clotted cream. You can also buy home-reared beef or learn more about the wood-fuel co-operative here. Self-catering accommodation also available. Check seasonal opening times.
→ Dartmoor, PL20 6SG, 0844 2880653
50.5431, -3.8751

23 RIVERFORD KITCHEN AND SHOP

No menu, just the best of what's in season and available on the day. Tours of the farm are offered and you can pick up produce to take home from the shop (on the Buckfastleigh–Staverton road).

→ Wash Barn, Buckfastleigh, TQ11 0JU, 01803 762059
50.4735, -3.7443

24 OCCOMBE FARM, PAIGNTON

Café and farm shop plus educational centre for food and farming with many activities.
→ Preston Down Road, Paignton, TQ3 1RN, 01803 520022
50.4566, -3.5867

25 CHURCH HOUSE, STOKEINTEIGNHEAD

Charming 13th-century pub that has been serving food and ale to weary travellers for the last 800 years. Food is traditional and seasonally-inspired: there is always some excellent local game or foraged bounty.
→ Stokeinteignhead, Newton Abbot, TQ12 4QA, 01626 872475
50.5242, -3.5306

26 BICKLEY MILL INN, KINGSKERSWELL

This converted old mill offers high-end menus based on fresh Brixham fish and local vegetables and meats.
→ Stoneycombe, Kingskerswell, TQ12 5LN, 01803 873201
50.4917, -3.6023

27 HOLNE VILLAGE SHOP & TEA ROOMS

Run as a community venture by friendly volunteers who serve up delicious home-made cakes and cream teas. Small shop selling local produce next door.
→ Holne, Ashburton, TQ13 7SL, 01364 631135
50.5113, -3.8264

28 GUARDHOUSE CAFÉ, BERRY HEAD

Short walk from the car park at Berry Head nature reserve. Enjoy freshly cooked, seasonal, local food in a relaxed environment with a stunning view. See also Berry Head ruins (see 18).
→ Berry Head Nature Reserve, Brixham, TQ5 9AW, 01803 855778
50.3991, -3.4878

29 THE MALSTERS ARMS, TUCKENHAY

Good, fresh food and local ales at this perfect creek-side location; once owned by chef Keith Floyd. There are moorings for your canoe and rooms if you want to stay the night. Good walks along the creek.
→ Tuckenhay TQ9 7EQ, 01803 732350
50.3941, -3.6643

ANCHORSTONE CAFÉ, DITTISHAM

Enjoy delicious local crab and mussels at this little blue shack overlooking the river Dart. Indoor and outdoor seating. Excellent crabbing is promised just off the river wall, so bring your bucket and line.

→ Manor Street, TQ6 0EX, 01803 722365
50.3820, -3.5971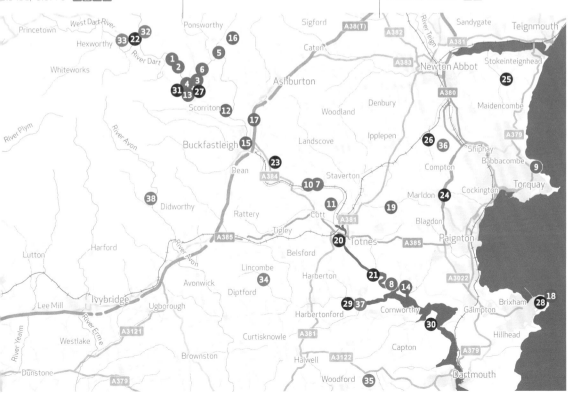

CHURCH HOUSE INN, HOLNE

Country inn with panelling and 18th-century arm settle. Roaring log fires, well-kept local ale and farm cider.

→ Holne, Newton Abbot, TQ13 7SJ, 01364 631208
50.5102, -3.8264

CAMP AND SLEEP

BRIMPTS FARM, DARTSMEET

Rustic camping in either Dolly's Cot or Crab Apple fields, situated on the lush banks of the East Dart. Campfires allowed and lovely tea rooms up at the farm. Self-catering options offered for larger groups.

→ Dartmoor, PL20 6SG, 0844 2880653
50.5451, -3.8770

33 HEXWORTHY BRIDGE CAMPSITE

Simple meadow on the banks of the West Dart by Huccaby bridge. No need for a shower block as there's a lovely river pool! The Forest Inn is 2 mins walk away.

→ Huccaby Farm, PL20 6SB, 01364 631533
50.5417, -3.8891

34 HAVEN MEADOWS YURTS

Lovely off-grid meadow sites set in 20 acres of secluded fields and woodlands. Order a holiday box from nearby Riverford Farm.

→ Beenleigh Meadows Farm, Harberton, TQ9 7NE, 01803 866864
50.4058, -3.7527

35 JACKSON'S CABIN, NR BLACKAWTON

Set in a wooded ridge W of Dartmouth, lovingly crafted family cabin with wood burner that looks out over pond and orchard. Tree houses and swings for kids and creative courses, such as furniture-making.

→ The Brake, Wadstray, Blackawton, Totnes, TQ9 7DE, 01803 712303
50.3488, -3.6538

36 LONG BARROW WINDMILL

Stay in this converted windmill, set on a hilltop in 5 acres of farmland with spectacular 360-degree views. Unfussy and cosy with winding stairs.

→ Moles Lane, N Whilborough, 01803 316191
50.4853, -3.5890

37 RIVERSIDE HOUSE, TUCKENHAY

Idyllic retreat with own slipway right on the Dart. Rent the whole house or stay as a B&B guest. Bring your own canoes or hire them.

→ Tuckenhay, TQ9 7EQ, 01803 732837
50.3931, -3.664

38 WILD CAMPING ON DARTMOOR

Wild camping is allowed on Dartmoor. Try the Avon valley, upstream from Shipley Bridge car park and toilets (50.4510, -3.8592, follow signs from South Brent). Or continue up to the beautiful wild area near Huntingdon Cross (50.4803, -3.8861). For camping on the Dart, drop down into Holne woods near Sharrah Pool (see 1), or canoe to a river beach on the estuary, such as Duncannon, near Ashprington (see 8).
50.4510, -3.8592

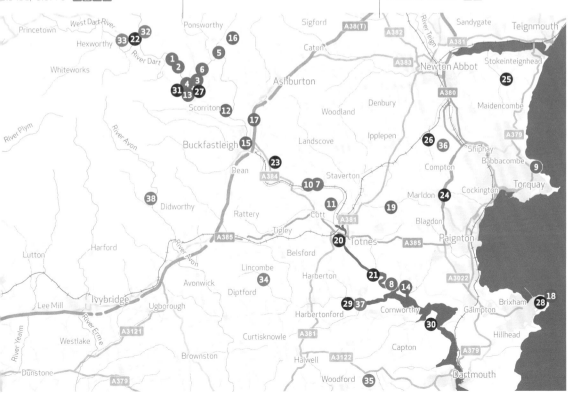

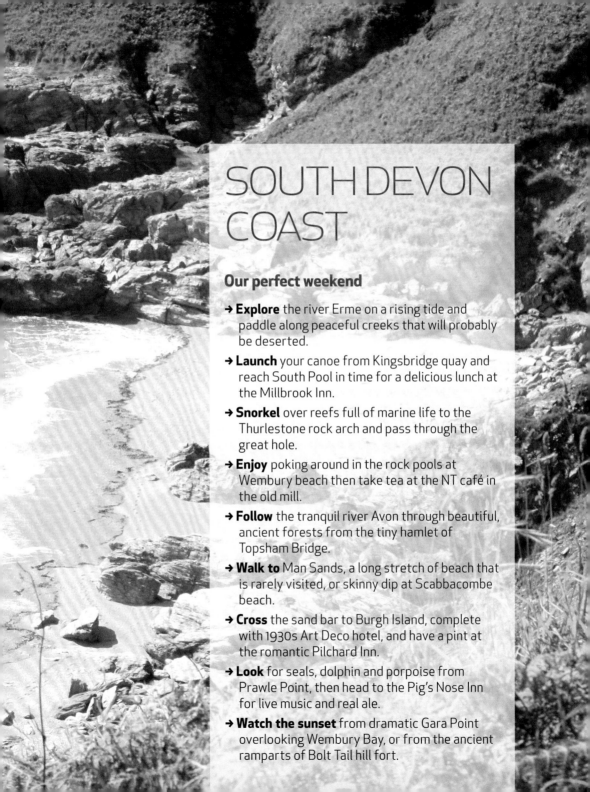

SOUTH DEVON COAST

Our perfect weekend

→ **Explore** the river Erme on a rising tide and paddle along peaceful creeks that will probably be deserted.

→ **Launch** your canoe from Kingsbridge quay and reach South Pool in time for a delicious lunch at the Millbrook Inn.

→ **Snorkel** over reefs full of marine life to the Thurlestone rock arch and pass through the great hole.

→ **Enjoy** poking around in the rock pools at Wembury beach then take tea at the NT café in the old mill.

→ **Follow** the tranquil river Avon through beautiful, ancient forests from the tiny hamlet of Topsham Bridge.

→ **Walk to** Man Sands, a long stretch of beach that is rarely visited, or skinny dip at Scabbacombe beach.

→ **Cross** the sand bar to Burgh Island, complete with 1930s Art Deco hotel, and have a pint at the romantic Pilchard Inn.

→ **Look** for seals, dolphin and porpoise from Prawle Point, then head to the Pig's Nose Inn for live music and real ale.

→ **Watch the sunset** from dramatic Gara Point overlooking Wembury Bay, or from the ancient ramparts of Bolt Tail hill fort.

Along Devon's most beautiful and enticing stretch of coastline, you'll find secret, sandy coves overlooked by wild cliff tops with breathtaking views at sunset. Four remarkable river estuaries give way to miles of secluded tidal creeks that are perfect for for canoeing and wildlife watching.

East of the Dart estuary, secluded Man Sands and Scabbacombe, which is part-naturist, have long bays with hidden coves, while Mattiscombe and Ravens coves are beautifully remote beaches below Start Point. At nearby Hallsands, an entire village was virtually washed away by storms in 1917. Today only 2 of the original 37 houses remain. For the best views, stay at one of the basic but stunningly located campsites a little further up the coast near Beesands and buy freshly caught fish at the Britannia Shack.

Prawle Point, the wildest headland, boasts a string of tiny coves like white pearls and an abundance of wildlife. Blue butterflies flutter on the breeze, buzzards circle high overhead and kestrels hover in search of small mammals. Moor Sands is an idyllic cove with silver sand or seek out Elender Cove, nestled in the corner of Gammon Head.

Bolt Head is wonderful for wild walks, and from Bolt Tail you can scan the sea for dolphins or just enjoy the neon blaze of an ocean sunset. On a warm day when the water is high, swim or snorkel out over the reef to Thurlestone Rock, the offshore arched stack. Swimming through the hole at high tide is a true rite of passage.

Heading west from Thurlestone beach, leave the summer hustle and bustle behind and find peace and tranquillity at Cowry Cove beneath the golf course and coast path. The shells on this wild, secluded beach are exquisite. And if you enjoy eating shellfish, try the Oyster Shack at Bigbury and sit outside in the sunshine. For liquid refreshment to the west of Bigbury and Burgh Island, visit the 13th-century Journey's End Inn above the silver rocks and shale of remote Aymer and Westcombe Coves. Two miles further, at Kingston, is the oak-beamed Dolphin with a track down to the sparkling sands of the Erme estuary.

For those who love canoeing, the greatest adventures along this coastline are to be found by journeying up the four stunning river estuaries, known as rias – valleys that were drowned by post-glacial sea level rises. The Kingsbridge ria is dendritic (branched), with nine little creeks to explore by canoe. The Yealm is perhaps the most impressive with steep, forested sides, but the Erme is the most peaceful, with not a yacht or other craft in sight, and probably the wildest and most peaceful river estuary in the whole of the South West.

SECRET COVES

CELLAR BEACH & GARA POINT

Small pebble sand beach on the shore of the river Yealm estuary. Great sunsets out over the Great Mew Stone from Gara Point.

→ From Noss Mayo car park (via Newton Ferres, B3186 SE of Plymouth) walk along the small road on the S bank of Newton Creek and then on to the path along the Yealm estuary. Note that part of the parking area is under water at high tide. Good sea bass fishing.
0 mins, 50.3098, -4.0644

WADHAM ROCKS, NEWTON FERRES

Tiny silver-sand cove with coloured rock formations and crystal-clear water. Naturist.

→ Entering Newton Ferrers on B3186 turn before church, towards Membland. After ½ miles turn L at T-junction, park, and find footpath on R between hedges after 500m. Bear R at coast path then descend L.
0 mins, 50.3054, -3.9968

ERME MOUTH, MOTHECOMBE

Beautiful sandy river mouth. Good for canoeing. Beware of rips when rough.

→ As for Wadham but continue on lane

from T-junction and turn R to Mothecombe after 2 miles. Park and walk down lane. Coast path leads S 500m to Meadowsfoot Beach. Continue on coast path to Bugle Hole (50.3050, -3.9640), a small inlet with a sea cave and tunnel. Other side of Erme is accessible from Kingston, which has a good pub (Dolphin Inn, Kingston, TQ7 4QE, 01548 810314) or by wading.
10 mins, 50.3116, -3.9478

4 AYMER COVE & WESTCOMBE

Very pretty walk down through remote NT Ringmore Valley. Path starts at an ancient orchard, currently being restored with traditional Devon apple varieties. Hidden Aymer Cove has silver rocks, or continue a little further W along the coast path for the even more secluded Westcombe Beach.

→ Find NT car park on edge of Ringmore, just off road to Challaborough. Good pub (Journey's End, see 36).
15 mins, 50.2937, -3.9102

5 BANTHAM SAND & BURGH ISLAND

Bantham is a well-known but beautiful beach at the mouth of the river Avon with low-tide sand and shallow lagoons. It's fun to walk along the sand bars from the ferry steps to

the beach at low tide, or the adventurous could wade across the river (take care) and head for the Pilchard Inn on Burgh Island (see 35).

→ On narrow lanes off the A379, S of Aveton Gifford.
5 mins, 50.2799, -3.8876

6 COWRY COVE, THURLESTONE

Little-visited stretch of sand, part-naturist, below Thurlestone golf course.

→ Follow the footpath 5 mins between the tennis courts at the S end of the village, or park just beyond the golf club and take the coast path 15 mins, dropping down just before the green changing hut at the end of golf course.
15 mins, 50.2666, -3.8679

7 THURLESTONE ROCK ARCH

From Thurlestone beach snorkel out across the reefs to the amazing offshore rock arch, a distance of 300m.

→ Best attempted at mid- or high tide, otherwise a tricky scramble over rock pools. Signed off A381 W of Kingsbridge.
20 mins, 50.2579, -3.8611

8

8 SOARMILL COVE, BOLT HEAD

Isolated NT cove below Soarmill Cove Hotel. There's also a little island to swim around at high tide and caves to explore at low tide.

→ From Malborough (A381, W of Salcombe) follow signs for Soar and then hotel. Pay for parking or eat at the hotel (TQ7 3DS, 01548 561566). If you have a kayak and it is calm you might like to head for beautiful Saltern Pike (50.2301, -3.8423) or Hugh's Hole (50.2341, -3.8526) 1 mile NW along the coast. Bolt Head and the sheltered, double coves of Starehole Bay are a 2 mile walk along the coast path (50.2147, -3.7861). Free parking at Bolt Head NT car park (continue through Soar village).
20 mins, 50.2229, -3.8275

9 MOOR SANDS, PRAWLE POINT

The best of a trio of wonderful coves along the dramatic and remote Prawle Point coastline. Beautiful, pale-coloured sand.

→ Entering East Prawle from the N turn R at water tower ½ mile before village (signed East Portlemouth/Cycle Route 2), then turn L after ½ mile at Vinivers Cross (signed East Prawle) then find bridleway on R at sharp corner. Descend for about 1 mile, keeping close to stream, then bear R. Also try Elender Cove tucked in on the E of Gammon Head, ½

mile to the E (50.2087, -3.7297, best in the morning). You can also park at Gara Rock hotel development and walk in from the W (TQ8 8PH, seasonal café and cove beneath). Good ales at the quirky Pig's Nose Inn, East Prawle (see 30).
20 mins, 50.2143, -3.7368

10 SUNNY COVE, EAST PORTLEMOUTH

Pretty cove on E side of Kingsbridge estuary, overlooking Salcombe Castle.

→ Park in East Portlemouth and drop down to Mill Bay and then on to Sunny Cove on coast path. Or access by ferry from South Sands, hire self-drive boat from Whitestrand Quay, Salcombe (TQ8 8ET, 01548 843818) or use your own kayak.
15 mins, 50.2280, -3.7707

11 LANNACOMBE BEACH, START POINT

Pretty sand and shingle cove.

→ ½ mile S of Kellaton find very narrow lane signed Lannacombe. Lovely B&B (1 double room) and seasonal camping at Lannacombe Farm B&B (TQ7 2NH, 01548 511158). Walk 500m W for more coves.
5 mins, 50.2228, -3.6807

12 MATTISCOMBE COVE, START POINT

Beautiful remote cove at Great Mattiscombe Sand on dramatic Start Point. Interesting Two Stones conical rock formation to the W.

→ Leave A379 at Stokenham, follow signs to Start Point and lighthouse and park. Take path in R corner, SW down through fields to beach ½ mile. Walk E 500m, around headland to find tiny shingle Raven's Cove with small cave and snorkelling.
15 mins, 50.2204, -3.6595

13 LANDCOMBE COVE

Small cove with a stream, 200m down from the coast path, only visited by boats.

→ ½ mile S of Blackpool sands on A379 find layby on corner at top of hill (50.3153, -3.6163) with parking for 2 cars. Continue on road 200m to find footpath L down to beach.
5 mins, 50.3142, -3.6159

14 WESTERN COMBE COVE

Small, rocky cove with secret access steps and sea caves.

→ Park at NT Little Dartmouth car park (1 mile E of Stoke Fleming/A379 on lanes). Head straight to coast path, then L for 400m to find steps down from W side of Combe Point.

ntinue on lower coast path ¾ mile NE to
note Compass Cove (down grass slope then
eps; sea-weedy rocks at low tide). Castle
ve (with bathing ledge) is 1 mile further
d there are tea rooms above at Dartmouth
stle (TQ6 0JN, 01803 833897).
  mins, 50.3264,-3.5728 [icons]

MAN SANDS, WOODHUISH

rge sandy bay on remote stretch of coast
tween Brixham and Dartmouth. Wetland
nd and old coastguard cottages.

From Kingswear N on B3205, turn R signed
leton Fishacre (NT house). After 1 mile
ar L (No Through Road, free range eggs/
at) and find first NT car park on R after
nile. (this leads down to part-naturist
abbacombe beach; can be rocky at low
e 50.3582, -3.5200). Continue through
oodhuish Farm to second NT parking on L
d continue down track to beach.
  mins, 50.3708, -3.5165 [icons]

ECLUDED CREEKS

YEALM RIA CANOEING

steep-sided, narrow and wooded stretch
kes this an impressive ria to paddle. The
per Yealm, which has oyster beds, is a
ture reserve with no yachts or landing
owed.

The public quay at Bridgend is the most
nvenient launch point. High water as for
mouth +15 mins.
ours return, 50.3140, -4.0327 [icons]

ERME RIA CANOEING

ere is no shoreline development or even
otpath access, and the river is too shallow
most other craft, so you will probably
ve this stretch to yourself. Keep quiet and
joy the best of the wildlife.

Wonwell beach, a mile SE of Kingston,
ovides the easiest launching, but the
rking is very limited. Mothecombe involves
ong walk back up hill. You could also launch
om Sequer Bridge on the A379 (50.351,
9240) above the weir. Can only be paddled
high water (as for Plymouth +15 mins).
ours return, 50.3122, -3.9403 [icons]

AVON RIA CANOEING

mainly sandy ria with sand bars at low tide
d plenty of surf at the river mouth.

Launch from or Aveton Gifford upstream
r park by roundabout, A379) or downstream
Bantham ferry or Bantham Sand (see 5).
gh water is 15 mins later than Plymouth.
ter heavy rainfall it may be possible to try

canoeing some of the upstream sections
around Topsham Bridge or Loddiswell New
Bridge (50.3145,-3.8009).
2 hours return, 50.3106, -3.8378 [icons]

19 KINGSBRIDGE RIA CANOEING

No main river, just nine small streams,
flowing into the Salcombe-to-Kingsbridge
nature reserve. The main harbour attracts
thousands of yachts each year, but Frogmore
and Southpool creeks provide solitude. Both
have pubs at their tips but the Millbrook Inn
at South Pool is our favourite. Much wildlife
and three wrecks, the *Resolute, Iverna*
and *Empress*, to see at low tide (see NT
Kingsbridge canoe map: buy or download).

→ Kingsbridge quay is the easiest place to
launch, signed 'The Quay long stay car park'.
High water is Plymouth +15 minutes and most
of the ria can be paddled 3 hours either side of
high water. Currents can reach 3 knots and are
strongest mid-tide, between Snapes Point and
Scoble Point, and downstream of Salcombe
and Mill Bay, particularly on The Bar at the
harbour mouth (breaking waves). Whitestrand
Boat Hire offers self-drive dinghies with
outboards (1 Strand Court, Whitestrand
Quay, Salcombe, TQ8 8ET, 01548 843818,
07528 410389) and Singing Paddles will hire

canoes or organise trips (Kingsbridge 0775
4426633).
5 hours return, 50.2797, -3.7753 [icons]

ANCIENT FOREST

20 TOPSHAM BRIDGE, AVON

Follow the river down towards Loddiswell
through idyllic, ancient woodland.

→ Topsham Bridge is signed L off the B3196
Loddiswell road. There is a small but deep
pool under the bridge with a ladder leading
down, possibly for swimmers (50.3468,
-3.7817). Or continue a mile downstream to
find a deep swimming spot on a right hand
bend after about a mile, or try above the
weir, a bit further down (50.3305, -3.7857).
Afterwards visit Blackdown hill fort and
earthworks, signed off B3196 3 miles before
Loddiswell. then continue to car park and
picnic site. (50.3547, -3.8012).
20 mins, 50.3333, -3.7816 [icons]

RUINS AND HILL FORTS

21 BOLT TAIL CLIFF CASTLE

These remains of this ancient Iron Age
fortification command spectacular views W
across the ocean. Perfect for sundown.

23

→ From Inner Hope (3 miles W of Marlborough /A381) lifeboat station follow coast path ½ mile, bearing R over earth ramparts at top. With luck, you'll catch sight of seals, dolphins and porpoises from the cliffs.
20 mins, 50.2422, -3.8699

22 HALLSANDS, START POINT
Ghostly ruins of a village that was all but washed away by the sea.
→ Turn L (signed North Hallsands, Muckton) 1½ miles before Start Point. Follow coastpath ½ mile S.
10 mins, 50.2342, -3.6585

23 ST ANDREW'S CHURCH, SOUTH HUISH
Romantic church ruins in a tiny hamlet, now cared for by Friends of Friendless Churches. St Andrew's was left to decay when a new church was built in Galmpton in 1860.
→ Turn R off A381 signed South Huish, just before R turn signed Outer Hope.
50.2563, -3.8328

WILDLIFE AND WILD FOOD

24 WEMBURY MARINE CENTRE
Family beach, good for rock-pooling.
→ Church Road, PL9 0HP, 01752 862538. 3 miles S of Plymstock, Plymouth.
50.3173, -4.0833

20

25 SEA FISHING, SALCOMBE
There's excellent deep-sea fishing along this coast, from Bolt Head to Start Point. Try your luck with bass, pollock, ray, sole, plaice, conger eel and mackerel.
→ Anglo Dawn (07967 387657, 01548 511500); Phoenix Charters (01548 842840); Whitestrand Boat Hire (01548 843818, 07528 410389); African Queen, Oxford Street, Dartmouth, TQ6 9AL (07885 246061).
50.2391, -3.7665

5

LOCAL FOOD

26 AVON MILL CAFÉ DELI, LODDISWELL
Plant nursery, licensed café and deli on the banks of the Avon serving locally sourced, organic and artisan foods.
→ Kingsbridge, TQ7 4DD, 01548 550338
50.3210, -3.7884

27 STOKELEY FARM SHOP, STOKENHAM
Local farm shop with butchery, deli, garden centre and café selling wonderful pizzas made in a traditional, wood-fired oven.

NO ENTRY
29

→ Stokeley Barton Farm, TQ7 2SE, 01548 581010
50.2737, -3.6634

28 BRITANNIA SHACK, BEESANDS
Enjoy freshly landed fish and shellfish at the charming café/fishmonger run by veteran fisherman Nick and his wife Anita. Perfect crab sandwiches.
→ The Viviers, Beesands, Kingsbridge, TQ7 2EH, 01548 581186
50.2528, -3.6578

29 THE OYSTER SHACK, BIGBURY
Quirky seafood restaurant serving freshly-caught fish and oysters. Have whatever's on the specials board and take a seat outside.
→ Millburn Orchard Farm, Stakes Hills, Bigbury-on-Sea, TQ7 4BE, 01548 810876
50.3078, -3.8521

30 PIG'S NOSE INN, EAST PRAWLE
Eccentric old smugglers' inn. Local ales and live music.
→ East Prawle, TQ7 2BY, 01548 511209
50.2152, -3.7098

31 KINGSBRIDGE FARMER'S MARKET
From oysters to local bread and honey, lots of delicious produce for sale on the first and third Saturdays of every month, 9am -1pm.
→ Town Square, Kingsbridge, TQ7 1HZ
50.2828, -3.7766

32 THE MILLBROOK INN, SOUTH POOL
Creekside location and excellent local food. Millbrook IPA is made especially for them by the local brewery and goes down a treat with the briliant bouillabaisse. Local veg is sold from the Veg Shed, an inspired solution to the lack of a village shop. Good pit-stop on a canoe trip from Kingsbridge.
→ Kingsbridge, TQ7 2RW, 01548 531581
50.2485, -3.7196

33 THE START BAY INN, TORCROSS
Offering the best fish and chips in the area, this pub does get busy, but you can sample the local ales while you wait. No bookings.
→ Nr Kingsbridge, TQ7 2TQ, 01548 580553
50.2678, -3.6526

34 WEMBURY OLD MILL CAFÉ
Locally sourced food, ales and home-made cream teas at this cosy NT corn mill right on Wembury beach. Glorious views and a great place for rock-pooling.

→ Church Rd, Wembury, PL9 0HP, 01752
462314
50.3201, -4.0795

5 PILCHARD INN, BURGH ISLAND

Worth stopping for a quick drink at this
very busy but romantic old inn, steeped in
smuggling history.

→ 35 Burgh Island, TQ7 4BG, 01548 810514
50.2804, -3.8984

6 THE JOURNEY'S END INN, RINGMORE

Hearty local food at this rural 13th-century
inn above Aymer Cove. A large garden for
sunny days, log fires in winter.

→ Ringmore Vean, TQ7 4HL, 01548 810205
50.2979, -3.8950

CAMP AND SLEEP

7 KARRAGEEN CAMPING, BOLBERRY

A well-run campsite just a mile from Hope
Cove. Opt for the lower valley, tent-only
areas. Fresh croissants and bread available
in the morning from the shop.

→ Kingsbridge, TQ7 3EN, 01548 561230
50.2386, -3.8397

38 PIPPIN THE GYPSY CARAVAN

Spend a romantic weekend in this beautifully
restored gypsy caravan, set in a quiet
orchard on Cleave Farm. Take a candlelit
walk to the cedar hot tub and in the morning,
munch your way through the breakfast
hamper.

→ Canopyandstars.co.uk, Cleave Farm,
Butterwells, Morleigh, Totnes, TQ9 7JS, 01275
395 447,
50.3674, -3.7736 camp

39 SUGAR PARK, BEESON

A tiny, very basic site with two small fields
but worth it for the views of Start Bay.

→ Richard Rogers, 01548 580696 580165
50.2553, -3.6623

40 OLD COTMOOR CAMPING

Tent-only field higher up the hill is open in
summer. Small, family-orientated site with
views over open country to Start Bay. Great
facilities include games room and separate
games field.

→ Stokenham, Kingsbridge, TQ7 2LR,
01548 580240
50.2616, -3.6792

41 BERYL'S FIELD, BEESON

Another basic camping field near the beach.
Lovely sea views. Hand made signs direct
you from the village.

→ Beryl Wotton 01548580527
50.2572, -3.6675

42 MAELCOMBE HOUSE, LANNACOMBE

Small, exposed, simple site but with glorious
views above the little cove.

→ A. Turley, TQ7 2NH, 01548511158/511521
50.222856, -3.681199

43 SOUTH ALLINGTON HS, CHIVELSTONE

Lovely site near Lannacombe Beach with
good facilities, duck pond and resident
sheep. Afternoon cream teas up at the main
house. No campfires. Also offers B&B.

→ Chivelstone, TQ7 2NB, 01548 511272
50.2345, -3.6955 camp

44 KINGSWEAR CASTLE, KINGSWEAR

Restored castle tower, dating back to 1481,
and right by the edge of the water. An
unforgettable place to stay – fall asleep to
the sound of crashing waves – but expensive.

→ www.landmarktrust.org.uk, 01628 825925
50.3418, -3.5600

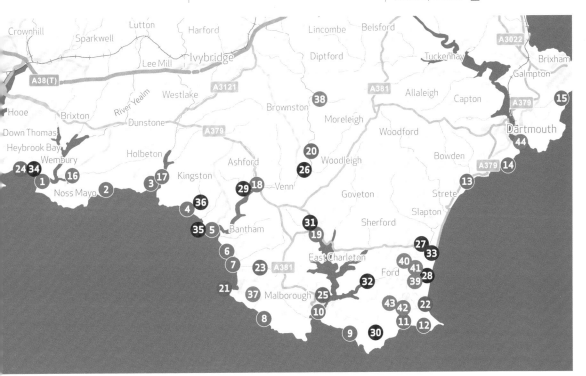

EAST DEVON

Our perfect weekend

→ **Sea kayak** around dramatic red sandstone sea stacks at Ladram Bay.

→ **Fish for** sea bass from the quay at Branscombe or take off on a deep-sea mackerel fishing trip from Beer.

→ **Follow** the ancient tree trail at Killerton or arrange a visit to the 900-year-old oak at Shute – its girth is astonishing.

→ **Try** your hand at cheese-making or building a wood-fired oven at River Cottage. And eat your fill at the River Cottage Canteen.

→ **Discover** the undercliff forests and amazing fossils at remote Charton Bay, scene of a massive landslip.

→ **Swim** in seclusion under red cliffs in the deep Otter pool at Colaton Raleigh.

→ **Cook fresh fish** for supper on a campfire at Weston Mouth, and watch the sun go down over the ocean.

→ **Celebrate** the night with glow-worms at Stoke Woods, nightjars on Aylesbeare Common, or stargaze at the old observatory near Sidmouth.

Often overlooked by tourists, East Devon has a long, wild coastline where dramatic red sandstone cliffs to the west give way to remote, undercliff beaches set far below wooded slopes. Inland, there are ancient forests to explore, and the oldest and biggest oak tree in the South West.

You have to make special arrangement to visit King John's Oak near Shute in Axminster, but you will be rewarded by the unforgettable sight of the aged, gnarled tree with a girth of more than seven arm spans. Tradition has it that the tree started life as an acorn planted by King John in 1199, when hunting nearby. Now, its great contorted boughs reach right down to the ground. You'll find more fine oaks on the ancient forest trail at Killerton Park and also at Ashclyst forest, near Exeter–a great place to see butterflies.

Some picturesque woodland valleys drop down to the sea, terminating in beautiful coves. A walk of about a mile, following a stream down through secluded woods, leads you to Weston Mouth, five miles west of Seaton. Easier to access is the charming National Trust beach at Branscombe, where you can head off on a deep-sea mackerel fishing trip. To the west, beyond Sidmouth, the profile of the coast changes and steep woods are replaced by spectacular, red sandstone cliffs. Ladram Bay has amazing stacks, sea caves and huge rock pools to explore. This same bedrock colours the pretty River Otter, which swirls beneath ivy-clad ciffs, forming secret river pools edged with red sand beaches. At its estuary you might come across red pebbles that split to reveal prehistoric, fossilised shells.

At the eastern extreme of this region, towards Lyme Regis, there is a particularly long, remote section of coastline. In 1839, after intense rain, a huge avalanche resulted in a 45-acre section of agricultural land breaking away to form 'Goat Island', complete with crops. The island became a tourist attraction and farmers charged for entry, but it has long disappeared. This special area is now known as the undercliff, a nature reserve with a unique geology and habitat, and accessible only by walking. The sandy beach far beneath, at Charton Bay, is hidden from sight by dense foliage. Miles from anywhere, this is one of the most beautiful wild bays in Devon and on a sunny day, you could almost be on a desert island.

SECRET BEACHES

LADRAM BAY SEA STACKS, OTTERTON

ed cliffs, stacks and sea caves, best
xplored by kayak or adventure swims:
round S headland 200m to Chiselbury Bay
r around N headland past stacks, to Sandy
ove (400m).

Access only via huge caravan park complex,
ear Otterton (off B3178, W of Sidmouth on
3052). Beach kiosk at bottom of slipway
res out kayaks.

mins, 50.6595, -3.2777

WESTON MOUTH, SIDMOUTH

T beach at bottom of secluded, steep valley
vith shingle, sand and rock pools.

There's a small NT car park in Weston
signed off A3052, E of Sidmouth). Follow path
long valley edge to coast then bear R down to
each. Also on cycle route 52.

0 mins, 50.6849, -3.1847

CHARTON UNDERCLIFF, ROUSDON

Remote, isolated, long sand beach below the
verdant coastal forest of the Dowlands Cliffs
nd Landslips. A National Nature Reserve
vhere there are many butterflies, grass
nakes, lizards and great-crested newts.

→ Access on coast path via long walk from
Lyme Regis or Axmouth (3 miles). When you
find 'Rousdon Cliff' and the ruins of Allhallows
pump station, cross gate/stile (warning sign)
and follow boardwalk down to beach.

60 mins, 50.7054, -2.9950

RIVER SWIMMING

4 COLATON RALEIGH, R OTTER

Lovely little beach and deep corner pool
beneath red cliffs strung with ivy and ferns.

→ Turn down Church Rd off B3178, opposite
Woods Village Shop. Pass church and follow
footpath from bottom of road (near farm) to
river and downstream for 5 mins. You could
also try the beaches 1 mile N at the bend
50.6862, -3.2957 (footpath off Church Rd).

10 mins, 50.6745, -3.2925

5 FLUXTON WEIR, TIPTON ST JOHN

Good pool above the weir in pastures S of
Ottery St Mary. Interesting old mill house
on way.

→ Follow signs for Tipton St John from
A3052/Sidmouth, pass Red Lion pub and
bridge and up Tipton Vale to find parking
behind bus stop (½ mile) and footpath beyond
on R. Weir is just under a mile, 5 mins beyond

Fluxton mill. Continue 1 mile (20 mins) up river
to a deep corner pool on the inside of a deep
hairpin bend/oxbow (50.7397, -3.2827).

20 mins, 50.7267, -3.2891

6 HIGHER WESTWATER WEIR, R YARTY

Small weir pool and salmon leap on bucolic
stream. Further paddling and picnic spots
upstream, as far as Beckford Bridge.

→ From centre of Axminster turn L at
George Hotel, and L again (Caste Hill, signed
Membury). Continue over river/railway line
a mile and turn L, signed Westwater. After
a mile, heading up hill, find lane to ford on L
(public byway). From ford follow footpath
upstream 400m.

10 mins, 50.7954, -3.0342

7 SQUABMOOR LAKE, BUDLEIGH

Lily pond and reservoir high on East Budleigh
Common.

→ Head N on B3179 from Budleigh Salterton.
About 1½ miles from roundabout (with
B3178) turn R at brown sign for 'reservoir'
(opposite 'farm shop'). Pass pretty Bystock
lily pond on L (nice walks) to find parking on R
and continue on track through trees down to
reservoir.

5 mins, 50.6486, -3.3592

17

ANCIENT TREES

8 KING JOHN'S OAK, SHUTE

The largest and oldest oak in the South
West, this tree has a massive a girth of
over 10 metres, and is thought to have been
planted by the young king (who held the
Manor of Axminster) in the 12th century.

→ The oak stands in private grounds in
Woodend Park, 1 mile to W of Shute. Group
visits can be arranged by contacting the
landowner John Bird (07845 909222).
Alternatively, there is a very fine ancient
Turkey Oak by the public footpath in the
grounds of Shute House (continue past
parking for Beacon House 300m to Haddon
Corner to find white gate and drive on R
leading to 50.7694, -3.0536).
15 mins, 50.7710, -3.0783

9 ASHCLYST FOREST, BROADCLYST

Ancient pollarded oaks, other broadleaved
and coniferous trees and lots of butterflies
in summer. Once part of Killerton Estate,
now NT. Lovely countryside around with
many thatched cottages.

→ Signed from Broadclyst (B3181, N of
Exeter, S of Cullompton).
20 mins, 50.7900, -3.4200

10 KILLERTON PARK, BUDLAKE

Follow the NT Killerton ancient tree walk
(downloadable) and discover an ancient
grove of tulip trees and gnarled sweet
chestnuts from the 1770s. Also good
tea rooms and a cycle trail. Farmers'
market every third Saturday of the month
10.30am–2.30pm.

→ Signed from Broadclyst (B3181, N of
Exeter, S of Cullompton).
10 mins, 50.7911, -3.4539

RUINED AND ANCIENT

11 COLUMBJOHN CHAPEL, KILLERTON

Diminutive chapel, on banks of pretty river
Culm on W edge of NT Killerton. Paddling.

→ Signed Columbjohn on R from Rewe, A396
N of Stoke Canon. Then L down track, after
river bridge, to farm and take footpath on L
through ruined gatehouse.
5 mins, 50.7895, -3.4772

12 HAYESWOOD HOLLOWAY, E BUDLEIGH

A good example of a Devonshire holloway
(sunken lane), once thronged with travellers,
drovers, miners, pedlars and thieves. Now
silent and forgotten, on Budleigh Common.

→ As for Squabmoor Lake but continue along
lane to next car park on R and follow paths
due E for ½ mile, connects to East Budleigh
and Knowle.
25 mins, 50.6511, -3.3483

13 CANNINGTON OLD VIADUCT, UPLYME

Set in a quiet valley, this viaduct opened in
1903 to carry steam trains on the branch
line from Axminster to Lyme Regis. It was
the first railway viaduct in the UK to be
constructed entirely from mass concrete
that had not been reinforced. Path along top.

→ Second R after Uplyme turning, down an
unsigned lane, about 2 miles W of Lyme Regis
on A3052. Footpath is on L, under the viaduct.
5 mins, 50.7273, -2.9692

SUNSET AND STARS

14 BEACON HOUSE, SHUTE

One of only two beacon houses remaining
in Devon, which were built to warn of the
approaching Spanish Armada. Fine views.

→ ½ mile E of Shute, on Haddon road (signed
Kilmington) find parking on L (Shute Hill wood)
and climb hill (300m).
5 mins, 50.7723, -3.0526

5 WOODBURY CASTLE, BUDLEIGH

Easily accessible ancient hill fort and a place to enjoy spectacular sunsets.

→ From Squabmoor Lake, Budleigh Common, head N on B3180 3 miles.

5 mins, 50.6779, -3.3692

6 NORMAN LOCKYER OBSERVATORY

Made from scrap metal and manned by volunteers, this working optical observatory has a 150-year-old telescope. An educational centre focusing on astronomy, meteorology, environmental and marine sciences, and amateur radio. Salcombe Mouth beach is 15 mins away on footpaths.

→ 1 mile E of Sidmouth on A3052, turn R at Trow (signed golf course, Salcombe Regis) and continue through village to find observatory on R after a mile (Salcombe Hill Road). Evening demonstrations from 7.30pm in summer. Entrance fee.

2 mins, 50.6885, -3.2202

7 AYLESBEARE & HARPFORD COMMONS

The woodland fringes, streams and ponds abound with butterflies, dragonflies and damselflies. Stay late on a warm summer evening to hear nightjars 'churring' at dusk.

→ Find car park on R (signed Hawkerland) off A3052 a mile W of Newton Poppleford.

20 mins, 50.6995, -3.3366

WILDLIFE

18 BUDLEIGH SALTERTON FOSSILS

The Otter estuary is a bird reserve but is also famous for its pebbles, which yield large numbers of fossilised shells when split. The pebbles were formed and carried along by a giant river that flowed during the Triassic period (240 million years ago). The same rocks and fossils can be found in Brittany, where the river probably had its source.

→ As you reach Budleigh Salterton sea front on the B3178, turn L to the large car park at the war memorial cross. A small hammer is all you need to split the pebbles. Look near the river edge (not the beach) for reddish-coloured fossiliferous pebbles and pebbles with shells showing on the surface.

2 mins, 50.6304, -3.3084

19 BRANSCOMBE MARINE LIFE

Branscombe is a delightful village, with NT old forge and mill, leading to shingle beach via a deep valley. Low-tide rock pools teeming with marine life including crabs, starfish and sea anemones. Divers and

snorkellers can explore low reefs, which run parallel to the beach, about 50 metres from the shore; also larger reefs further out to sea as well as the remains of wrecks. Hire a boat during the summer season and try your luck at mackerel fishing out in the bay, or cast straight from the beach for sea bass.

→ Signed from the A3052 between Seaton and Sidmouth. For fishing trips (on the iconic, orange Branscombe Pearl) and self-drive boats contact beach superintendent John Hughes on 01279 680369 or 07971 519163. The Masons Arms is good for food and accommodation (see 26).

5 mins, 50.6873, -3.1232

20 STOKE WOOD GLOW-WORMS

Ancient forest and hillfort where glow-worms are sometimes seen.

→ Signed 'Skirmish Paintball' on L off A396 approaching Exeter from Stoke Canon. Also check www.glowworms.org.uk.

20 mins, 50.7546, -3.5177

21 BEER MACKEREL FISHING

White pebble beach, cliffs and the ideal starting place to go mackerel fishing.

→ Turn up on the beach to book a mackerel fishing tip or arrange deep-sea and half-day

angling trips through Beer Fish Shop (Sea Hill, Beer, EX12 3NE, 01297 20297). Rent self-drive wooden boats by the hour and catch enough mackerel for the campfire (Butler Boats, 07771 924857).

5 mins, 50.6961, -3.0912

LOCAL FOOD

22 LOWER BRUCKLAND LAKES AND CAFÉ

Two idyllic crystal-clear lakes on either side of the mown meadow public footpath. Grassy banks, little jetties and places for picnics. The owners have turned it into a nature area and it's a wonderful place to watch the sunset and a very tempting place to take an

illicit dusk dip. The Lakeside café serves lots of homemade treats.

→ Signed off the A3052, a mile E of Colyford. Holiday cottages available on the farm (EX13 8ST, 07851 247 320).

50.73246, -3.03495 🏊

23 FORAGING AT RIVER COTTAGE

Experience one of the many courses at the famous River Cottage, including making cheese and building a wood-fired oven.

→ Park Farm, Trinity Hill Road, Musbury, Axminster, EX13 8TB, 01297 630300

50.7443, -2.9881 🍴

24 RIVER COTTAGE CANTEEN

The stalwarts of fine seasonal and local produce continue to serve up innovative and delicious food. Visit on a Thursday, which is market day in the square and recreate simple dishes back at camp.

→ Trinity Square, Axminster, EX13 5AN, 01297 631862

50.7822, -2.9987

25 WET FISH SHOP, BEER

Pick up fish straight from the boat. NB Amazing fan shells on beach, great for kids.

→ Sold on the beach in Beer.

50.6961, -3.0912 🏖🏊🍴

26 MASONS ARMS, BRANSCOMBE

Gorgeous, 14th-century village inn serving fish landed from the nearby beach and meat spit-roasted in front of you on the fire. Good local ales and well-appointed rooms.

→ EX12 3DJ, 01297 680300

50.6937, -3.1293 🍴📱

27 JOSHUA'S HARVEST CAFÉ AND DELI

Behind the gift shop is a café where you can order tasting platters of local, artisan cheeses and organic meats sold in the deli. Started 20 years ago by organic farmers and continues to champion good, local food.

→ Gosford Road, Ottery St. Mary, EX11 1NU, 01404 815473

50.7612, -3.2731

28 THE SEA SHANTY, BRANSCOMBE

Enjoy local crab sandwiches and the freshest battered fish, or a cream tea at this rustic beach café with garden.

→ EX12 3DP, 01297 680577

50.6903, -3.1249 🍴📱

29 THE WHEELWRIGHT INN, COLYFORD

Sit in the flowery garden and choose good, local food in season from the menu. The interior is cob-walled, beamed and cosy.

→ Nr Seaton, EX24 6QQ, 01297 552585

50.7274, -3.0617 📱

30 DELI SHACK, YEARLSTONE VINEYARD

Enjoy simple, seasonal platters on the sunny terrace as you sample the wines. Planted over 35 years ago, the vineyard is beautifully located with views over the Exe valley.

→ Tiverton EX16 8RL, 01884 855700

50.8622, -3.5091

31 OTTERTON MILL BAKERY AND CAFÉ,

Artisan bread from flour milled in the ancient millhouse and a menu with foraged and wild food, including rabbit and grey squirrel. There are courses, a café and award-winning cream teas.

→ Mill House, The Green, Budleigh Salterton EX9 7HG, 01395 568031

50.6596, -3.3035

32 A LA RONDE TEA ROOMS, EXMOUTH

The shell grotto in the quirky A La Ronde house is amazing, but entry is free to sample the best Devon produce at this lovely NT tea room. Enjoy cream teas on the lawn overlooking the wildflower meadow or eat your own picnic in the orchard.

→ Summer Lane, Exmouth, EX8 5BD, 01395 265514

50.6417, -3.4088

33 MILLERS FARM SHOP, AXMINSTER

A family-run farm shop selling high-quality produce from their own and surrounding farms. Delicious cheeses and treats, and a great fish stall.

→ Gammons Hill, Axminster, EX13 7RA, 01297 35290

50.7786, -3.0305

34 THE LYME BAY WINERY, SHUTE

Traditional country drinks and preserves: wines, fruit liqueurs, cider, cider brandy, vinegars and preserves, all made on site.

→ Shute, Nr Axminster, EX13 7PW, 01297 551355. Turn L for Shute 2 miles W of Axminster on A35, then turn R in village (signed).

50.7632, -3.0657

JACK IN THE GREEN, ROCKBEARE

...varding-winning gastro pub specialising in ...cal produce.

→ Nr Exeter, EX5 2EE, 01404 822240
...7504, -3.3932

THE SEAFOOD PLATTER, BEER

...gendary local seafood platters and home-...ade, organic food.

→ Fore Street, Beer, EX12 3EQ, 01297 20099
...6978, -3.0924

CAMP AND SLEEP

7 CUCKOO DOWN, OTTERY ST MARY

...ree yurts and a safari tent with ...oodburner and composting loo in a large ...eadow. Comfortable beds and bunting ...lore with access to wild woods. Campfires.

→ Lower Broad Oak Road, West Hill, Ottery ...aint Mary, EX11 1UE, 07974 66080
...7365, -3.3112 ⛺

38 COOMBE VIEW, BRANSCOMBE

Although there are static caravans here, the feel is rural feel with views of rolling fields and the sea. Enjoy a campfire at night or head to the Masons Arm's (see 26).

→ Seaton, EX12 3BT, 01297 680218
50.7060, -3.1334 🏕️

39 HUNGER HILL, YURT HOLIDAYS

Laze in the hammock and eat fresh duck eggs every morning. Five fully equipped kilim-filled yurts set in a quiet orchard location on the edge of the Aylesbeare nature reserve.

→ Hollytree, Hunger Hill, Newton Poppleford, EX10 0BZ, 01395 568454
50.7021, -3.3098

40 GREAT SEASIDE, BRANSCOMBE

A charming thatched 16th-century farmhouse B&B just minutes walk from Branscombe beach. Inglenooks, flagstones, beams, woodburning stove and sea views.

→ Great Seaside Farm, Branscombe, Seaton
EX12 3DP, 01297 680470
50.6892, -3.12347

41 BILLINGSMOOR FARM, CULLOMPTON

Enjoy the rustic comfort of tent life on this organic dairy farm in the heart of Devon. There's a sweat lodge in the woods, a forest school for the kids and moonlit wood-fired hot tubs.

→ Butterleigh, EX15 1PQ, 01884 855800
50.8502, -3.4612 🏕️

42 HOOK FARM CAMPING, UPLYME

Set in the beautiful Lym valley and only 1 mile over the style to Lyme Regis. Easy access to beaches and fresh croissants in the morning. Aim for a site at the top of the hill and enjoy glorious sunsets.

→ Gore Lane, DT7 3UU, 01297 442801
50.7335, -2.9589 🏕️

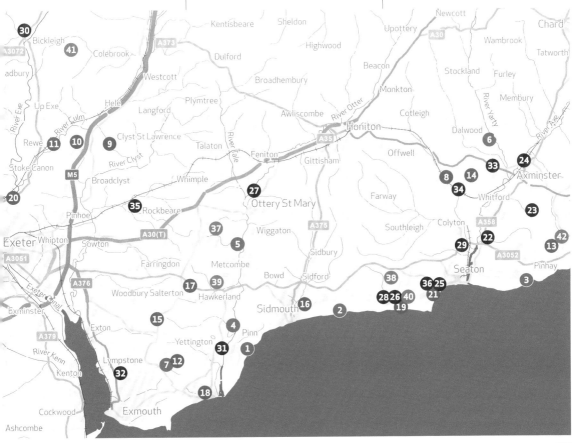

CENTRAL EXMOOR

Our perfect weekend

→ **Scramble** down to secret Selworthy Sands, revealed only at low-tide, after camping out in Porlock Bay.

→ **River tube** down the Lyn from Rockford to Watersmeet, exploring pools and avoiding waterfalls, or dip in from the footpath.

→ **Dip** in the pool above Tarr Steps, explore the ancient woodland and enjoy a delicious lunch at the Tarr Steps Farm Inn.

→ **Explore** tunnels and ruins on the path to Culbone church, England tiniest, tucked away deep in woodland, by the sea.

→ **Search** for ancient oaks in Horner Wood, and pay your respects to 'The General', the oldest of them all, at Cloutsham.

→ **Sample** wine from the vineyard at Wootton Courtenay or enjoy tea and panoramic views at NT Holincote.

→ **Follow** the river Barle from Simonsbath to Cow Castle. Plunge in the pool and watch the sunset from the top of the hill fort.

→ **Cook** supper over the fire at the back-to-nature woodland campsite at Pool Bridge, high in the Horner Valley.

→ **Star gaze** from the remote Great Rowbarrow cairn near Dunkery Beacon. Listen out for nightjars and red deer.

This sweeping landscape of high, flat hills grazed by wild ponies is Britain's least-visited National Park. Exmoor was also made Europe's firs International Dark Sky Reserve for its remoteness and low light pollutio Its precipitous, cliff-edged coastline is particularly rich in marine life.

Exmoor's coastline – surely one of the wildest places in Britain today – is often hard to reach and the few paths down the steep cliffs are mainly use by rock climbers or wild-beach hunters. If a scramble down to the shore appeals, look closely in the rock pools and find three types of sea anemon (beadlet, strawberry and snakelocks), as well as velvet swimming crabs an porcelain crabs. Exploring the dramatic low-tide coastline is a delight, but take care not to get cut off by rising tides.

This remote stretch has always attracted those seeking solace and rugge beauty. Coleridge retreated to an isolated Exmoor house to write his unfinished poem, *Kubla Khan*, and a tiny pre-Norman church still stands in the fairytale woods at Culbone, with the ruins of Ada Byron Lovelace's romantic mansion nearby. The heather-strewn hills, tumbling waterfalls and wooded valleys prompted the Victorians to name Exmoor the 'Little Switzerland of England'. For a taste of this era visit Watersmeet, originally a 19th-century fishing lodge, now a quaint National Trust tea shop, set in magical woodland with river pools that are perfect for a dip. Explore the river upstream as far as Rockford, with its microbrewery and inn, or continue to Malmsmead and Oare, the heart of *Lorna Doone* country.

Nearby Cloud Farm, beside the river Badgworthy in the Doone Valley, is a great place to camp, with pools for paddling and pony trekking trips. Further east, at the more remote Pool Bridge campsite in Horner Wood, you'll find more streams and pools, and some of the best natural woodland on Exmoor. To the south is the moor's highest point, Dunkery Beacon, wher you can watch the sunset then stay to gaze up at the vast, starry sky.

For those who love wild swimming, the river Barle is a paradise. Landacre Bridge has shallow and deeper pools for invigorating dips, and further alon the enchanting valley the enterprising Withypool post office sells rubber dinghies. Heading south-east through quiet woodland valleys, you come to the famous clapper bridge, constructed from megalithic flat stones, at Tar Steps, and a perfect place for lunch – or another cream tea.

SECRET BEACHES

SILLERY SANDS, LYNTON

hingle and sand beach with a backdrop of steep cliffs. Part-naturist.

→ Leave Lynmouth on steep A39 coast road, ir Minehead. After ¾ mile, about a third of ay up hill, park in small lay-by on R, cross ɔad and climb down to coast path 20m below. ollow lower path E (R) for 500m, dropping own steep, difficult, zig-zag path to beach. ough return. Take care not to get cut off if ou head up beach.

:0 mins, 51.2332, -3.8065

EAST PORLOCK BAY, BOSSINGTON

luge, wild pebble beach. Good jumps and ives from Hurlstone Point at high tide.

→ Pretty walk besides stream from car ark in Bossington (signed from E side of orlock, A39). Strong tow back on the steep each. Exmoor Owl and Hawk Centre is also Bossington at West Lynch Farm. Daily owl how and flying display, 01643 862816.

5 mins, 51.2303, -3.5795

SELWORTHY SANDS & HURLSTONE

ow tide only stretch of sands beneath ossington Hill. Amazing sunsets from Hurlstone Point look-out. If you like scrambling, find the cave (Gull Hole) and follow its route through and under the point.

→ As for Porlock, but climb up around Hurlstone Point, past the ruined coastguard tower. After 300m find path to beach, a steep scramble down scree, with a rope.

30 mins, 51.2328, -3.5667

WATERFALLS AND POOLS

4 LONG POOL, ROCKFORD/BRENDON

Lovely, deep, long pool in a small, verdant ravine beneath a waterfall. Just off the path, and feels very secluded. Some good jumps for the brave.

→ There are paths on both L and R banks of the beautiful East Lyn stream and the pool can be accessed from either Watersmeet NT tea rooms, or Rockford - turn onto B3223 from A39, just N of Lynton, then immediately L up steep narrow lane (cycle route) for 1 mile. Head downstream on R bank from Rockford (cross opposite the excellent Rockford Inn) exploring several more good pools with jumps at valley bottom. If you reach Ash Bridge you have overshot by 500m. Continue to Watersmeet on foot, or for a real adventure do the whole route in wetsuits with rings, but beware the various waterfalls and drops.

15 mins, 51.2203, -3.7873

5 WATERSMEET, LYNMOUTH

A fine series of pools and falls. The NT tearoom has been serving teas in the old fishing lodge since 1901: try the Exmoor speciality, whortleberry jam. A good location to watch salmon leaping, see otters, red deer and buzzards, too. Bluebells in May.

→ 300m upstream there are a series of rocky pools down beneath the path on R. Another ½ mile, before Ash Bridge, find several beachy areas and deep corner pools. Lots of paddling for kids. Another 1½ mile upstream leads to Long Pool. Watersmeet House is a mile S of Lynmouth on the A39.

5 mins, 51.2262, -3.7908

6 BADGWORTHY POOL, MALMSMEAD

Charming but small plunge pool underneath shallow waterfall and big tree in popular Doone Valley woodland walk.

→ Malmsmead is a tiny village off A39 Lynmouth-Minehead road and is at the heart of Doone country (tea rooms). Park here or drive ½ mile up to Cloud Farm campsite to use their shop or campsite. From here cross

footbridge, follow path 1 mile upstream until woods clear and path bears R up onto moor. On L, under a lip of bank, find small pool by large tree.

20 mins, 51.1951, -3.7285 🌊🗑️🚻👣

7 PINKERY POND, CHALLACOMBE

High, lonely, open stretch of moor known as The Chains. Pinkery Pond lake was created for landowner John Knight in 1830 by damming the headwaters of the river Barle. A canal was then dug to power a large waterwheel, which would assist the operation of an inclined railway carrying iron ore from Exmoor to Porlock Weir. Neither the canal nor the railway were ever built and John Knight retired to Rome.

→ Between Challacombe and Simonsbath (B3358) find gate and tarmac track off road at bridge (Pinkery ENPA) and follow for a mile. The Long Stone megalith can be found on moor, a 1½ mile boggy trudge to the NW.

20 mins, 51.1658, -3.8275 🏞️🏕️⛪🌊

8 WITHYPOOL & DOWNSTREAM, BARLE

Withypool is a popular and bucolic paddling spot: even the village post office sells inflatables. Walk downstream 1½ miles (Two Moors Way) through open meadows and along wooded banks to find a small weir, island and pool, just before footpath turning signed Winsford Hill.

→ Signed off B3223 N of Winsford Hill. Continue walk down to Tarr Steps 30 mins and return via Parsonage Down and lanes.

30 mins, 51.0919, -3.6351 🌊🏊🏃👣

9 COW CASTLE, BARLE

Remote, small pool in the babbling river Barle at foot of the impressive Cow Castle hill fort, halfway between Simonsbath and Landacre Bridge. Pass the interesting ruins at Wheal Eliza, before reaching the castle. There are several secret and idyllic places to bivouac.

→ From Simonsbath (good pub Hunter's Inn, 01643 831506) take footpath opposite and follow river's L bank for 2 miles.

40 mins, 51.1237, -3.7254 🏞️🏕️🏃🌊

10 LANDACRE BRIDGE, BARLE

Stone bridge, grassy river banks and popular Exmoor spot for paddling.

→ For deeper pools continue up moor road and take track on R after 500m and follow down to river 500m (Sherdon Hutch, at confluence with a smaller stream 51.1119, -3.7078). Signed Landacre/S Molton off B3223 near Exford, just N of turning for Withypool.

2 mins, 51.1121, -3.6922 🌊🚻

11 TARR STEPS, BARLE

Ancient stone clapper bridge, in deep wood at end of lane. Very popular with children for paddling. Deeper pool with open grassy banks about ½ mile (15 mins) upstream through woods on L bank, on corner below footbridge.

→ Signed off B3223 (Liscombe). Very good food and accomodation at Inn by waterside. Tarr Farm Inn, Dulverton, TA22 9PY, 01643 851507

15 mins, 51.0820, -3.6291 🌊🗑️🚻🍴🏄

12 BRUSHFORD HOLLOW OAK

A record of this aged tree in St Nicholas's churchyard, near Dulverton, exists from the reign of Elizabeth I. Described as hollow with timber props under its large limbs. The largest limbs have gone, but the oak is still considered the oldest tree on Exmoor.

→ 2 miles S of Dulverton, B3222

3 mins, 51.0208, -3.5420

13 'THE GENERAL' OAK, CLOUTSHAM

Wonderful area of ancient oaks along East Water. The General, the most venerable at well over 500 years old, has an enormous girth, gnarled branches and fissured bark. The tree's splits, hollows and dead branches provide a unique habitat for a host of rare fungi and other species.

→ Start from Aller Combe meadow, a pretty area of stream-side woodland meadow with parking near Cloutsham (N side of Dunkery Beacon, 51.1761,-3.5820). Follow lane down to ford/footbridge (200m), passing several old pollarded oaks, and take track on L just before ford. Continue up on to open heath and follow path on contour around for about 500m to find a faint path L leading up to some scree/bare rocks on slopes above you. A lovely walk, even if you don't manage to find the tree, and you can also continue on to (or start at) Webber's Post car park, off Dunkery Hill, with fine sunset views (51.1841, -3.5707).

10 mins, 51.1807, -3.5764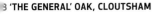

SUNSET AND STARS

14 ROWBARROWS, DUNKERY BEACON

Sweeping vistas reward those who make it to Exmoor's summit at sunset. As night falls, you might hear churring nightjars and see bats swoop. While Dunkery Beacon is the highest point at 519m, Great Rowbarrow, 1 mile to the W, features Bronze Age cairns, is wilder, has better views, and is only 9m lower. The parking is closer too!

→ 10 mins from the tiny wild car park at the top of Stoke Pero Common/Lang Combe Head (51.1653, -3.6164, 3 miles above Webber's Post, Cloutsham). Webber's Post car park also has great views for those who are feeling 'nesh' visit 'The General' Oak (see 13). Or why not be dropped off at the top with your bike and enjoy the long descent home? Moor Rover from A T West, 01643 709701

10 mins, 51.1619, -3.6096

15 SHOULSBURY CASTLE, HIGH BRAY

Isolated Iron Age hillfort commanding the western approaches to Exmoor. Not as prominent as Cow Castle but the far-reaching views make up for it.

Cycle route 3.

→ About 4 miles SW of Simonsbath, on the Brayford road, turn R signed Challacombe (cycle route 3), and park at hairpin after 3 miles on R (51.139, -3.8346), bear L on track

and approach from the W. Also, Setta Barrow for the keen (51.1281, -3.8234).

10 mins, 51.1366, -3.8515

SACRED AND RUINED

16 BURGUNDY CHAPEL, SELWORTHY

Ruined chapel and hermitage in steep, wooded, coastal combe. The area around Selworthy Beacon is good for rare fritillary butterflies in summer, and sunsets.

→ Follow signs to Selworthy Beacon/North Hill from central Minehead. Continue 2½ miles onto moor. Park at first gravel car park (500m before first summit) and follow path down into the combe (500m). Continue along road for the Beacon summit (51.2209, -3.5490).

15 mins, 51.2230, -3.5081

17 CULBONE CHURCH & STONE

Tiny church, deep in fairytale coastal woods and only accessible by foot. The route passes through two tunnels constructed by the husband of Ada Byron Lovelace (Lord Byron's daughter) so tradesman would not be seen approaching their now ruined home, Ashley Combe. Ada also had a private bathing pool built in the cliff. Hidden in woodland nearby is a 7th-century inscribed standing stone.

17

17

3

4

14

→ Follow coast path from Porlock Weir W (via the quirky thatched Worthy toll house), then 1½ miles through woods and the tunnels. For the stone, turn off A39 at The Culbone (TA24 8JW, 01643 862259, top of Worthy toll road), and continue 300m to find track on L. Follow 200m through low forest to stone row and the Culbone stone, to one side (5 mins, 51.2135, -3.6737).

30 mins, 51.2211, -3.6591

WILDLIFE WONDERS

18 SNOWDROPS, WHEDDON CROSS

Snowdrops carpet the woodland banks of the Avill stream in North Hawkwell Wood in February. A beautiful spectacle.

→ A Park and Ride scheme runs from Wheddon Cross every half an hour in February to the start of the valley walk. Path passes the site of an old sawmill. During the season, refreshments are offered at the 'Snowdrop Cafe', run by volunteers in the Moorland Hall.

30 mins, 51.1480, -3.5423

19 EXMOOR PONIES AND RED DEER

Only found on Exmoor this unique species roams, semi-feral, across the moors. The pony has remained unchanged for a million years and is closely related to prehistoric horses. The main focus of the Pony Centre's work is looking after abandoned filly foals.

→ Exmoor Pony Centre, Ashwick, Dulverton, TA22 9QE, 01398 323093

5 mins, 51.0612, -3.5858

LOCAL FOOD

20 ROYAL OAK, WINSFORD

Constantly changing, seasonal menu with produce from local suppliers.

→ Royal Oak Inn, Winsford, Exmoor National Park, Winsford TA24 7JE, 01643 851455

51.1111, -3.5576

21 ROCKFORD INN, BRENDON

Quirky pub, microbrewery and good river pools in Brendon.

→ The Rockford Inn, Brendon, Lynton, EX35 6PT, 01598 741214

51.2131, -3.7792

22 PERIWINKLE COTTAGE TEA ROOM

Set on the picturesque NT Holincote Estate, this quaint, thatched cottage offers perfect West Country cream teas, with moorland views.

→ Selworthy Green, Minehead, TA24 8TP, 01823 451587

51.2100, -3.5487

23 TARR STEPS FARM INN

Exmoor lamb, Devon beef and local venison and game are all on the menu. Enjoy lunch outside by the River Barle, or inside by the fire. Great cream teas, but busy in summer.

→ Tarr Steps, Dulverton, Somerset, TA22 9P 01643 851507

51.0773, -3.6171

24 HIDDEN VALLEY PIGS

Get a taste of the good life on this off-grid smallholding with rare-breed pigs. Self-sufficiency practitioner and expert, Simon Dawson, offers courses in pig butchery and smallholding management. Appointment only.

→ Hidden Valley Pigs, Barbrook, EX35 6PH, 01598 753545

51.2056, -3.8472

25 ETHEL BRAITHWAITE'S, LYNTON

Stock up on picnic supplies or sample some Exmoor ice cream at this local produce emporium.

→ 1 Castle Hill, Lynton, EX35 6JA, 01598 753721

51.2297, -3.8333

26 THE EXMOOR FOREST INN

On the main road but a perfect resting place for the weary traveller returning from Cow Castle or Pinkery Pond. Serves local game and ales.

→ Simonsbath, TA24 7SH, 01643 831341

51.1397, -3.7548

27 THE MASONS ARMS, KNOWSTONE

Hidden away behind the bar of this 13th-century, thatched pub in rural Exmoor (just off A361) is a Michelin-starred restaurant. Enjoy your cider by the fire or treat yourself to exceptional locally-sourced cuisine.

→ Knowstone, EX36 4RY, 01398 341231

50.9948, -3.6733

28 DUNKERY VINEYARD, WOOTTON

Who would have thought such a harsh terrain could produce red wine? Support this small vineyard with a tasting tour of its seven acres of beautiful Exmoor vines.

→ Wootton Courtenay, TA24 8RD, 01643 841505

51.1797, -3.5161

9 CLOUD FARM, MALMSMEAD

Popular family site with babbling stream and pools up in the wooded Doone Valley. Accessed by a farm track.

➜ Nr Lynton, EX35 6NU, 01598 741278
51.2161, -3.7283

0 HALSE FARM, WINSFORD

A peaceful campsite right on the moor on a working beef-cattle and sheep farm. Some caravans, but there's plenty of space and lots of wildlife to watch, including hedgehogs and Exmoor ponies.

➜ Minehead, TA24 7JL, 01643 851259
51.0978, -3.5785

1 POOL BRIDGE, HORNER WOOD

At the top of the beautiful Horner Valley, this is a lovely, remote woodland campsite with stream and pools. No booking.

➜ Turn L in Porlock by museum, signed Doverhay. Take second (hard) R after a mile, up steep narrow lane, and continue 2 miles to the hairpin bend/stream. TA24 8JS, 01643 86252
51.1906, -3.6142

32 BURROWHAYNES FARM CAMPSITE

Camp in the heart of Exmoor in the lovely Horner valley and woods. Hire ponies from the stables or just let the kids play in the stream.

➜ West Luccombe, Porlock, Minehead, TA24 8HT, 01643 862463
51.2040, -3.5781

33 DOONE VALLEY/CAROL'S CAMPSITE

Closer to Malmsmead, this is a level field by a shallow stream perfect for paddling. Enjoy fishing and campfires. Close to the Buttery tea rooms (01598 741106).

➜ Oaremead Farm, Oare/Malmsmead, EX35 6NU, 01598 741267
51.2164, -3.7311

34 WESTERMILL FARM, EXFORD

Lovely, quiet campsite set in a secluded valley by a stream. Catch fish from the river for your supper and get local eggs and bacon for breakfast. Campfires in the fourth field.

➜ Nr Minehead, TA24 7NJ, 01643 831 238
51.1457, -3.6841

35 LOWER RODHUISH FARM

Six luxury Featherdown Farm tents, spread across two paddocks, with ponies, pond dipping and good views.

➜ Minehead TA24 6QR, 01984 640254
51.1462, -3.4062

36 DOVERHAY FARM, PORLOCK

Shepherd's hut, B&B, rare-breed pigs and home-reared bacon for breakfast.

➜ Porlock, TA24 8LJ, 01643 863416
51.2070, -3.5921

37 MILLSLADE CAMPING, BRENDON

Great basic site with campfires along the River Lyn, not far from Rockford pools/ Watersmeet swims. A minute's walk to Fox and Hounds or a mile from the Rockford Inn.

➜ Nr Lynton, EX35 6PS, 01598 741322
51.2202, -3.7648

38 HINDON ORGANIC FARM, MINEHEAD

Working organic hill farm with B&B, cottage rental and home-reared meats.

➜ Minehead, TA24 8SH, 01643 705244
51.2098, -3.5287

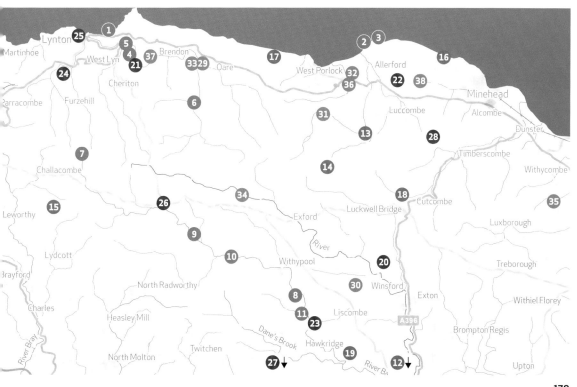

QUANTOCK & BLACKDOWN

Our perfect weekend

→ **Walk** the old drovers' way from Triscombe Stone to Wills Neck summit, then drop down to the Blue Ball Inn for refreshment.

→ **Forage** for whortleberries on Quantock Common and picnic among the ancient beech, ash and oak trees.

→ **Pay homage** to the 3,000-year-old yew at Ashbrittle and take afternoon tea at romantic Cothay Manor.

→ **Follow** the river Culm to a woodland bathing spot, enjoy a dip, then laze on the grassy banks.

→ **Visit** the great yew at Bicknoller, complete with village stocks, then climb the ancient beech-lined track to Thorncombe Barrow.

→ **Cycle round** Wimbleball Lake, stopping to look out for herons, or for a dip at a secluded spot on the eastern shore.

→ **Drink** from the holy love well at Cothelstone, stroll through the parkland and then enjoy a drink at the Rising Sun.

→ **Listen** for nightjars and tawny owls on Staples Plain, after watching the sunset from Beacon Hill.

→ **Camp** at Hunstile organic farm for the wonderful views and enjoy a delicious breakfast at the café.

Three beautiful and very different sets of hills encircle the Vale of Taunton. The Brendon Hills form Exmoor's eastern fringe, while the wilder Quantocks create a distinct chain north to Bridgwater Bay. To the south, at the border of Devon and Somerset, lie the peaceful Blackdown Hills.

While the Blackdown Hills, with their woodlands, lakes and steep escarpments, were one of the most recent places to be designated an Area of Outstanding Natural Beauty, the Quantocks were the first, back in 1956. Renowned for their combination of lush, rolling pastures, wild heathland and hilltop panoramas, the Quantocks also boast a magnificent herd of red deer, which browse the heather and roam through ancient oak and beech woods.

These hilly landscapes have a timeless atmosphere, and the trees and woods feel very ancient. A great avenue of gnarled beeches lines the estate drive at Holford, and there are more beautiful old beeches along the ridge-top drovers' road at Triscombe and Thorncombe. At Bicknoller, the massive yew, although supported, has been standing for over a thousand years, and at Dunster you will find a 60-metre-high fir, Britain's tallest tree.

The hills, valleys and parklands of this part of Somerset are perfect walking country. The great poet Coleridge, a keen walker, once lived in Nether Stowey and his long wanderings through the surrounding landscape were a rich source of inspiration for his poetry. The Coleridge Way, a long-distance walk, starts in the Quantocks, then passes through the Brendon Hills.

Sunset vantage points abound on the western flanks of the Quantocks and offer magnificent views to Exmoor and the sea. To the north, the shoreline along Bridgwater Bay to the Bristol Channel is remote and rarely visited. Here you will find giant wave-cut rock platforms, great stone cobbles, marshland, fantastic birdlife and the ghostly remains of a ruined harbour.

In the far south of this region, the river Culm meanders through bucolic countryside and offers good, secluded swimming. And don't miss the quirky local pub in the Culm valley: the food is delicious. High on the western edge of the Blackdown Hills sits a beautiful Elizabethan beacon – a glorious place to watch the sun's last rays, looking down on deepest Devon and Somerset.

7

SECRET BEACHES

KILVE CHURCH & BEACH
Follow the track from St Mary's church and
its ruined 14th-century chantry, down to
the great, grey wave-cut platforms on the
Bristol Channel. There's no swimming from
this beach.

→ Turn L at the Hood Arms in Kilve (A39), 4
miles E of Watchet.
10 mins, 51.1889, -3.2213 †🖼️

LILSTOCK CHURCH & RUINED HARBOUR
Tiny St Andrew's church sits in a pretty
paddock and a lane leads down to this
remote foreshore of cobbles and cliff. There
was once an 18th-century pier, harbour and
warehouse here. Hinkley Point nuclear power
station is visible on the horizon.

→ From A39, just N of Holford, turn R at
corner and follow signs for Kilton and Lilstock.
5 mins, 51.1975, -3.1933 †🖼️⛰️

STEART POINT, BRIDGWATER BAY
Long, wild spit of sand and marshland at the
estuary of the River Parrett. Climb the Tower
of the Winds hide to see wild sea birds and
enjoy far-reaching views.

→ Turn into Cannington 3 miles W of
Bridgwater (A39), go though village and follow
signs for Otterhampton/Steart (6 miles)
15 mins, 51.2134, -3.0319 ⛰️🐾

RIVERS AND LAKES

4 RIVER CULM, CULMSTOCK
Riverside woodland and meadow with places
to paddle and dip.

→ Take the footpath by the bridge, opposite
the Culm Valley Inn (01884 840354) and
follow the river downstream for up to a mile, to
Hunkin Wood. About 8 miles from M5, J27 via
A38/B3391.
15 mins, 50.9157, -3.2845 🐟🏊

5 WIMBLEBALL LAKE, UPTON
Large reservoir lake on the fringes of
Exmoor. The W edge has a campsite, visitor
area and easily accessible shore. The E shore
is secluded, shallower and more gently
shelving – enjoy a discreet dip if there are no
fishermen. There's also a lakeside cycle path
and cycle hire. Good place to see herons,
kingfishers, buzzards and kestrels.

→ On the lane between Upton and the
causeway (which crosses the lake on the N
end) turn down the 'No Through Road' (cycle
route sign) to find a small car park at the end.
From here you can explore along the wooded S
shoreline. Or continue along the road/track to
Upton Farm, remains of St James' church, and
more wooded, secluded shoreline. Bike hire
behind the café (Alex, 01398 371156).
10–30 mins, 51.0617, -3.4473 🚴🏊🐾

6 OTTERFORD LAKES, ROYSTON WATER
Hidden spring-fed lake reservoirs on the S
slopes of the Blackdown Hills, created as
part of the Otterhead estate in the mid-19th
century and now a nature reserve. Here you
will see dippers, kingfishers, grey wagtails,
and, if there are no fishermen, it's a good
spot for a dip. Managed by Wessex Water.

→ Otterford is signed off the B3170, on the S
side of the Blackdown Hills, S of Taunton. From
the woodland car park follow track 5 mins to
top lake. Another 15 mins brings you down to
the more secluded and larger Royston Water
(also accessible from S on Bishopswood road
E from Churchstanton).
15 mins, 50.9188, -3.1037 🏊

9

SUNSET HILLTOPS

7 STAPLE PLAIN & BEACON HILL

The car park at Staple Plain is a wonderful place to watch the sunset over the Bristol Channel, and then view the stars, with little light pollution. Listen out for red deer, tawny owls and the churring of the nightjar at dusk on still summer evenings. In late summer, the northern Quantocks are ablaze with heather and gorse, or visit in autumn when the beech and sweet chestnut woods below turn golden. The path leads up to Beacon Hill (51.1615, -3.2530).

→ Staple Plain is signed from the centre of West Quantoxhead village (E of Watchet on A39).

2 mins, 51.1623, -3.2645

8 THORNCOMBE BARROW & BEECHES

An ancient trackway up a beech-lined combe passes the Trendle Ring settlement and leads up to the burial barrows on one of the Quantocks' most impressive high points.

→ 200m S of the turning for Bicknoller, turn L off A358 down tiny Chilcombe Lane. After ½ mile the lane reaches Quantock Moor farm. Follow the R bearing footpath from here up on to the moor via Long Combe, along an ancient

line of beech and to Thorncombe Barrow.
30 mins, 51.1477, -3.2487

9 TRISCOMBE STONE & QUARRY LAKE

A tiny lane leads up to the Quantocks ridge and this Bronze Age stone. It marks a meeting place on the old drovers' way, part of King Alfred's Way, which runs along the top of the ridge. Gnarled, shallow-rooted beech trees line the route up to Wills Neck view point. You can peer down into Triscombe quarry, an amazing blue lagoon backed by steep red-stone cliffs.

→ Signed Triscombe Stone off the lane that connects Nether Stowey to Plainsfield. You can drive right to the top. Also accessible as a 20-min walk from the Blue Ball Inn (see 24) which is close to the gated quarry entrance.
5 mins, 51.1167, -3.1958

10 CULMSTOCK BEACON

A stone roundhouse atop a hill with stunning views. One of a chain of Elizabethan beacons built to warn of approaching ships and a potential Spanish invasion from the coast.

→ Signed Woodgate/Beacon R off the B3391, 1 mile N of Culmstock.
15 mins, 50.9279, -3.2673

RUINS AND FOLLIES

11 CONYGAR TOWER, DUNSTER

Built by Henry Fownes Luttrell of Dunster Castle in 1775 as a folly. A picturesque 'ruined' gatehouse can also be found in the woods to the W of the tower. NB Bat walks at NT Dunster Castle on August evenings.

→ Turn into Dunster village off the A39 E of Minehead and there is a path after 100m. Fin footpath up into the woods from here.
15 mins, 51.1872, -3.4440

12 GLEBE SHAFT, NETHER STOWEY

A lonely old mine engine house stands alone in a field by a spreading oak.

→ About 1½ miles W of Nether Stowey on A39, turn R at brow on hill signed Didington. The ruin is through gate on the R, after 150m
2 mins, 51.1538, -3.1804

13 WILLETT TOWER, ELWORTHY

Sham, picturesque ruined church tower, built in 1820, perched high on a forested hill top.

→ Heading N on B3224, 1 mile before Elworthy, find Forestry Commission sign/gate for Willett's Hill on L. Follow track up ½ mile.
15 mins, 51.0939, -3.2922

19

ANCIENT TREES

14 DUNSTER WOOD TALLEST TREES

Dunster's Douglas fir, the tallest tree in the UK, is higher than Nelson's Column. There's a marked 'Tallest Trees' trail and several cycle routes through the conifer forests.

→ Take A396 W from Dunster (direction Timberscombe). Turn L after a mile, signed Luxborough, and bear R for the Nutcombe Bottom car park.

15 mins, 51.1718, -3.4627

15 HOLFORD BEECHES, HODDER'S COMBE

Ancient beech trees line the lower part of the path from Holford up Longstone Hill. The trees are set behind Alfoxton House (now a hotel), where Wordsworth once lived.

→ From Holford follow the signs through narrow lanes down to car park in woods by the green. Bear R and continue another 200m to the old dog pound. Take the bridleway on the L and continue about ¾ mile to find the beech avenue descending on the R. Or head up the beautiful Hodder's Combe with woods and stream (51.1554, -3.225) directly from the car park, and make a circular walk taking in Longstone Hill.

20 mins, 51.1653, -3.2236

16 ASHBRITTLE CHURCHYARD YEW

Reputed to be 3,000 years old, this tree was standing when Stonehenge was in use, and it pre-dates the adjoining church of St John the Baptist by millennia. It is thought to be one of the oldest living things in Britain.

→ Ashbrittle is signed ('Westleigh Quarry') off the A38, 5 miles W of Wellington (M5, J26). Follow the lanes and signs via Greenham for about 4 miles. Cothay Manor is 3 miles to the E with fine gardens and teas (entrance fee).

2 mins, 50.9835, -3.3514

17 WELLINGTON WOODS

This well-known giant obelisk and viewpoint leads to ancient woodland on the N escarpment of the Blackdown Hills.

→ Signed 'Monument' from Rockwell Green, A38 Wellington (M5, J26), and continue 3 miles to ridge top. Turn R at top for monument, or L for the Woodland Trust nature reserve.

5 mins, 50.9477, -3.2296

18 BICKNOLLER YEW & STOCKS

Bicknoller's churchyard is dominated by this 1,000 year old hollow yew. Supported on great crutches with the medieval village stocks set beneath. A path from here leads up to Thorncombe Barrow (see 8).

→ Signed off the A358, 5 miles S of Watchet. There is a further impressive yew in Combe Florey churchyard, 7 miles further S on A358 (51.0735, -3.2130) and another yew with stocks at West Monkton (NE of Taunton, 51.0515, -3.0524).

3 mins, 51.1470, -3.2723

19 DEAD WOMAN'S DITCH

Deep, dark, twisted ancient forest clad Quantock Common. There are defensive earthworks and a hillfort in the woods

→ About 1½ miles W of Nether Stowey on A39 turn L at brow on hill signed Crowcombe. Climb up narrow lane through deep wood 2 miles to the large parking areas at the top. Head ¾ mile N to find Dowsborough hill fort deep in the forest (¾ mile, 51.1456, -3.2016) or ¾ mile W to Wilmot's Pool where ponies sometime gather.

20 mins, 51.1376, -3.1988

SACRED AND ANCIENT

20 COTHELSTONE WELL & PARKLAND

Young women came to secluded St Agnes' holy well to learn the name of their future lover, and it was also a wishing-well of some repute. After you have done your magic,

continue across field to the parkland behind the grand medieval manor house. There are ancient oaks to picnic under and a gate to L leads through to a secret lake, where we enjoyed a dip.

→ From Bishops Lydeard (A358) head N along the village high street, past the Co-op, to reach the splendid gatehouse of Cothelstone Manor on the L, after 1 ½ miles. The footpath to the parkland (trees and lake, 15 mins, 51.0822, -3.1738) is on L by the postbox in wall. The footpath to the holy well is 200m further along lane on L. Continue along lane another mile, up into woods, to find footpath to Cothelstone Woods on R, with good sunset views and sparse remains of a folly tower on summit (51.0880, -3.1550). The Manor offers luxury B&B (01823 433480).

15 mins, 51.0801, -3.1663

21 CROWCOMBE PAGAN CARVINGS

Fine 16th-century pagan carvings on the bench-ends in this village church. Continue down narrow lanes to Triscombe for the Blue Ball Inn and up to the Triscombe Stone (9).

→ Crowcombe is off the A358 between Taunton and Watchet.

2 mins, 51.1234, -3.2293

SLOW FOOD

22 WHORTLEBERRY FORAGING

Also called bilberries, these are common on Quantock Common in August. Hunt out the low-lying bushes with their small, purple-blue berries. Delicious in a pie and smothered in local cream.

→ See Dead Woman's Ditch (see 19).

51.1376, -3.1988

23 THE CAREW ARMS, CROWCOMBE

A rustic yet lively 16th-century village pub with stags' heads and wooden settles. Sit by the fire or enjoy local ales in the garden.

→ Crowcombe, TA4 4AD, 01984 618631

51.1237, -3.2323

24 BLUE BALL INN, TRISCOMBE

Winding lanes lead up to this charming and remote pub, serving seasonal and local organic food. Inside it's a cosy wooden labyrinth with tartan carpets and fires. Outside is a sweet garden with converted outbuildings where you can stay the night. Triscombe Stone and the quarry lake are a climb up the ridge behind.

→ Triscombe, TA4 3HE, 01984 618242

51.1126, -3.2063

25 TORRE CIDER FARM

Home-made scrumpy heaven.

→ Washford, Watchet, TA23 0LA, 01984 640004

51.1515, -3.3649

26 CULM VALLEY INN, CULMSTOCK

Dogs and cats wander about or laze by the fire in this cosy pub, and the local food will exceed your expectations. Pretty walks down the river Culm.

→ Culmstock, EX15 3JJ, 01884 840354

50.9166, -3.2783

27 HALBERTON COURT FARM, TIVERTON

A community farm shop and tea room selling good-value, local produce, light lunches and cream teas. Lovely views.

→ High Street, Halberton, Tiverton EX16 7AW, 01884 829543

50.9085, -3.4147

28 THE RISING SUN INN, W BAGBOROUGH

Nestled under the W edge of the Quantock ridge, with local ales, red ruby beef, game in season and excellent black pudding. Rooms to stay in, too.

→ West Bagborough, TA4 3EF, 01823 432575

51.0940, -3.1861

29 THE FARMERS ARMS, SLOUGH GREEN

Good food, ciders and beers in an 18th-century converted barn with luxurious rooms. Outside, the garden has far-reaching rural views and overnight parking for a few camper vans. Bickenhall churchyard, a peaceful, sacred spot with ancient yew and orchard, is nearby (50.9720, -3.0157).

→ Higher West Hatch, TA3 5RS, 01823 480980 (Follow signs to RSPCA centre from S-bound A358).

50.9729, -3.0373

CAMP AND SLEEP WILD

30 ROBIN HOOD'S HUT, HALSWELL

Hilltop folly with wonderful views out across the Quantock Hills and Bridgwater Bay.

→ Landmark Trust, Halswell, Goathurst, TA5 2DH, 01628 825925.

51.0946, -3.0657

31 HUNSTILE FARM, GOATHURST

A 14th-century, picture-postcard organic working farm with two small fields for tents, a bow-top gypsy caravan, shepherd's hut and farmhouse B&B. The views from the farm are

agnificent, there's an on-site café serving
rm produce, and the owners run sausage-
aking and bee-keeping courses.

Goathurst, TA5 2DQ, 01278 662358
.0973, -3.0483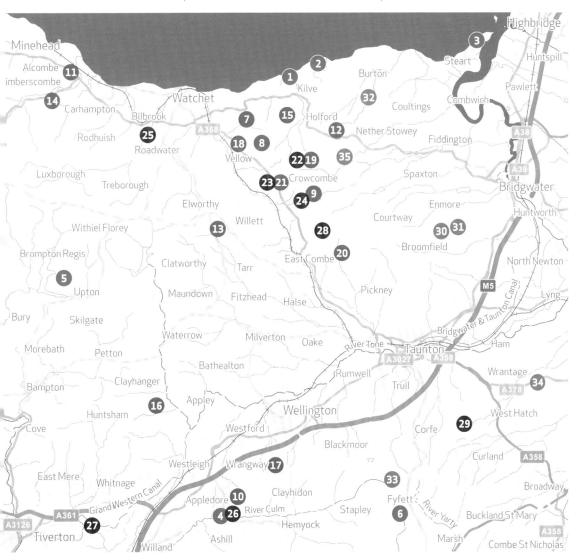

STOGURSEY CASTLE

king of your own castle in this restored
th-century gatehouse surrounded by a
oat. The main castle is long gone but you
ve exclusive access to its grassy ruins.

Castle St, Stogursey, TA5 1TG, 01628
5925, Landmarktrust.org.uk
.1770, -3.1415

33 HOLLY BUSH, OTTERFORD

Quiet campsite up on the Blackdown Hills
surrounded by ancient woodland, with
excellent walking and cycling. Although you
will find mostly caravans, your tent won't
feel overwhelmed – there's plenty of room
for everyone.

→ Culmhead, TA3 7EA, 01823 421515
50.9399, -3.1120

34 BALL HILL FARM, NR TAUNTON

Simple camping with glorious views on an
old cider farm under apple trees. No showers
but there is a composting loo, or you can rent

the appealing bow-top gypsy caravan with
woodburning stove.

→ Ball Hill Farm, Wrantage, TA3 6DN, 01823
490460
51.0015, -2.9648

35 PARSONAGE FARM, OVER STOWEY

A lovely relaxed farmhouse B&B serving
food from the bee-filled walled garden and
orchards. There are pottery classes, a wood-
fired pizza oven and wonderful walks on your
doorstep.

→ Parsonage Farm, Over Stowey, TA5 1HA
51.1400, -3.1651

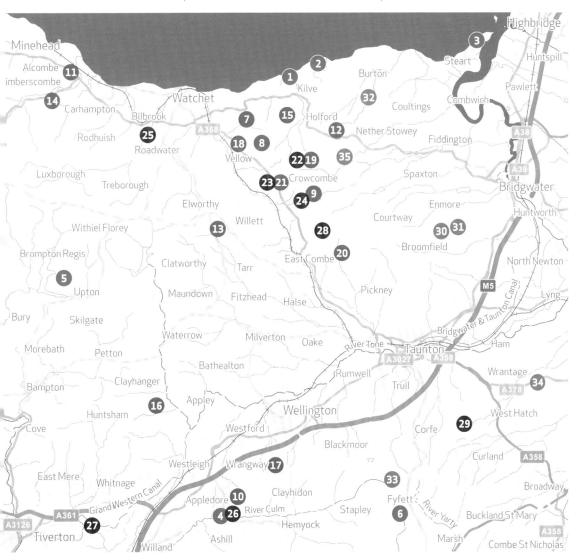

SOMERSET LEVELS

Our perfect weekend

→ **Cycle** the 'Orchards and Cider' route from Langport, visiting the famous cider-brandy distillery and eel smokery along the way.

→ **Marvel** at the fabulous sunset sky patterns created by huge starling flocks at Westhay, Shapwick or Ham Wall.

→ **Picnic** on the banks of the River Parrett at Muchelney ruined abbey, and enjoy a refreshing dip.

→ **Canoe** through the Levels from Parchey Bridge, enjoying the peace and quiet as you float under vast empty skies.

→ **Swim** at Baltonsborough Flights, a wonderful pool beneath cascades on the River Brue.

→ **Find** the thousand-year-old oaks of Avalon near Glastonbury Tor, or seek out the mystical zodiac symbol on Dundon Beacon.

→ **Swing** in trees at Montacute House, climb the tower on top of St Michael's Hill, then take tea in the courtyard café.

→ **Sleep** in a beautifully restored gypsy caravan parked in an old apple orchard, or try a converted horse wagon.

The Somerset Levels, a flat, low-lying wetland dominated by mysterious Glastonbury Tor, extends east from the Mendips to Taunton. This fertile landscape, criss-crossed by dykes known as 'rhynes', is rich in birdlife and ancient cider orchards – perfect for exploring by bike or canoe.

Somerset, literally 'land of the summer people', once was an area inundated in winter and accessible for farming only during the summer. Yet the neolithic community who settled here around 6,000 years ago constructed a complex system of raised sand and wooden trackways for fishing, hunting and foraging in the wetter months. One of the oldest existing trackways, The Sweet Track dating from about 3800 BC, can still be explored.

Wildlife is abundant in the levels and there are several nature reserves, including Shapwick and Westhay. Habitats range from secluded fenland to lush wildflower meadows and a mosaic of lakes, fringed with rustling reedbeds and busy with otters. In the magical winter landscape, the great skies come alive with huge flocks of starlings that create extraordinary, spiralling patterns agains the vast horizons

One of the most popular attractions in this part of Somerset is Glastonbur Tor, but there are other, quieter holy places, such as the ruined church up on Burrow Mump, or the two hills on each side of Compton Dundon –home to a revered, aged yew tree. You might also like to seek out Gog and Magog, two ancient oaks thought to be the only survivors from a 2,000-year-old avenue that once stretched from Glastonbury to King Arthur's hill fort at Cadbury.

And no visit to this part of Somerset, the home of traditonal scrumpy, would be complete without a trip to one of the old cider orchards, beautiful when laden with blossom in spring or with ripening fruit in summer and autumn. Stock up with supplies of still or sparkling cider from the cider-brandy distillery at Burrow Hill, near Kingsbury Episcopi, or at one of the traditional cider-making farms. Add delicious local cheeses, smoked fish, bread and salad, and enjoy a lazy picnic lunch by the river Parrett.

14

WEST LYDFORD, RIVER BRUE

pretty stretch of river running by the
hurch lawns from the road bridge to the
eir, with rope swing.

 West Lydford is just off the A37, near the
3153 junction (Lydford-on-Fosse). Footpath
uns through churchyard to weir and then
ootbridge. Also access via track on opposite
ank. If you use the churchyard please don't
icnic, sunbathe or leave litter.

mins, 51.0846, -2.6236

BALTONSBOROUGH FLIGHTS

arge, stepped weir cascade on River Brue
ith pool beneath, in fields off the lane.

ollow river footpath downstream from
ast Lydford 2 miles or, heading S out of
altonsborough on the Barton St David lane,
nd footpath through fields on R after ¾ mile,
efore Catsham.

mins, 51.1019, -2.6473

PARCHEY BRIDGE, CHEDZOY

ing's Sedgemoor 'drain' is actually a very
leasant river, albeit straight and a bit
uddy, that runs through a huge empty part
f the Levels. Head downstream (walk or

cycle) and take a dip opposite Pendon Hill or
canoe/walk upstream towards Glastonbury
and you will see no-one for miles. This is a
great stretch of water for easy canoeing.

→ From M5 J23 (Bridgewater) follow A39
Glastonbury, then turn R at lights, A39
Bridgewater. Turn L signed Chedzoy after a
mile. Turn L in Chedzoy at the T-juction (Front
Street) and continue 1 mile. You can also pick
up Cycle Route 3 here and complete a lovely
circuit via Catcott. The upstream path reaches
Greylake Bridge (A361, 51.1061, -2.8617)
after 4 miles, and continues another 6 miles to
Somerton beyond that.

5 mins, 51.1353, -2.9278

4 MUCHELNEY ABBEY, RIVER PARRETT

Visit the NT abbey and ruins then take a
picnic down the River Parrett footpath and
find a quiet place for a dip. Lovely views back
to the abbey.

→ Muchelney is signed, 1 mile S of Langport.
As you enter, turn R by the church/abbey,
signed Drayton, to find river and downstream
path after ¼ mile on R. Also on the Parrett
Trail footpath and 'Orchard and Cider' cycle
trail (see 13).

10 mins, 51.0201, -2.8214

5 MONTACUTE HOUSE AND TREE SWINGS

Stunning NT Elizabethan house with tree
swings, good café and local-produce market.

→ The house is signed on A3088 between
Yeovil and Stoke-sub-Hamdon. There is a big
2-person chair swing on the Cedar Lawn or
jump over the wall into the parkland to find
tree swings under the great sweet chestnuts.
The courtyard café offers local produce meals
and there are occasional farmers' markets in
the grounds.

10 mins, 50.9513, -2.7154

6 OAKS OF AVALON, GLASTONBURY

Two massive, dying oak trees, more than
1,000 years old, named after legendary
giants Gog and Magog. They formed part of a
long ceremonial avenue that was said to lead
to the Tor from Wells Cathedral, and then to
King Arthur's castle at South Cadbury.

→ Descend on the NE side of Glastonbury Tor,
bear R and follow No Through Road, Stone
Lane (Cycle Route 3) for ¾ mile then take
footpath on L, towards Old Oaks caravan park
(BA6 8JS, 01458 831437). Also accessible via
A361 Edgarley, then signs to Wick.

20 mins, 51.1497, -2.6848

7 GREAT YEW OF DUNDON AND HILL FORT

Ancient yew, well over 1,000 years old, dominates the churchyard and is revered by New Age followers. The neighbouring hills of Lollover and Dundon Beacon both have wonderful views and, for some, mystical significance– they represent Gemini in Glastonbury's landscape zodiac.

→ Dundon is 5 miles S of Glastonbury (B3151 to Somerton). Lollover Hill ¾ miles to W is bare and grassy with sunset views (51.0892, -2.7524). Follow the footpath from the No Through Road sign leading to the church. Dundon Beacon, ¾ mile to E (51.0873, -2.7372), is a nature reserve with ancient oak woodland (path off School Lane).

2 mins, 51.0898, -2.7441

RUINS AND FOLLIES

8 BURROW MUMP, OTHERY

A perfect round hillock rises from the levels and is crowned with the ruins of St Michael's church. A smaller, less crowded version of Glastonbury Tor.

→ There's a small car park signed on the R, just 2 miles SW of Othery on A361, before King Alfred pub / traffic lights in Burrowbridge.

5 mins, 51.0704, -2.91610

9 ST MICHAEL'S TOWER, MONTACUTE

18th-century lookout tower atop the conical hill that gives the village its name (literally 'steep hill'). There is a small fireplace and chimney at the top of the 52-step spiral staircase and, allegedly, a secret tunnel that connects to the main house.

→ As for Montacute House (see 5) but the path to St Michael's Hill is signed from the end of the lane behind the church/Kings Arms pub. Or extend the adventure and follow Cycle Route 33 through quiet lanes to NT Barrington Court (10 miles).

20 mins, 50.9499, -2.7221

SACRED AND ANCIENT

10 SWEET TRACK, SHAPWICK RESERVE

6,000-year-old, elevated causeway footpath that ran for almost 2 miles across the Somerset Levels. Claimed to be the oldest road in the world, it extends between what was once an island at Westhay and a ridge of high ground at Shapwick. An amazing place to see starlings roost in autumn.

→ Follow Shapwick Road SW from Westhay for 1 mile, past the Peat Moor/Avalon Marshes centre (pop in for some additional history, BA6 9TT, 01458 860697) to the bridge, and

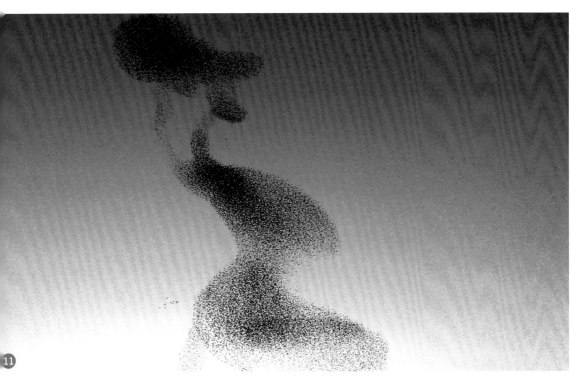

11

---

nd Shapwick Nature Reserve, signed on L.
nter reserve and the trackway can be seen
n R after 300m. Or follow Cycle Route 3 from
lastonbury.
mins, 51.1655, -2.8229

MEADOWS AND WILDLIFE

1 WESTHAY MOOR, MEARE
ne of the best places to see massive flocks
f starling 'murmurations' at sunset, from
utumn to February. Thousands of birds
woop, loop and funnel, making incredible
hapes in the dusk sky. Also, a good reserve
or otter spotting on summer evenings, in
articular in the lakes off London Drove.

5 miles NW of Glastonbury on B3151. ½
ile after Westhay village turn R on corner
signed Godney) and continue 1 mile to find
ar park on R, at the junction with Daggs Lane
rove.
mins, 51.1898, -2.7794

2 HAM WALL RSPB, MEARE
nother superb place to see starlings roost
n winter.

In Meare, W of Glastonbury on B3151, turn L
own Ashcott Rd and continue 1½ miles, past
he Railway Inn (BA6 9SX, 01458 860223) to

find car park on R after bridge.
10 mins, 51.1533, -2.7890

CIDER ORCHARDS

13 ORCHARDS AND CIDER CYCLE TRAIL
13-mile flat route taking in Muchelney Abbey
and pottery, Brown & Forrest Smokery,
Burrow Hill Cider and Somerset Distillery at
Stembridge.

→ Hire bikes from the visitor centre in
Langport, by bridge on A378 (TA10 9RB,
01458 250350).
60 mins, 51.0359, -2.8358

14 CIDER BRANDY, KINGSBURY EPISCOPI
Awarded the first full cider-distilling licence
in 1989, Somerset cider brandy is delicious.
Take a walk around the traditional sheep-
grazed orchards and see the beautiful copper
stills where cider has been made for 150
years. Open 9am–5pm, Monday–Saturday.

→ Burrow Hill, Stembridge, Kingsbury
Episcopi, TA12 6BU, 01460 240782
5 mins, 50.9763, -2.8343

13

26

15 BRADLEY ORCHARDS, GLASTONBURY

Learn how to plant and maintain your own orchard or learn the art of West Country cider making. Annual apple blossom and apple-scrumping days.

→ West Bradley Orchards, Glastonbury BA6 8LT, 01458 850154

2 mins, 51.1307, -2.6258

16 WILKINS CIDER FARM, WEDMORE

Traditional CAMRA award-winning farmhouse cider with a rustic tasting-bar and a small farm shop selling unpasteurised cheddar, local vegetables and eggs. Cider has been made here by the same family for generations. It's a nice walk from here to Westhay to see the starlings roost.

→ Mudgley, BS28 4TU, 01934 712385

5 mins, 51.2075, -2.7837

17 PERRY'S CIDER MILLS, ILMINSTER

A charming farm making artisan cider using wild yeasts and Somerset apples. On-site farm shop, café and a small museum in the 16th-century thatched cider barn.

→ Orchardland, Dowlish Wake, Ilminster, TA19 0NY, 01460 55195

2 mins, 50.9104, -2.8895

LOCAL FOOD

18 DEVONSHIRE ARMS, LONG SUTTON

Smart old pub with locally-sourced pub grub.

→ Nr Langport, TA10 9LP, 01458 241271

51.0256, -2.7582

19 RED BARN FARM SHOP, MUDFORD

A lovely third-generation family farm shop selling home-grown heritage vegetables, over 30 varieties of potatoes, asparagus, raw milk and other seasonal produce.

→ Hinton Farm, Mudford, Yeovil, BA22 8BA, 01935 850994

50.9838, -2.6084

20 BROWN & FORREST SMOKERY

For over 30 years this family-run smokery has been producing delicious smoked eel, salmon and meats in small batches using only wood smoke. There is a simple restaurant serving food straight from the smokery, accompanied by local cheeses and vegetables.

→ Bowdens Farm, Hambridge, Langport, TA10 0BP, 01458 250875

51.0001, -2.8594

21 THE APPLE TREE, WEST PENNARD

Chef Lee Evans and his family bake the bread, cook the food, serve the drinks and run the accommodation at this cosy inn.

→ Glastonbury, BA6 8ND, 01749 890060

51.1544, -2.6189

22 QUEEN'S ARMS, CORTON DENHAM

Just a couple of miles off the A303 down a small lane is a charming 18th-century pub serving delicious local game, meats and vegetables often sourced no further than the village boundary. A muddy-boots-and-dogs pub with excellent selections of real ales and ciders, rooms to stay in and lovely walk from the doorstep.

→ Corton Denham, DT9 4LR, 01963 220317

51.0012, -2.5217

23 LORD POULETT ARMS

Enjoy a drink in the beautiful walled garden sit in a hammock in the orchard, dine in the wildflower meadow or take a seat on an old oak settle by the fire. Luxurious and comfortable rooms if you want to extend your stay.

→ High Street, Hinton St George, TA17 8SE, 01460 73149

50.9102, -2.8245

24 BARLEY MOWS FARMSHOP, CHARD

Good farm shop with local supplies, campsite and fine far-reaching views. Off A30 on W side of Chard.

→ Snowdon Hill Farm, Chard, TA20 3PS, 01460 62130

50.8766, -2.9881

25 THE PILGRIMS REST INN, LOVINGTON

Relaxed, high quality slow-food restaurant, with rooms, serving a range of local, organic Somerset food and drinks. Cheeses come from 30 miles, vegetables from the local organic co-operative and chef and co-owner Jools bakes bread using locally milled flour.

→ Nr Castle Cary, BA7 7PT, 01963 240600

51.0830, -2.5855

CAMP AND SLEEP

26 LOVESTRUCK, EAST PENNARD

Charming converted horsebox lorry with two double beds and a woodburner, parked in a magical, secluded spot under two oak trees backed by woods and overlooking apple orchards. Separate eco loo and shower. Wonderful bluebells and apple blossom in April and May.

Pennard House, East Pennard, Shepton
Mallet, BA4 6TP, 01275 395447
canopyandstars.co.uk/the-lovestruck-at-
pennard-house
51.1366, -2.5745

7 YE OLDE BURTLE INN
Said to be haunted, this 16th-century pub
makes cider from apples in the orchard and
serves home-made food using local produce.
Log fires, views of Glastonbury Tor and the
Polden Hills, simple camping in the orchard,
and cycle hire are all on site.
→ Catcott Broad Drove, TA7 8NG, 01278
722269
51.1837, -2.8574

28 BRIDGE FARM, GLASTONBURY
Low-key camping on a simple flat, grassy
field on a working dairy farm with views
of Glastonbury Tor. Watch the cows being
milked and bring bicycles to tour the area.
→ Bridge Farm, West Bradley, Glastonbury,
BA6 8LU, 01458 850431
51.1241, -2.6421

29 SHEPHERD'S HUT, CREWKERNE
Four yurts and two modern shepherd's huts
set in quiet fields on an organic dairy farm
overlooking Castle Hill and a lake.
→ Ford's Croft Farm, Fordscroft, TA18 7TU,
07773 505671
50.8913, -2.8182

30 GYPSY CARAVAN, COMPTON DUNDON
Perfectly restored, bow-topped Gypsy
caravan in an old cider-apple orchard.
Composting loo and shower. Eggs and meat
from farmhouse or Pitney farm shop.
→ Bartlett's Farm, Hayes Road, Compton
Dundon, TA11 6PF, 01458 274944
51.0918, -2.7524

31 GREENACRES, NORTH WOOTTON
Large, family-friendly grassy site with views
of Glastonbury Tor and lots of animals, slides
and swings. No caravans and no dogs.
→ Barrow Lane, North Wootton, Shepton
Mallet, BA4 4HL, 01749 890497
51.1716, -2.6409

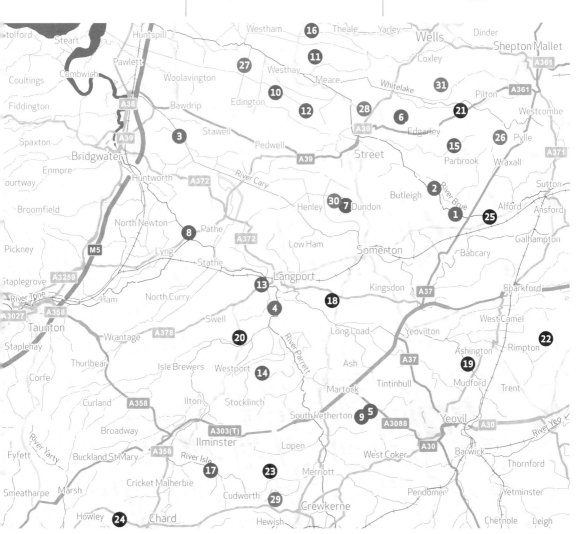

MENDIP HILLS

Our perfect weekend

→ **Make** a dawn splash at Wookey Farm campsite, where there are no showers, just the pretty River Axe.

→ **Walk** the Cheddar Gorge skyline for fantastic views from 400 feet up, taking in the Pinnacles, Pulpit viewpoint and Jacob's Ladder.

→ **Descend** into Goatchurch cavern, its entrance found deep in a wooded combe.

→ **Experience** the full force of the wind and sea at Brean Down ruined fort, explore the caves beneath, then lunch at the National Trust café.

→ **Sample** traditionally made, award-winning ciders at Brent Knoll farm, after climbing up the knoll and working up a thirst.

→ **Explore** Ubley Warren's historic lead-mine workings and find the location of the Roman amphitheatre near Charterhouse.

→ **Spot** slow-worms and grass snakes at Velvet Bottom.

→ **Fly kites** and watch the sun go down over Glastonbury Tor from Deer Leap, one of the Mendips' finest viewpoints.

→ **Wild camp** on remote Westbury Beacon after stocking up with delicious, local provisions from Priddy Farm shop.

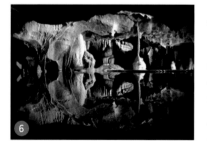

Up on the grassy heights of the Mendips, where ancient hill forts surmount the steep limestone escarpment, there are some of the best views in Somerset down to Glastonbury Tor and the Levels. This great, high plateau is scored through by vast gorges, pitted with underground caves and rich in Roman, Iron Age and prehistoric remains .

Formed over a million years ago during the last Ice Age from great torrents of glacier melt water, Cheddar Gorge is England's largest canyon. In places it is 400 feet deep, and a staggering three miles long. A walk along its cliff-top 'skyline', among its weathered crags and pinnacles offers magnificent panoramas and the chance to spot peregrine falcons swooping below.

It's not surprising that this extraordinary landscape inspired artists and writers: it is said that Gough's Cave was the inspiration for Helm's Deep in Tolkien's *The Two Towers*. If you visit only one show cave in the Cheddar complex, make it this one. The spectacular cavern was scooped out when the melt waters of the Cheddar Yeo worked their way underground. Cheddar Man, Britain's oldest complete skeleton, was also found here, as well as the country's earliest evidence of cannibalism.

There are hundreds of miles of wild caves in the Mendips, but most are gated and only accessible to caving clubs. A few remain open to the casual explorer however. Monster Cavern is in the gorge itself or head north to Goatchuch Cave, once a Victorian show cave, now hidden among undergrowth in the woods of Burrington Combe. To the east, Ebbor Gorge, a scaled-down and wilder version of Cheddar, has rock shelters where human, reindeer and cave bear bones have been discovered.

According to some sources, the richness of the lead ore deposits in the Mendips was one of the reasons the Romans invaded Britain in AD 43. At Ubley Warren, there is abundant evidence of lead mining from Roman times, and even the remains of an amphitheatre. Ruins and strange shaped furrows abound and in Velvet Bottom the worked lead seams, known as 'rakes', are now home to bee orchids, slow-worms and lizards.

As the day draws to a close, leave the underground caves, mines and passageways of the Mendips behind and make for the hilltops. High up on the slopes around Ebbor and Priddy are some of the best vantage points in Somerset – perfect places to fly kites and watch the sun go down. There are magnificent views out across the Bristol Channel, Wales and Glastonbury Tor, wonderful places to enjoy a summer dusk and camp wild.

17

WILD COAST

1 BERROW DUNES

Take a dusk walk through Berrow Dunes nature reserve and observe rare moths on your way down to the 7-mile-long beach. Good sunsets.

→ From M5 (J22) head into Burnham-on-Sea and follow signs R for Berrow/sea front/B3140. After 3 miles, park at St Marys church, Berrow, and follow footpath through dunes to beach.

5 mins, 51.2666, -3.0159

2 BREAN DOWN FORT AND CAVES

Like a great dragon's back, the headland juts out into Bristol Channel. High cliffs, secret coves and caves, a ruined Victorian fort and fantastic views out to Steep Holm and Flat Holm islands. Bluebells in spring. A superb location, especially on a windy day! Good NT café with hearty traditional British fare.

→ As for Berrow (see 1) but continue another 5 miles, through Brean, to NT café (TA8 2RS, 01643 862452) and car park at the very end. You'll find the caves on the N side of the down. Beware the currents around Brean Down: they are some of the most powerful in Britain.

30 mins, 51.3280, -3.0339

LAKE SWIMMING

3 EMBOROUGH POND, LECHMERE WATER

Easy-access lake by side of lane, bordered by woodland. Beautiful bluebells in spring. A lovely but rather muddy place for a discreet dip. Nearby is the pretty white church of the Blessed Virgin Mary. *Reported closed 2016.*

→ Turn L off A37 2 miles N of Gurney Slade (B3139 signed Radstock) then first L (unsigned) after ¾ mile. Take the next R (signed Chewton) for the white church.

2 mins, 51.2567, -2.5524

4 WALDEGRAVE POOL, STOCKHILL WOODS

Wild, open lake on heathland by roadside. Great for an early-season swim; can get weedy later in the summer.

→ From A39 S of Chewton Mendip, turn R on B3135, signed Cheddar. After 3 miles turn L (B3134, signed Upper Milton) to find lake on R, just before Stockhill Woods car park.

2 mins, 51.2608, -2.6502

5 LITTON RESERVOIR

A footpath follows the N shores of this secret lake on the upper Chew. Primroses, wood anemone, violets and red campion in spring. A quick dip is possible if there are no fishermen. Or paddle in the stream at pub.

→ Coming from Chewton on B3114, take the second R down Back Lane, shortly after the Kings Head in Litton (pretty stream-side garden and gastro-dining, BA3 4PW, 01761 241301). Take R at end, and find footpath on L after 200m (after stream).

10 mins, 51.2921, -2.5821

CAVES AND CAVERNS

6 GOUGH'S CAVE, CHEDDAR

The best of the commercial caverns, with impressive stalactites, and one of the most important and best-preserved cave shelters in Britain.

→ Can't miss them. At the bottom of the gorge road (BS27 3QF, 01934 742343).

5 mins, 51.2821, -2.7655

7 GOATCHURCH, BURRINGTON COMBE

Large deep, dry cavern with many chambers. Once a Victorian show cave with old railings and steps, and still quite popular. Take a head torch and helmet.

→ As for Aveline's Hole (see 23) but continue 200m further up road and find good footpath on R. Follow into woods and along stream and after ¼ mile climb, take steep path up

to L, via steps, to find the signed entrance to Goatchurch on L. For Dolebury take the path up on R instead.

15 mins, 51.3207, -2.7536 🇻🅿🚹

8 READ'S CAVERN, DOLEBURY WARREN

A stream cascades down a deep, steep passageway and though you can descend you shouldn't go too far in unless you are experienced.

→ As for Goatchurch, but take path up on R towards Dolebury Warren (about 1 mile). After ½ mile, however, look out for green metal post and gate into little overgrown combe. Follow the stream down to the narrow entrance. It is marked with a metal name sign and emergency numbers – take care!

30 mins, 51.3225, -2.7645 🇻

9 MONSTER CAVERN, CHEDDAR GORGE

Impressive cleft in the rock face, also called Great White Spot and Great Fissure cavern. Opposite Reservoir Hole – recently discovered and believed to contain Britain's largest cavern.

→ About 50m above and to the L of the bus turning circle, about halfway down the gorge just after a small parking area on R.

2 mins, 51.2865, -2.7556 🚌

10 BANWELL CAVES AND TOWER

In 1824 a huge cavern was discovered containing hundreds of bison and bear bones. The Bishop of Bath felt this was conclusive proof of Noah's flood and it was opened as a show cave. Also, various follies in the grounds.

→ Open three times a year (in May and September), and to groups by arrangement. There is also a folly tower to climb. Heading W from Banwell on A371 turn L into Well Lane (signed Christon Road) and follow this up to the top of the hill to find house, 'The Caves' on L (BS29 6NA). (Contact johnatthecaves@btinternet.com, 01934 820516).

5 mins, 51.3252, -2.8884 ⛪✝

FOREST AND NATURE

11 EBBOR GORGE & CAVES

A smaller but wilder version of Cheddar Gorge. 200,000 years ago the huge cavern that formed the gorge collapsed and left behind a number of small caves with names such as Bracelet Cave, Lion's Shelter and Eagle's Nest. The remains of reindeer, cave bear and wolf have been discovered within. There are several bear sculptures made of willow throughout the woods.

9

Entering Priddy from the A39 N of Wells,
turn sharp L and pass the Queen Victoria Inn
(BA5 3BA, 01749 676385). Continue along
lane to edge of escarpment and picnic car park
(amazing sunset views) and continue down hill
to find Ebbor Gorge car park on L. The main
path descends steeply into the woods and then
up into the gorge with some rock shelters, but
bear R from the car park, and stay high (parallel
to the lane) and you will find several deeper
caves in the steep, wooded hillside. Bracelet
Cave (late Bronze Age jewellery was found
here) is at 51.2322, -2.6847 with a slippery 4m
drop into two chambers.

5 mins, 51.2331, -2.6876

2 BLACK ROCK, CHEDDAR GORGE
A sheltered glade with high cliff faces
popular with climbers. A wooded walk leads
up to Velvet Bottom nature reserve. Or
make Black Rock your starting point for the
spectacular cliff-top, circular walk around
the edge of the gorge and its pinnacales.
Look up for peregrines and down for
dormice, great crested newts, basking
adders, slow-worms and grass snakes. In
nearby Long Wood there are several cave
systems and good blackberries in late
summer.

→ Limited parking at Black Rock Gate (NT),
by the bus stop, at the very top of B3135
Cheddar Gorge road. The cliff walk climbs up
on the N side, then along the cliff edge and
down to Lion Rock via a wooded descent,
through the village and up again via Jacob's
Ladder, the lookout tower, then back on S side
of the cliff edge.

5 mins, 51.2876, -2.7442

13 DRAYCOTT SLEIGHTS, STOKE CAMP
There are wildflowers (including orchids)
and butterflies in abundance at this nature
reserve, with its ancient hill fort. Fine sunset
views over the Somerset Levels, across
the Bristol Channel to Wales, and south to
Glastonbury Tor and Dorset.

→ Following the B3135 from the A39, take
the second R after Priddy, signed Gliding Club.
About ½ mile after the club find footpaths on
L and R, and some narrow parking on the side.
Head L (and back up the hill) to the hill fort
or R for Draycott Sleights nature reserve. Or
from Draycott, turn up New Road by the old
Methodist Chapel (now flats) and continue
¾ mile.

15 mins, 51.2592, -2.7373

14

14 CROOK PEAK, COMPTON BISHOP
An extraordinary vantage point, with views
out over Brent Knoll and the Severn Estuary.
The M5 resembles a tiny ribbon, far below.

→ Heading S on A38 turn R at the New Inn, by
Axbridge turn-off (signed Webbington), then
½ mile after Compton Bishop, as road climbs
and bends to R, find NT sign and parking on R,
opposite a narrow turning on L. Look out for
Denny's Hole cavern immediately as you enter
the woods (51.2907, -2.8666) and then start
climbing!

30 mins, 51.2983, -2.8798

15 DOLEBURY WARREN

Iron Age hill fort surrounded by grassland, limestone heath and ancient field systems. Beautiful walks on to Burrington Combe passing through ancient copses with caves.

➔ ½ mile S of Churchill on A38, as hill begins to climb, find a footpath by side lane ('Dolebrrow'), at post box and parish noticeboard. Some limited parking opposite. Or use the direct bus service from Bristol.

20 mins, 51.3274, -2.7869

16 DEER LEAP, PRIDDY

Remote picnic and parking spot on the Mendip escarpment with very fine views. Paths lead down onto Cook's Field and Lynchcombe nature reserves.

➔ As for Ebbor Gorge (see 11) but car park on R before descent.

5 mins, 51.2403, -2.6908

17 WESTBURY BEACON HILL FORT

Perhaps the most remote point on the Mendips to enjoy the sunset.

➔ As for Draycott Sleights but take first L after Priddy, signed Westbury-sub-Mendip Park by the grassy hump (a concealed reservoir), head down the hill and enter the next field on the R (50m) with gate and 'access land' sign.

10 mins, 51.2539, -2.7173

18 BRENT KNOLL, BURNHAM-ON-SEA

Hill fort, Jubilee stone and great views over the Severn Estuary.

➔ Footpath leads up from behind St Michael's church, Brent Knoll village (signed off B3140 to Burnham).

20 mins, 51.2541, -2.9455

RUINS AND FOLLIES

19 UBLEY WARREN, CHARTERHOUSE

Unique, lead-mining landscape dating from the Roman occupation, and possibly earlier. Deep pits and ridges are everywhere - the undulating 'gruffy' ground left by open-cast mining. Among them are the more recent ruins of Victorian smelting tunnels. The earthworks of a Roman amphitheatre can also be seen near Charterhouse, an indication of how important this settlement was.

➔ Climb up and out of Burrington Combe on B3134 (see 7) and turn R after 2 miles, signed Charterhouse. First R leads to site of the amphitheatre 51.3054, -2.7203, but otherwise continue past wooden-spired St

Hughes' church and descend into the little valley and park. Bear up L for Ubley Warren, o down R for Velvet Bottom.

10 mins, 51.2966, -2.7135

20 PAVEY'S LOOKOUT TOWER, CHEDDAR

The eccentric Roland Pavey built the origina wooden watchtower, calling it his Mystic Tower. Climb the 274 steps of Jacob's Ladde and 48 more to the top of the lookout. Best explored at the halfway point on the skyline cliff-top walk from Black Rock (see 12) to avoid Cheddar village congestion.

20 mins, 51.2806, -2.7704

21 SMITHAM CHIMNEY, EAST HARPTREE

Impressive 1850s brick-and-stone chimney stack in woods – all that remains of a thriving Victorian lead-smelting complex.

➔ Between the Castle of Comfort pub (BS40 6DD, 01761 221321) and East Harptree. Find Forestry Commission signboard and track leading to parking.

5 mins, 51.2890, -2.6405

SACRED AND ANCIENT

22 NINE BARROWS, PRIDDY

Ancient burial place, made up of 17 barrows over two low ridges in grazing pasture. Most are in good condition although they were all opened in the 18th century.

➔ Heading through Priddy village from E, turr R signed Nine Barrows Lane, and continue ¾ mile to find a track and a kissing-gate. Follow the footpath up onto the field 500m to the great row of barrow mounds (Ashen Hill barrows). From here you can bear R and follow the footpath to near the Nine Barrows (51.2612, -2.6628).

5 mins, 51.2657, -2.6620

23 AVELINE'S HOLE, ROCK OF AGES

Small cavern by roadside containing the earliest human cemetery in Britain, at around 8,400 years old. Also contains one of the few known examples of cave art in the UK. The Rock of Ages opposite is where Blagdon curate Augustus Toplady wrote the famous hymn while sheltering in a storm.

➔ Burrington Combe (B3134) is signed off A368, W of Blagdon. Pass Burrington Inn and park in first car park on L. Rock of Ages is opposite and Aveline's Hole is by roadside, 200m up on L. Watch out for busy road.

2 mins, 51.3248, -2.7533

4 WEST CROFT CIDER, BRENT KNOLL

aste the award-winning artisan cider made
oak casks with home-grown apples and
ose from neighbouring farms. The farm is
ost to the lively village wassail in January.
→ West Croft Farm, Brent Knoll, Highbridge,
A9 4BE, 01278 760762
1.2566, -2.9629

5 WILKINS CIDER, MUDGLEY

aste and buy proper old-school traditional
der from this family-run cider farm that
as been making cider for generations. Fresh
cal vegetables, eggs and unpasteurised
heeses are also for sale in the rustic barn.
→ Land's End Farm, Mudgley, Wedmore BS28
TU, 01934 712385
1.2075, -2.7845

6 NYLAND HILL FARM SHOP, NR
HEDDAR

lovely rural farm selling poultry and meat
rom this family-run rare-breed cattle. Excellent selection
f local vegetables, dairy produce and cakes
rom neighbouring farms. Good views from

the top of the hill if you want to burn off a
cake or two!
→ Decoy Pool Farm, Nyland, Cheddar, BS27
3UD, 01934 744802
51.2533, -2.7725

27 PRIDDY GOOD FARM SHOP

Will Simmons' family have been farming in
Priddy for over 300 years. Buy home-reared
beef and lamb and other locally sourced
produce. The burgers, pies and cakes are
delicious.
→ Townsend, Priddy, Wells, BA5 3BP, 01749
870171
51.2636, -2.6849

CAMP AND SLEEP

28 WARREN FARM, CHEDDAR

Enjoy luxury Featherdown camping with
awesome views towards Cheddar Gorge.
Come in spring and see the lambing and
calving. A 45-minute walk takes you to the
gorge itself.
→ Blagdon, Charterhouse, BS40 7XR,
01420 80804
51.2910, -2.7154

29 WOOKEY FARM, NR WELLS

A family-run goat farm with glorious views of
the Mendips. This is lovely, low key camping
with campfires, rope swings and a small
farm shop selling home-reared meats, goat's
cheese and milk. There are no showers, only
a refreshing plunge in the River Axe.
→ Monks Ford, Wookey, Wells, BA5 1DT,
01749 671859
51.2096, -2.7061

30 GARDEN END FARM, NR WELLS

Camp under the apple trees and enjoy fine
Mendip views. Cooked breakfasts can be
delivered directly to your tent!
→ Garden End Farm, Panborough, Wells, BA5
1PN, 01934 712414
51.2080, -2.7577

31 CASTLE FARM CAMPSITE, WEDMORE

Alpacas in the fields and glorious views
from your tent towards the Levels and
Glastonbury Tor.
→ Castle Lane, Heath House, Wedmore, BS28
4UH, 01934 712267
51.2130, -2.8317

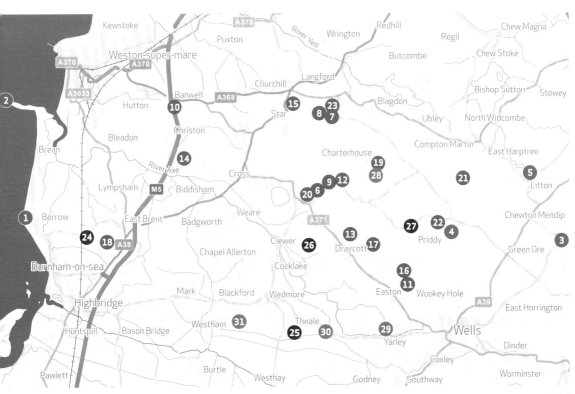

SOMERSET AVON

Our perfect weekend

- → **Escape** on a boat trip to Steep Holm island and explore the ruined fortifications with panoramic views of the Severn estuary.
- → **Descend** into the Giant's Cave and gaze out from its mouth into the Avon Gorge, or meet the hermit at Burwalls Cave.
- → **Feast** on award-winning, ethical food at the Ethicurean, set in stunning walled gardens near Blagdon Lake.
- → **Wild swim** or canoe safari along the river Avon, from picturesque Bradford-on-Avon as far as Claverton Weir.
- → **Climb** Little Solbury Hill, or gaze out from Kelston Round Hill or Rainbow Woods for sensational views of the Bath skyline.
- → **Explore** Brown's Folly and tree swings, then enjoy a superb supper at the Kings Arms in Monkton Farleigh.
- → **Watch** the sunset from the craggy headland at Sand End, pick rock samphire and cook it on a fire at Hope Cove.
- → **Sleep** high up in the trees after relaxing on your own leafy veranda of the magical treehouse in East Harptree.

This northernmost part of Somerset encompasses the beautiful Avon valley, from picturesque Bradford on Avon through to the Severn estuary. Despite the proximity of Bristol and Bath, there are meandering rivers, picturesque lakes and ancient woodlands just waiting to be explored.

Perhaps the most dramatic way of escaping Bristol is to take the small boat out to Steep Holm island and explore the ruined Victorian gun batteries and World War II lookout stations perched precariously on the cliffs. Another place to appreciate the swirling vastness of the Severn estuary is Sand Point, where sea caves and a secret cove await, and there are spectacular sunset views.

The precipitous limestone cliffs of the Avon Gorge offer caves and caverns for exploration and the same craggy rocks were used to create circles and burial chambers at the quiet sites of Stanton Drew and Stoney Littleton. It is, perhaps, not surprising that this region was the birthplace of modern geology. William Smith, who lived in a small cottage at Tucking Mill, worked out the geological processes that formed the Earth and calculated its true age. Smith arrived at his final conclusions by surveying the nearby Somerset Coal Canal at Combe Hay. Its fascinating old ruins now lie abandoned and overgrown.

The lush valley lakes of Chew and Blagdon, to the south of Bristol, are wonderful places to cool down in the heat of summer. These fishing lakes do attract picnickers and swimming is not officially allowed, although a discreet swim may be possible. But if you follow the Chew river downstream, there are several places to dip after an alfresco lunch.

Along the river Avon, in the heart of north Somerset, there are wonderful opportunities for canoeing, wildlife-watching and wild swimming. The river pools are deep, the water quality is good, and most places are easily accessible by cycle and train. The most beautiful stretch is the Limpley Stoke valley from Bath through to Bradford on Avon, a tranquil boat-free zone where herons, kingfishers and otters abound.

COAST AND ISLAND

SAND POINT AND MIDDLE HOPE

he steep, wild headland of Sand Point has a
ecret cove and offers spectacular views out
ver the Severn estuary. You can find Rock
amphire here, a tasty wild-food treat.

→ Continue up along Sand Bay via Beach Road
om Kewstoke (pass Kewstoke Hospital) on N
de of Weston-Super-Mare. Then continue up
nto the headland, bearing E for Hope Cove,
/ for caves. Hill fort fans might also like to
xplore Worlebury and Weston Woods.
5 mins, 51.3895, -2.9682 🏖️🪧🚶🏃

STEEP HOLM ISLAND

teep, craggy island in the middle of the
evern estuary. Famed for its muntjac deer
nd wild peonies, which flower in May. It is
lso home to the remains of a 12th-century
ugustinian priory, six Victorian gun
atteries (with intact cannons) and a host of
ntriguing World War II remains. Fantastic,
60-degree views of the Bristol Channel and
he Somerset and Welsh coastlines.

→ Access is via a 12-person 'rib' which leaves
p to 4 times per day from Knightstone
auseway, Weston-Super-Mare (01934
22125). The trip includes a boat tour of the

island. On the N side there are gun batteries,
rocket-launcher sites and the ruin of a cliff-
edge searchlight station, reached by a set of
perilous steps.
20 mins, 51.3396, -3.1032 🏖️🪧👁️▼

3 CHEW VALLEY LAKE, BISHOP SUTTON

Warm, wide and shallow this is a beautiful
place to take a dip, if you are discreet.

→ 1 mile S of Bishop Sutton on A368 find No
Through Road on R, opposite Hillside Farm,
with parking at end, leading to lake shore and
fishing hut.
3 mins, 51.3301, -2.6115

4 BLAGDON LAKE, BUTCOMBE

Nestled in the folds of a long lush valley,
with the Mendip escarpment rearing up
opposite. There is a beautiful meadow on the
lake shore. Early in the season it is a blissful
place to swim and paddle, but then the water
levels fall and the weeds proliferate.

→ Follow the shore path from the N end of the
dam road. After about 10 mins, having crossed
two footbridges, and passed through some
woodland, find a lakeside meadow on R. It's a
lovely cycle ride out here from Bristol via Long

Ashton, Barrow Gurney and Felton. Do not
disturb the fishermen.
15 mins, 51.3427, -2.7039

5 RIVER YEO, YATTON

Small meandering river with steep grassy
banks and a great place to sunbathe out of
sight. The water is clear, silky and reedy –
perfect for a long swim.

→ Heading into Yatton from A370, pass
railway station and then turn L at mini-
roundabout (Wembersham Lane/Horncastle
Chapel) and continue the to the end (1¾
miles). Follow footpath straight ahead (along a
ditch) to reach the river after 300m, then bear
R downstream for 5 mins. Cycle Route 26.
10 mins, 51.3827, -2.8587 🏊🏖️⛰️

6 DUNDAS AQUEDUCT, AVON

Descend the steps to this bucolic stretch
of the river Avon, which is perfect for
secluded riverside picnics and swims. Or hire
a Canadian canoe/electric boat and pootle
along the canal.

→ Follow the A36 from Bath S for 5 miles and,
just beyond Claverton, turn L at the traffic
lights onto B3108 (signed Limpley Stoke). The
Canal Centre is immediately on L (BA2 7JD,
01225 722292). From the aqueduct descend

to the boathouse below. The path continues as far as Claverton weir (1 mile). Buses 264 and 265 half-hourly from Bath stop at the Old Viaduct Inn.

5 mins, 51.3613, -2.3104 ⚊⚊

7 CLAVERTON WEIR, AVON

Long curving weir with cascade by beautiful meadows. Find the old ferryman's steps below and a long deep stretch above. Very popular but very limited parking. Best reached on the cycle path from Bath or from Dundas aqueduct, or via Bus 264/265.

→ 3 miles E of Bath on A36, turn L at Claverton, down Ferry Lane, just before sign for The American Museum on R. Cross railway to field on R.

10 mins, 51.3772, -2.3003 ⚊⚊⚊

8 PUBLOW, RIVER CHEW

Large pretty pool with shelving beach and rope swing, next to church, just downstream of the road bridge.

→ Publow is off the A37, S of Bristol. Also nice pools upstream of Pensford. Follow narrow lane next to the Rising Sun pub, under the viaduct and down through Culvery Wood (51.3730, -2.5534).

1 min, 51.3754, -2.5433 ⚊⚊

9 WOOLLARD, RIVER CHEW

Secluded pool beneath old weir on edge of meadow.

→ E of Publow, off A37. From E side of Woollard bridge (opposite Brook Cottage) follow footpath over stream and into meadow, to find pool on R.

3 mins, 51.3767, -2.5297 ⚊

10 ABBOT'S POOL, ABBOTS LEIGH

A large, dark lily-pad pool in the woods with a little stone grotto. Originally a fishpond.

→ From Abbots Leigh (A369) turn down Manor Road, by the George Inn, and find track on R after about 1 mile (signed to the pool).

5 mins, 51.4566, -2.6690 ⚊⚊

11 AVONCLIFF WEIR, BRADFORD ON AVON

Large, fun river-pool above weir, with rope swing. There's a long deep stretch upstream leading to a willow maze. Continue further into Barton Farm riverside park to find several more places to swim en route to the Tithe Barn in Bradford on Avon.

→ Alight from train at tiny Avoncliff station, cross aqueduct (Cross Guns riverside pub, 01225 862335, also accessible by road from Westwood.) and continue 200m along canal

to find a path on L that drops down through woods to the weir. The maze is ½ mile further upstream (51.3426, -2.2599). Or a 20-min walk downstream from Bradford on Avon, (where you can hire open canoes or cycles at TT Cycles, BA15 1LE, 01225 867187).

5 mins, 51.3391, -2.2797 ⚊⚊⚊⚊⚊⚊

12 AVON VALLEY PARK, SALTFORD

Grassy picnic riverside area, by old railway bridge. There's a wooden landing stage and it's fun to jump in.

→ In fields next to the cycle route, where the bridge crosses the river. 1 mile N of Saltford or 1 mile S of Bristol edge on A4. The Jolly Sailor in Saltford is also a popular swimming spot with a good rope swing on the opposite bank, above the weir. Don't play on the weir.

20 mins, 51.4171, -2.4600 ⚊⚊⚊⚊

13 TUCKING MILL, MONKTON COMBE

Pretty fishing lake where Willam Smith, the father of modern geology, lived. At this spot the new Two Tunnels bike path emerges into daylight from Bath.

→ On narrow lane between Midford (B3110) and Monkton Combe, 2 miles S of Bath.

5 mins, 51.3526, -2.3386 ⚊⚊

19

ANCIENT FOREST

4 GOBLIN COMBE, CLEEVE

Ancient yews and beech and a wild craggy lookout point with sunset views. Many Bronze Age remains.

→ Heading S on A370, turn L at Cleeve, signed Village Hall, and park at top of hill (½ mile). Follow footpath signs down Plunder Street, bearing L up steps once you are in the woods.

10 mins, 51.3852, -2.7620 🖼️🐾🚶

5 LEIGH WOODS, BRISTOL

Ancient woodland with yews, the ramparts of Stokeleigh Camp hillfort and views over the Avon Gorge. Night-time son et lumière performances by the Whispering Wood Folk.

→ Heading to Abbots Leigh from Ashton Court, turn R off the A369 just after gate house (Leigh Woods/Forestry Commission board) and park at end, after 800m. You'll find several yews growing out of crags just beyond on L. Or continue 15 mins SE to the hill fort (51.4572, -2.6364). The Whispering Wood Folk stage night time folk tales featuring fire, song and trapeze artists hanging from the trees (whispering-wood-folk.co.uk).

5 mins, 51.4639, -2.6438 🐾

16 ASHTON COURT, BRISTOL

Ancient oaks in public parkland with fallow deer. Great place for tree climbing and home of the International Tree Climbing Festival. Our favourite part is Clerken Coombe (for the pollarded oaks) and the Old Deer Park on the W/Long Ashton side of the park.

→ The Ashton Road car park is on B3128 next to the Dovecote pub (BS41 9LX). There's a local-produce market here on the third Sunday of each month.

15 mins, 51.4433, -2.6486 🐎🍴🚶

SUNSET HILLTOPS

17 LITTLE SOLSBURY HILL, BATH

Wonderful grassy plateau made famous by Peter Gabriel. Far-reaching views over Bath and the Avon valley.

→ Turn off Batheaston High Street opposite the White Hart, signed St Catherine's. Take first L up single track Solsbury Lane, then turn R up dead-end lane to park at end.

5 mins, 51.4104, -2.3344 🚗

18 RAINBOW WOODS, BATH

Wonderful views over Prior Park and the dreaming spires of Bath from beechwoods on the Bath 'skyline' walk.

→ From Claverton Down Road (Coombe Down) find gates opposite Shaft Road/Oldfield RFC. For best views bear L off the path, across playing fields, and continue along escarpment, eventually arriving at NT purple shepherd's caravan.

15 mins, 51.3692, -2.3364 🚶🚶

19 SUTTON WICK HILL FORT

Meadow plateau with far reaching W views over Chew Valley Lake. Superb sunset spot and a great place to watch hot-air balloons.

→ Take Sutton Hill Lane (signed Top Sutton) from Red Lion pub in Bishop Sutton (A368). At top of hill (1 mile) turn R down rough track and continue to parking at far end. Walk down track to hill fort escarpment in fields to L.

5 min, 51.3243, -2.6020

20 MAES KNOLL HILL FORT, WHITCHURCH

Great Wansdyke is a 45-mile-long series of giant earthworks built in the 5th century. This hill fort forms its W extremity and is one of the best places to see the sunset S of Bristol.

→ Follow footpath just N of Norton Malreward, off the A37 near Pensford (close to Stanton Drew, see 27).

10 mins, 51.3923, -2.5752 ⛰️

21 KELSTON ROUND HILL, KELSTON

The ancient tumulus atop this perfect conical hill is visible from miles around and affords superb views.

→ Heading out of Kelston village towards Bristol (A431) find a lane on R just after the telephone box. Walk up this for 15 mins, bearing round to the R of Coombe Barn.
20 mins, 51.4059, -2.4172

RUINS AND FOLLIES

22 BROWN'S FOLLY, BATHFORD

Built in 1848 to provide local employment during an agricultural recession, this great tower sits on the edge of woods with views over the river Avon. Farly Quarry lies below, with many miles of tunnels and caverns. Some of the locals know the routes down.

→ From A363 Bathford, follow signs through village towards Kingsdown, then turn R up Prospect Place to find car park up hill on R. Follow path through woods (see tree swings on L) to folly tower and views. (Or climb up Beckford's Tower on other side of Bath, open weekends 10.30am–5pm, Lansdown Road, BA1 9BH, 01225 460705, 51.4066, -2.3788).
20 mins, 51.3938, -2.2968

23 COAL CANAL, COMBE HAY

The beautiful overgrown remains of 22 stone locks built in 1794 are located in these woods, S of Bath. See if you can find the site of the extraordinary 'Hydrostatic Caisson lock', a 60-foot-high water-filled stone vault.

→ Take the lane E from Combe Hay (direction Midford) and find footpath on L (opposite Bridge Farm) after ¾ mile. Follow the path under bridge to find first of the old locks.
5 mins, 51.3436, -2.3693

CAVERNS AND CAVES

24 GIANT'S CAVE, AVON GORGE

A 600-metre tunnel (built in 1837) leads down from the observatory to St Vincent's Cave and opens out onto the cliff face, 250 feet above the floor of the Avon Gorge.

→ Near suspension bridge. Clifton Observatory, Clifton Down, Bristol, BS8 3LT 0117 9741242.
5 mins, 51.4567, -2.6279

25 BURWALLS CAVE, AVON GORGE

One of several large caverns in the rocky gorge. Often occupied by a hermit and used for meditation.

→ Crossing Clifton suspension bridge, turn first L down Burwall Road (past the Burwall Centre) and find NT Leigh Woods entrance on L in fence after 200m. Bear L and follow rough path due N, keeping about 10m below the edge of the Centre boundary, to come to top of cave. Some climb discreetly over the wall the wooden-clad information centre on Clifton suspension bridge.
5 mins, 51.4537, -2.6289

26 REDCLIFFE CAVES, BRISTOL

Huge underground cavern system, created by excavating fine sand for glass-making, between the 15th and 18th centuries. Guided tours can be organised for a fee.

→ Iron bar doors on the waterfront under Redcliffe Parade West (01761 452288, bristoltours.com/Redcliffe). Near Ostrich pub.
2 mins, 51.4486, -2.5924

SACRED AND ANCIENT

27 STANTON DREW STONE CIRCLE

Third largest collection of standing stones in England, yet attracts surprisingly few visitors. Three prehistoric circles and a three-stone 'cove', spread over fields, all part of a more elaborate ritual site.

→ The cove is located in the garden of the Druid's Arms pub. The circles are in fields just E of village (B3130, off A37 en route to Chew Magna). Follow brown signs.
2 mins, 51.3672, -2.5757

SLOW FOOD

28 BEESE'S RIVERSIDE TEAS, CONHAM

Established in 1846 by the wife of the ferry man, Mr Beese, there is still a tea room here to this day (albeit rebuilt in the 1960s) with a little boat that will come and collect you from the opposite bank of the Avon. You can also swim from the ferry steps.

→ Signed Avon Valley Woodlands from Conham, E Bristol (BS15 3N). Or via Wyndham Crescent (BS4 4SX, 0117 9777412).
51.4448, -2.5349

29 THE ETHICUREAN, WRINGTON

One of our favourite places for a long lunch, this restaurant has a big pile of awards for its innovative, local, and lovingly made food and drink. The setting is the old glasshouse in a restored, walled vegetable garden.

→ Barley Wood Walled Garden, Long Lane, Wrington, BS40 5SA, 01934 863713
51.3629, -2.7484

YEO VALLEY ORGANIC GARDEN

njoy an organic cream tea or lunch
verlooking Blagdon Lake. This is the only
rtified ornamental organic garden in
e UK and the wildflower meadows are
eautiful. Entrance fee.
→ Holt Farm, Bath Road, Blagdon, BS40 7SQ,
1761 461650. Off A368, E of Blagdon.
1.3294, -2.6981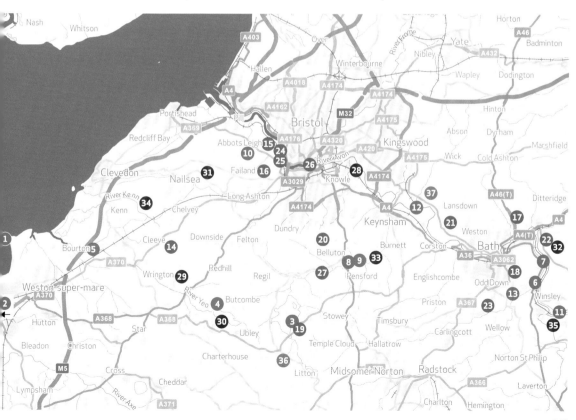

1 THE COW BARN KITCHEN, TYNTESFIELD

it and eat in the Victorian cow stalls, now
NT café with free entry. Most of the food
omes from the estate gardens or from
ithin a radius of 30 miles.
→ Nr Bristol, BS48 1NT, 01275 461900
1.4367, -2.7101

2 KINGS ARMS, MONKTON FARLEIGH

isteria-clad village pub with leather sofas
nd fires. Delicious local food including
ome-made scotch eggs and steak frites.
→ Nr Bath BA15 2QH, 01225 858705
1.3881, -2.2827

33 COMPTON INN, COMPTON DANDO

A cosy pub at the heart of village life serving
only home-made local produce. Enjoy a
pickled egg and a pint of real ale in the
garden after a long walk.
→ BS39 4JZ, 01761 490321
51.3785, -2.5107

34 THE BLUE FLAME INN, NAILSEA

An eccentric, yet earthy and old-fashioned
locals' pub with stuffed badgers, and cider
straight from the barrel.
→ Netherton Wood Lane, Nailsea, BS48 4DE,
01275 856910
51.4180, -2.7941

35 IFORD GARDEN TEAS

One of the most beautiful Italianate gardens
in England with an old-fashioned kitchen
providing teas and large chunks of lovely
home-made cake.
→ Signed off A36, 7 miles S of Bath.
51.3291, -2.2873

CAMP AND SLEEP

36 TREEHOUSE & YURT, EAST HARPTREE

Watch the sunset from the veranda of your
treehouse then soak in your own copper
bath. Or stay in a three-pod yurt full of
antique furniture with a woodburner in the
bathroom.
→ Canopyandstars.co.uk, Whitecross Road,
East Harptree, BS40 6AA, 01761 221729
51.3007, -2.6218

37 MANOR FARM, UPTON CHEYNEY

Simple farm camping with home-made curry
from the farm's own chillis and meat. Great
farm shop and café, and there's lots of
wildlife. Access to Bath and Bristol via the
nearby cycle track.
→ Upton Cheyney, Bitton, BS30 6NQ, 0117
9328800
51.4279, -2.4439

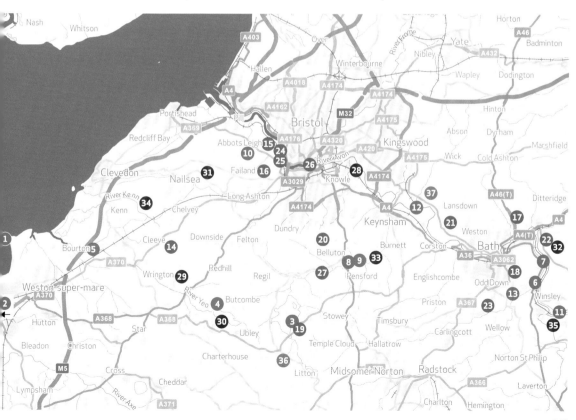

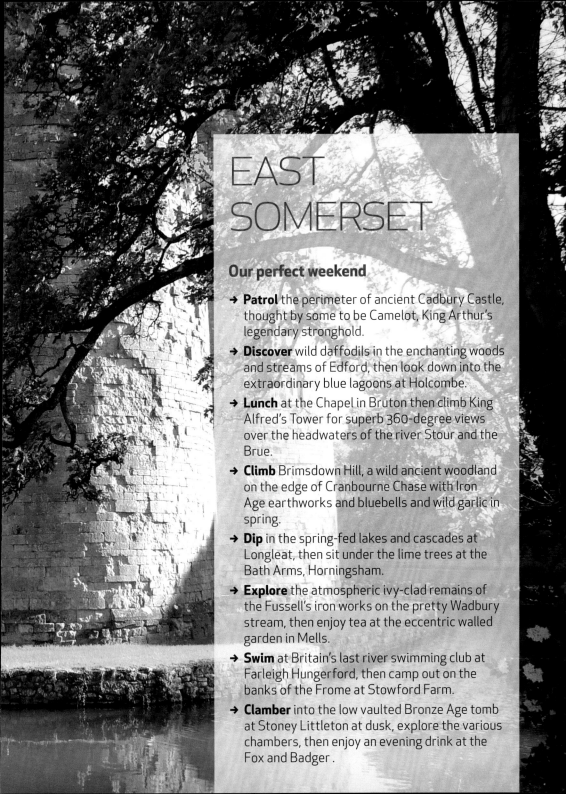

EAST SOMERSET

Our perfect weekend

→ **Patrol** the perimeter of ancient Cadbury Castle, thought by some to be Camelot, King Arthur's legendary stronghold.

→ **Discover** wild daffodils in the enchanting woods and streams of Edford, then look down into the extraordinary blue lagoons at Holcombe.

→ **Lunch** at the Chapel in Bruton then climb King Alfred's Tower for superb 360-degree views over the headwaters of the river Stour and the Brue.

→ **Climb** Brimsdown Hill, a wild ancient woodland on the edge of Cranbourne Chase with Iron Age earthworks and bluebells and wild garlic in spring.

→ **Dip** in the spring-fed lakes and cascades at Longleat, then sit under the lime trees at the Bath Arms, Horningsham.

→ **Explore** the atmospheric ivy-clad remains of the Fussell's iron works on the pretty Wadbury stream, then enjoy tea at the eccentric walled garden in Mells.

→ **Swim** at Britain's last river swimming club at Farleigh Hungerford, then camp out on the banks of the Frome at Stowford Farm.

→ **Clamber** into the low vaulted Bronze Age tomb at Stoney Littleton at dusk, explore the various chambers, then enjoy an evening drink at the Fox and Badger.

The lively river Frome runs through this tranquil region, with fine picnic spots in the flowery meadows or leafy glades along its banks. The great chalk escarpment of Cranbourne Chase rises to the east, while to the south there are magnificent views from the summits of ancient hill forts.

Two grand estates lie just on the region's eastern border, abundantly supplied with water from the Wiltshire Downs. Stourhead is one of England's finest landscaped gardens and its peaceful lake, ornamented by classical, pillared buildings, was created by damming the river Stour. The great river rises here, just below King Alfred's tower – it's well worth climbing the monument's 200 steps-flowing into secluded, spring-fed pools in Six Wells Bottom before passing through Dorset down to the sea.

Nearby Longleat, the other great estate, features a series of beautiful spring-fed lakes. Its lower waters are now part of the safari park and home to hippopotamuses and sea lions, but the upper pools are crystal clear and lie in a quieter area of the parkland.

Heading west from the Wiltshire border, is the region's main river, the Frome. One particularly bucolic stretch is occupied by the Farleigh Hungerford swimming club, and is a wonderul place for a dip. The Frome powered numerous industries, such as the Fussell family's iron works during the late 18th and early 19th centuries. The highly successful business produced scythes, sickles, spades, shovels and other agricultural implements in the headwaters around Mells. Now the great works lie derelict and wreathed in ivy, but the wooded vale is deeply atmospheric, with the constant background gurgle of the stream.

You can explore more of Somerset's ancient ruins, including the perfect tiny castle of Nunney, and the ancient stone barrow on a remote hillside below Wellow. Or pay a visit to the venerable Wyndham's Oak, which may have been a gallows tree, on the boundary of what was once a royal forest. Its massive trunk is now hollowed, and most of its great branches are gone, but step inside and imagine all the history this tree must have witnessed.

To the far south are the great earthern ramparts of Cadbury Castle, thought by some to be the true Arthurian court of Camelot. The views are sensational and it is a wonderful place to capture the last hours of a summer day and watch the colours fade across the landscape.

13

RIVERS & LAKES

FARLEIGH HUNGERFORD, RIVER FROME

his deep, narrow, pleasant stretch of the
rome, above a weir, is home to England's
est river-swimming club. There are lawns,
teps and a changing hut. Close by is a
uined castle, and good campsite
st upstream.

→ Descend into the village from A36 (signed
rowbridge), over two bridges then enter field
nmedately on R.

mins, 51.3179, -2.2810

LONGLEAT UPPER LAKES

lear chalk springs from the Wiltshire downs
eed this series of beautiful lakes that flow
own towards Longleat House. Wonderful
arkland to explore and lovely pub close by.

→ Take the B3092 S of Frome and after 3
iles turn L (Horningsham). At the Bath Arms,
ark and turn L down to the large arched
atehouse (300m). Turn immediately R down
o the bridge and cascades at bottom of field,
vith parkland beyond. Fishermen tend to use
he lower lakes, so please be discreet.

0 mins, 51.1775, -2.2669

3 TELLISFORD, RIVER FROME

Large weir pool with medieval packhorse
bridge and pillbox ruin. Lovely, leafy pastoral
aspect. Popular with local kids.

→ Continue on from Farleigh 1 mile and
turn R (B3109 Rode). After 1½ miles turn R
(Tellisford Bridge), park at end and continue
down hill to river. Admire bridge and micro-
hydro scheme then head upstream through
field 300m to weir.

10 mins, 51.2975, -2.2807

4 ORCHARDLEIGH LAKE, LULLINGTON

Large lake, with wooded shore, in parkland.

→ From Oldford (1 mile N of Frome on B3090),
turn L signed Lullington/Stapleton. 600m
after bridge find wooden kissing gate on L and
follow the path up to the lake, 500m.

10 mins, 51.2570, -2.3144

5 SIX WELLS BOTTOM, STOURHEAD

Descend from the headwaters of the Stour,
past the ancient pumphouse, to three
spring-fed ponds, and eventually to the main
Stourhead garden lakes. There is a hill fort in
the woods above to the right.

→ Heading S on the B3092 towards Stourton,
turn R shortly after the Red Lion Inn, signed

Alfred's Tower. Turn first L (Alfred's Tower) and
find small car park on L after ¾ mile. Bear R
out of car park and descend into the grassy
valley. The pools are ¾ mile further on, at the
bottom. On your R as you descend there is an
iron age hill fort in the woods. If you enter the
gardens at the bottom, look out for the grotto
tunnel and ice house with its deep ice pit. For
refreshment, the Red Lion (BA12 6RP, 01985
844263) and the smarter Spread Eagle (in
Stourton, BA12 6QF, 01747 840587) offer
good local, seasonal food.

20 mins, 51.1096, -2.3312

6 HOLCOMBE QUARRY LAKE

Immense quarry lake with clear blue water
and high cliffs. Usually closed and fenced
off, but still used by locals.

→ Travelling S on A367 from Radstock,
pass through Stratton-on-the-Fosse, pass
first turning to Holcombe and descend hill.
Near bottom turn L, signed Stoke Bottom/
Holcombe. Continue 1 ¾ miles to crossroads.
Continue straight over to find quarry gates
and fence on L after ½ mile.

5 mins, 51.2281, -2.4713

ANCIENT FOREST

7 BEACON HILL, SHEPTON MALLET
Old beeches, Bronze Age barrows, quarry pits, standing stones and the great Roman road, the Fosse Way. During World War II the highly secret Auxiliary Unit had bunker here.
→ Heading S on A367, 2 miles before Shepton Mallet, turn L signed Stoke St Michael / Waggon & Horses. After ¾ mile find gate on R.
5 mins, 51.2115, -2.5200

8 WYNDHAM'S OAK, SILTON
Ancient hollow oak, over 1,000 years old and still an inspiring sight.
→ From Bourton (A303) take the Gillingham road and pass under A303. Take next R (after 200m) and follow to Silton (1 mile). The oak is in field behind church (footpath by entrance).
5 mins, 51.0633, -2.3099

9 WHITECLIFF DOWN, MAIDEN BRADLEY
Rolling hilltops with earthworks, ancient woodland, glades, bluebells. Wild, remote.
→ Heading S on B3092, turn L in Maiden Bradley (signed Warminster) and find footpath on R, just after Baycliffe Farm.
30 mins, 51.1511, -2.2487

10 LONGLEAT FOREST, EAST WOODLANDS
Longleat is the largest expanse of woodland in Somerset and Lower Woods is one of its most remote pockets.
→ Travelling S on A361 (Frome bypass) turn L just before B3092 roundabout, signed East Woodlands, then R after a mile to Woodlands Church. Bear L at church, down the track, and find paths off to R, into woods, after 300m.
15 mins, 51.1938, -2.2994

SUNSET HILLTOPS

11 WHITE SHEET HILL, STOURTON
Neolithic camp and spectacular lookout on W escarpment of Cranbourne Chase. Chalk grassland rich in wild flowers and butterflies
→ Travelling S on the B3092 towards Stourton, turn L on tiny unsigned lane alongside the Red Lion Inn. Continue ¾ mile up to car park, then another ½ mile to hilltop.
20 mins, 51.1101, -2.2809

12 CADBURY CASTLE "CAMELOT"
Impressive hill fort with far-reaching views and strong Arthurian connections.
→ Heading S on A359, turn L (N Cadbury) just before the A303. Pass through N Cadbury

village, into S Cadbury, and 200m beyond the Camelot pub find Castle Lane and track on R.
15 mins, 51.0254, -2.5299

MEADOWS

13 EDFORD WOODS, HOLCOMBE

One of the best early spring displays of wild daffodils in Somerset, in an idyllic streamside setting. Great for paddling.
→ As for Holcombe quarry lake (see 6), but find entrance to wood on L by bridge/stream, ½ mile before crossroads. You can also stop off at Harridge Wood on R, ½ mile before, with large oaks and bats too. Old St Andrew's church in nearby Holcombe (continue on and turn L, 51.2549, -2.4759) has delightfully unspoilt interior.
5 mins, 51.2335, -2.4849

SACRED AND ANCIENT

14 STONEY LITTLETON LONG BARROW

Neolithic tomb in a field on the hillside. You can crawl into the central gallery tunnel and explore three pairs of side chambers.
→ Due S of Bath, off A367. From Wellow school descend Mill Hill to the ford, then bear R (100m) and take the bridleway on R (100m) and continue 15 mins to the barrow. You can continue on 10 mins to cross the stream on R and return via lane and path on L bank of stream, passing a couple of nice paddling and plunge spots (e.g. 51.3159,-2.3800). Fox and Badger in the village is a good pub.
20 mins, 51.3133,-2.3816

RUINS AND FOLLIES

15 NUNNEY CASTLE, NUNNEY

A perfectly picturesque 14th century, French-style ruined castle with a pretty, circular moat.
→ Signed off the A361 at Nunney Catch services, W of Frome on the Shepton road. Free entry. There are lovely walks around the village and Nunney Brook.
5 mins, 51.2107, -2.3784

16 FUSSELL'S IRON WORKS, MELLS

Huge, ruined, early 19th-century iron works by the Wadbury stream, complete with ivy-clad workers' houses, pumping stations, fabrication halls and the old weir. Remote, beautiful and little visited.
→ Leave Mells (W of Frome) on the Great Elm road (second R just after the post office) and find an iron gate and footpath after 300m on R. Follow this for 15 mins along the stream to

find the beginning of the ruined works. They extend along the stream for almost ¼ mile.
20 mins, 51.2393, -2.3712

17 KING ALFRED'S TOWER, BRUTON

Magnificent, three-sided folly tower, completed in 1772 in honour of the English king. You can climb up to the top via the dark, spiral staircase, which has 205 steps, to enjoy fine views out over the wooded escarpment.
→ Heading S on the B3092, turn R shortly after the Red Lion Inn signed Alfred's Tower. Turn first L (Alfred's Tower).Continue and find tower and car park after 1 ½ miles. Open 9am–5pm during summer.
10 mins, 51.1148, -2.3650

SLOW FOOD

18 BATH ARMS, HORNINGSHAM

Most of its food is sourced from within 50 miles, the pigs are bred next door, and there is organic ale and vodka. Beautiful lime trees in the garden and rooms for overnight stays. Great for exploring Longleat park and lakes.
→ Horningsham, BA12 7LY, 01985 844308
51.1734, -2.2727

19 STAPLETON ARMS

Funky, country gastropub. Local-produce menus with fine pork pies and ales. Comfy sofas and rooms for overnight stops.
→ Church Hill, Buckhorn Weston, Gillingham, SP8 5HS, 01963 370396
51.0214, -2.3472

20 TUCKERS GRAVE INN, FAULKLAND

Eccentric tiny bar. Barrels of cider and beer are piled up in what looks like the front room of someone's house.
→ Radstock, Avon BA3 5XF, 01373 834230
51.2952, -2.3579

21 THE TALBOT INN, MELLS

This charming 15th-century courtyard coaching inn is full of character and serves excellent local food and ale.
→ Selwood St, Frome BA11 3PN, 01373812254
51.2414, -2.3917

22 AT THE CHAPEL, BRUTON

The high street site is not exactly a wild location, but we love this converted chapel. Excellent pizzas, brunches and roasts, with breads baked in their wood-fired oven. Afterwards, take a walk up to the strange, ruined dovecote tower on the hill to the S.

28 High Street, BA10 0AE, 01749 814070
..1117, -2.4547 🏛️

3 MELLS WALLED GARDEN

ovely 17th-century walled garden where
stainable cut flowers are grown for
le. Delicious pizzas from a wood-fired
ven are served at weekends, and simple
as and lunches every day in season. The
eenhouses have been converted to cosy
ating areas, with a small library.
➜ Selwood St, BA11 3PN, 01373 812597
1.2409, -2.3909

4 THE OAKHILL INN

cosy village pub with rooms. After a long
alk, retreat to the fireside and tuck into
elicious game and local produce, sourced
thin walking distance.
➜ Fosse Road, Oakhill, Radstock, BA3 5HU,
1749 840442
1.2228, -2.5209 🅿️

CAMP AND SLEEP

5 THE BELL, BUCKLAND DINHAM

quirky, characterful and friendly pub,
ith the added bonus of wonderful, simple
amping in the field behind. Real ales, hearty
es and lovely hosts, Jeremy and Lucy.
➜ Frome, BA11 2QT, 01373 462956
1.2599, -2.3565 🅿️⛺

6 STOWFORD MANOR, FARLEIGH HUNGERFORD

dyllic, family-run riverside camping on a
arm dating back to medieval times and
ome to England's last swimming club (see
. Enjoy fairtrade cream teas in the gardens
n summer made with fresh cream from the
arm's Jersey cows. B&B also available.
➜ Farleigh Hungerford, BA14 9LH, 01225
52253
1.3175, -2.2729 🏊⛺

7 MOLLIE'S HUT, TRUDOXHILL

Candlelit shepherd's hut in its own paddock
ith a cosy woodburner. Breakfast is
elivered in a hamper every morning,
ncluding the farm's own eggs.
➜ Belle Vue Farm, BA11 5DW, 01373 836213
1.1880, -2.3601

28 GILCOMBE FARM, BRUTON

uxury 'Featherdown' camping with glorious
ountryside views, and acres of rolling
ills, woods and streams to explore. Enjoy
elicious unpasteurised milk from the onsite

farm shop, as well as organic meats, cheeses
and ciders. Treat yourself to lunch At The
Chapel in Bruton.
➜ Gilcombe, Bruton BA10 0QE, 01420 80804
51.1266, -2.4358

29 ORCHARD CARRIAGE, UPTON NOBLE

Colourfully restored railway carriage
complete with roll-top bath and woodburner.
Lovely setting in an organic orchard.
➜ Canopyandstars.co.uk, BA10 0JW
51.1464, -2.3868

30 BATCOMBE VALE CAMPING

Perfect camping under trees among streams
and ponds with views of the rolling hills.
Rowing boats, fishing and lovely walks to
nearby pubs.
➜ Batcombe, BA4 6BW, 01749 831207
51.1399, -2.4576 ⛺

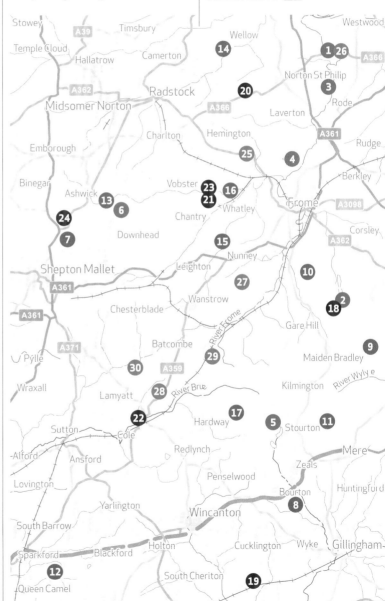

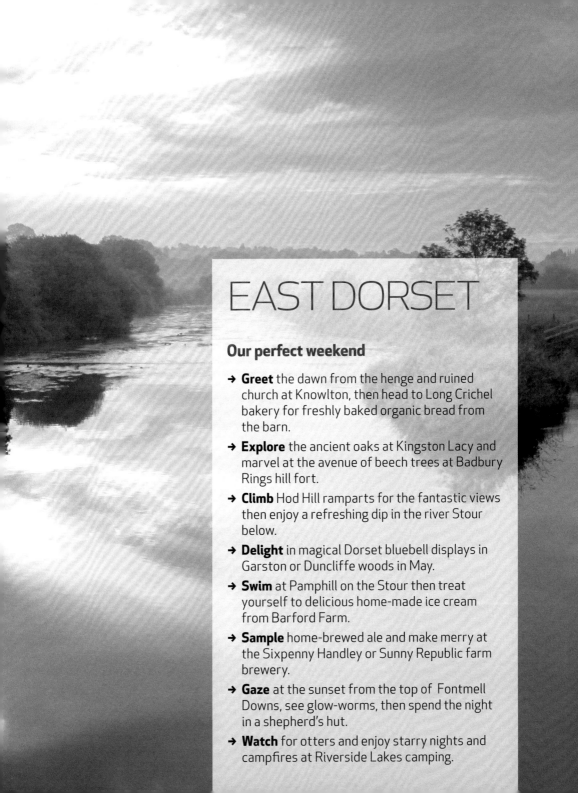

EAST DORSET

Our perfect weekend

→ **Greet** the dawn from the henge and ruined church at Knowlton, then head to Long Crichel bakery for freshly baked organic bread from the barn.

→ **Explore** the ancient oaks at Kingston Lacy and marvel at the avenue of beech trees at Badbury Rings hill fort.

→ **Climb** Hod Hill ramparts for the fantastic views then enjoy a refreshing dip in the river Stour below.

→ **Delight** in magical Dorset bluebell displays in Garston or Duncliffe woods in May.

→ **Swim** at Pamphill on the Stour then treat yourself to delicious home-made ice cream from Barford Farm.

→ **Sample** home-brewed ale and make merry at the Sixpenny Handley or Sunny Republic farm brewery.

→ **Gaze** at the sunset from the top of Fontmell Downs, see glow-worms, then spend the night in a shepherd's hut.

→ **Watch** for otters and enjoy starry nights and campfires at Riverside Lakes camping.

This eastern corner of Dorset, part of the ancient kingdom of Wessex, is irrigated by the river Stour. It is a beautiful, undulating landscape of chalk escarpments and downland dotted with wild flowers, ancient forests and mysterious neolithic earthworks.

Starting high up on the western downs, the six-mile-long cursus, an avenue with parallel earth banks, was built around 5,500 years ago, possibly as a processional route that linked to the nearby earth henge at Knowlton. Here around the ruined Norman church that sits in the earthworks, ancient yews – trees worshipped long ago as deities – survive as a reminder of how our pagan and Christian sites are sometimes inextricably linked.

For more recent history, make for the old Roman ford on the Stour at Pamphill, a crossing point on the main route from Dorchester to Salisbury. Beneath the footbridge, find a large pool for dipping, or you can seek out other picnic spots along this picturesque river. On a hot day, enjoy a paddle in the Tarrant stream and explore the pretty church at Tarrant Crawford.

Further upstream, the massive earth ramparts of Hod Hill and Hambledon Hill are pretty impressive. These hill forts were built to guard the banks of the river Stour. You can also visit Badbury Rings, another important Iron Age fort on the meeting of two Roman roads. Its magnificent avenue of 365 ancient beeches is a glorious sight in the quiet of an early summer morning.

Flour is still ground in the traditional way near Shaftesbury and supplied to local bakeries, so it's one of the best places to taste real bread. At Long Crichel bakery you can eat mouthwatering organic bread, savoury pastries and cakes still warm from the oven, while over at the Old Rectory at Semley Jemma sells bread and jams from her kitchen. The local microbreweries are also not to be missed.

Those who seek solitude will find it here – high on Martin Down, walking through the ancient woods at Garston and Duncliffe, or searching for glow-worms in the uplands of Melbury Down under a starry, summer sky.

5

RIVER SWIMMING

WHITE MILL, STURMINSTER MARSHALL

River pool downstream of a beautiful medieval arched bridge and mill. Follow the lane upstream and find the quiet riverside footpath that leads up to Shapwick church.

→ Signed Sturminster Marshall from the B3082 at Badbury Rings. Cycle Route 25.
mins, 50.8048, -2.0613

PAMPHILL, WIMBORNE MINSTER

wide, popular river pool with a riverside each, footbridge and a small weir. There are good walks or swims upstream, leading to an old Roman ford.

→ Heading W out of Wimborne on the B3082 Blandford road, turn L down Cowgrove Rd, signed for the football club. Continue ¾ mile to find small parking area and river on L.
mins, 50.8000, -2.0076

CANFORD MAGNA, STOUR

Large weir pool in meadow opposite Canford School.

→ Turn R for Canford Magna on A341 from Bournemouth (Wimborne direction). Follow brown signs for the parish church ('No Through Road' to school). Cross river by footbridge and turn R to river pool below weir. In the school grounds stands one of the oldest chestnut trees in the country (50.7884, -1.9529).
10 mins, 50.7903, -1.9568

4 TARRANT CRAWFORD CHURCH

Tiny hidden church up a little track next to clear chalk stream, with shallow pool and rope swing.

→ Heading from Wimborne to Blandford, turn L off B3082 at the True Lovers Knot pub (signed Tarrant Crawford), then L at the T junction (Spetisbury) and take the first track on the L (unsigned) after 300m, alongside the Tarrant stream ½ mile up to church.
3 mins, 50.8311, -2.1110

TREES AND MEADOWS

5 BADBURY RINGS BEECHES AND OAKS

Wonderful views from this Iron Age fort ringed with concentric earth works – now peaceful woodland. Dating from 150BC, it lies at the crossing of two important Roman roads. The adjacent tree-lined avenue, now the B3082, has 366 beeches along one side, to represent a leap year, and 365 along the other. The trees were planted by William John Bankes in 1835 as a gift to his mother. There are also over 80 ancient pollarded oaks on the 8,500-acre Kingston Lacy estate, especially in The Oaks, a 14th-century woodland ½ mile to the N of the Rings.

→ The Rings are signed off the Wimborne/Blandford B3082 and you can do a circular walk around the Rings via King Down Farm/The Oaks (50.8344, -2.0478) and along the roadside for the beeches. See Kingston Lacy NT Walk 2.
20 mins, 50.8267, -2.0520

6 GARSTON WOOD BLUEBELLS

Hazel woodland carpeted with wood anemones and primroses, then bluebells, in spring. Many birds including turtle doves.

→ From Sixpenny Handley (off A354), take the Bowerchalke road (Deanland) for 1½ miles to the RSPB car park. You might also like to explore Chase Woods and find Chase Avenue, a magnificent old beech 'ride' that runs through it (50.9759, -2.0399). Turn L for Deanland before reaching Garston.
10 mins, 50.9730, -2.0022

7 ABBOT STREET COPSE, KINGSTON LACY

Ancient fern and ivy-clad holloway leads

through a copse with a sea of bluebells in spring. The wider Kingston Lacey estate is also famous for its wild daffodils in spring.

→ Turn L and L again out of the main Pamphill car park (near the church end of the oak avenue) into Abbott Street. After 200m, by No 542, turn L again down All Fool's Lane, which crosses the Old Sarum Roman road after 300m. See Kingston Lacy NT Walk 3.

10 mins, 50.8052, -2.0204 ▣▣🚶

8 DUNCLIFFE WOOD BLUEBELLS

Straddling two hilltops, the region's largest area of ancient woodland has fantastic bluebells. The coppiced stools of small-leaved lime may be Dorset's oldest living things. Filled with butterflies in summer.

→ From Shaftesbury, take the A30 towards Sherborne and after approximately 3½ miles, turn L signed Stour Row (opposite the Kings Arms Inn). The entrance to Duncliffe is after ½ mile on L.

20 mins, 50.9993, -2.2619 ▣

9 FONTMELL DOWNS, MELBURY ABBAS

A fantastic place to spot butterflies and orchids, with skylarks singing overhead. Wonderful sunset views over the Blackmoor Vale and dancing glow-worms at night.

→ From Shaftesbury head S on B3081 and follow signs to and through Melbury Abbas. Car park on the R at the top of Spread Eagle Hill, 1 mile beyond the village, just before the left turn to Compton Abbas airfield. A path from here also runs N to Melbury Down (this path is the best place to see glow-worms during June and July if the weather is good) and along a wildflower-edged path down to Compton Abbas village, which has a ruined church.

20 mins, 50.9680, -2.1635 ▣▣🐄🦋

SUNSET HILLTOPS

10 WIN GREEN, CRANBORNE CHASE

The highest point on Cranborne Chase with fine views of rolling downland in all directions. Crowned by a stand of trees growing on a Bronze Age bowl barrow.

→ Signed on L, 4 miles SE of Shaftesbury on B3081. Fontmell and Melbury Downs are 1 mile to the W.

5 mins, 50.9850, -2.1077 ✝▣🌳🔾

11 HOD HILL FORT & RIVER STOUR

Dorset's largest hill fort with stunning views, and surrounded by downland rich in wild flowers, butterflies and wildlife. The Stour runs through woods below. There are five entrances through the earth ramparts – two Iron Age, two Roman and one medieval. Once inside the fort you'll see remains of building and property boundaries in the form of circular hollows and ridges.

→ From Blandford Forum take the A350 and after Stourpaine turn L (Hanford/Child Okefor) and find small parking area on L afte ½ mile. Take the lower woodland path along the river if you fancy a dip (though the banks are steep). Hambledon Hill is 1 mile to the N.

20 mins, 50.8956, -2.2068 ▣🔾🚶

12 HAMBLEDON HILL FORT

Although not the largest, this is considered one of Dorset's most dramatic Iron Age hill forts for its series of steep earth ramparts. Fine views from the fort's N end.

→ You can ascend from Hod Hill, Child Okefor or Shroton/Iwerne Courtney, although the latter has the best pub for the return journey. If you approach on the S flank (Hod Hill) then look out for the dense stand of ancient yew woodland below (50.9042, -2.2153).

30 mins, 50.9127, -2.2212 ▣

8

13 KNOWLTON RUINED CHURCH

Remains of a 12th century church in the centre of a neolithic ritual earth henge. The juxtaposition symbolises the transition from pagan to Christian worship. Look out for the remnants of an ancient yew avenue.

→ Turn L off the B3078 signed Brockington, 7 miles N of Wimborne Minster. At Wimbourne St Giles there are several ancient old yews that pre-date the church. The yew avenue may have stretched to Knowlton from Wimborne St Giles church and the old cemetery at All Hallows (50.9129, -1.9681).

1 min, 50.8920, -1.9671

14 MARTIN DOWN & DORSET CURSUS

The starting point of a mysterious 6-mile processional avenue (cursus) built in 3500 BC, which then headed SW. Little of it remains, but there are downland butterflies and wild flowers, including orchids, to enjoy.

→ Parking can be found on A354, 3 miles N of the Sixpenny Handley roundabout.

10 mins, 50.9740, -1.9430

15 HORTON TOWER, HORTON

An imposing, rather sinister, three-sided ruin that stands sentinel over the countryside.

→ On the S edge of Horton (just off B3078 near Knowlton) towards Chalbury Common, find bridleway on L and follow it for 300m.

5 mins, 50.8602, -1.9584

SLOW FOOD

16 CANN MILLS, SHAFTESBURY

Buy stoneground flour to take home from this working watermill, or join one of Paul Merry's courses on making bread by hand.

→ Cann Mills, SP7 0BL, 01747 823711

50.9871, -2.1833

17 QUANGLE WANGLE, SEMLEY

Drop in at the Rectory on a Wednesday to buy Jemma's brilliant home-made bread, jelly and jam. Her artisan breads are also available at De-Liz in Tisbury, Indulge in Shaftesbury and Ludwell Stores (Wednesday delivery) .

→ Mrs Jemma Morgan, The Rectory, Semley. SP7 9AU, 01747 830174

51.0403, -2.1562

18 BARFORD FARMHOUSE ICE CREAM

Stroll around the gardens and enjoy award-winning ice cream made on the farm using only milk from the Jersey cows and fruit from local growers. Gluten-free and diabet options too.

→ Sturminster Marshall, Wimborne, BH21 4BY, 01258 857969

50.8040, -2.0521

19 LANGTON ARMS, TARRANT MONKTON

Popular thatched pub by a pretty ford selli real ales and Dorset produce, including the own Tarrant Valley beef (which you can buy to take home).

→ Nr Blandford, DT11 8RX, 01258 830225

50.8785, -2.0803

20 LONG CRICHEL BAKERY

Charming artisan bakery in a converted ba selling organic bread, simple pizzas and pastries, all made from local ingredients. This is slow food at its best – eaten straigh out of the wood-fired oven.

→ Wimborne, BH21 5JU, 01258 85728

50.8936, -2.0382

21 THE MUSEUM INN, FARNHAM

An upmarket pub with rooms that still retains a local feel. Good selection of real ales and ciders, and high-quality local food with lots of game from nearby estates.

→ Blandford Forum, DT11 8DE, 017255162

50.9355, -2.0602

22 SIXPENNY BREWERY & BAR

Possibly the smallest pub in the UK, selling brilliant, home-brewed beers. Popular with locals, especially before lunch and in the early evening on weekends. Situated right i the centre of the farm next to the vats.

→ Manor Farm, Sixpenny Handley, SP5 5NU, 01725 762006

50.9493, -2.0023

23 GOLD HILL, CHILD OKEFORD

Choose from an impressive range of super-fresh vegetables grown on Dorset's first organically certified farm. On-site café.

→ Ridgeway Lane, DT11 8HB, 01258 86029

50.9195, -2.2426

24 PAMPHILL DAIRY FARM SHOP

Dairy, café, butcher and farm shop combine

→ Wimborne, BH21 4ED, 01202 857131

50.8080, -2.0146

CAMP AND SLEEP

5 RIVERSIDE LAKES, HORTON

There's a drop-off only policy for cars at this quiet campsite set among three lakes. Look out for the otters (who have polished off all the stock in these former fishing lakes) and enjoy starry nights and campfires.

→ Slough Ln, Wimborne BH21 7JL, 01202 821212
50.8643, -1.9204

6 OLD FORGE, COMPTON ABBAS

Stay in 'Rosie,' the beautiful 1930s Romany caravan, or in 'Sam', the newly restored cosy shepherd's hut with woodburner. Both look out over the buttercup meadows. Horses, free-range chickens and great breakfasts.

→ Canopyandstars.co.uk, The Old Forge, Compton Abbas, Shaftesbury, SP7 0NQ
50.9662, -2.1859

27 NORTHWEST FARM BREWERY

Bring your own tent or stay in one of the lovingly restored, wooden shepherd's huts set on this quiet working farm. Enjoy a Friday evening drink at the Sunny Republic brewery, housed in the Georgian barn, or come in the spring for a lambing weekend.

→ West Street, Winterborne Kingston, DT11 9AT, 01929 471 600 / 07810 505180
50.7787, -2.2100

28 THE INSIDE PARK CAMPING

Although predominantly a caravan park, the pitches are laid out over 14 acres of ancient parkland. Camp under a venerable tree, take midnight walks in the woods and let the kids play in the large adventure playground.

→ Fairmile Road, Blandford DT11 9AD, 01258 453719
50.8404, -2.1959

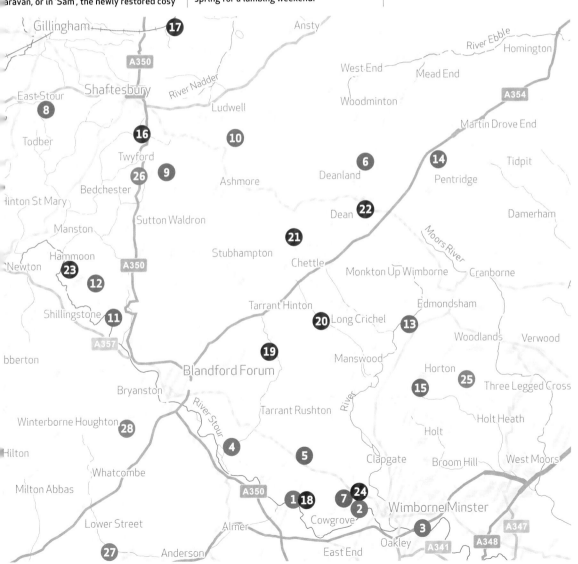

DORSET PURBECK

Our perfect weekend

→ **Swim** through Durdle Door or explore the amazing grotto, sea caves and tunnels at Stair Hole.

→ **Stroll** through wildflower meadows and see spring and summer orchids on the downland at Durlston or Corfe Common.

→ **Collect** picnic fare from Clavell's Farm shop then relax on the secluded shores of Worbarrow Bay.

→ **Snorkel** and swim in the crystal-clear lagoons of Winspit and Seacombe, then explore the cliff-edge caverns.

→ **Enjoy** local food and ale with a side order of museum curiosities at the Square and Compass in Worth Matravers.

→ **Paddle** in the ford and play Pooh Sticks at Moreton, then take cream tea at the award-winning tea shop.

→ **Follow** the Kimmeridge trails and discover an abundance of marine life, or try sea kayaking at Studland Bay.

→ **Camp** at Downshay and enjoy sunset views over Corfe castle or sleep in a luxury bell tent at Knaveswell Farm.

The rugged Purbeck shoreline is one of the wildest and most beautiful stretches on the south coast, punctuated by huge sea arches, limestone caves, and secluded coves with natural rock pools. In the waters around Poole, wildlife thrives and orchids bloom on the chalk downlands.

Much of this wonderful region has managed to remain relatively unscarred by development. To the west and south of Poole, one of Europe's largest natural harbours, parts of the shoreline and the islands are wildlife havens, with three designated nature reserves. Inland, army firing ranges, although forcing the abandonment of hamlets such as Tyneham, have left large swathes of grassland untouched and rich in wild flowers and butterflies.

On a hot, sunny day, Stair Hole is an idyllic azure grotto with small caves and tunnels leading out to the ocean. For many, however, the greatest attraction along this coast is the ancient, gnarled archway of Durdle Door. Swim through this vast opening at dusk or dawn for a truly memorable experience. Along this coastline there is abundant evidence of quarrying, which was carried out during the 18th century to supply building stone for London's Georgian squares. In some places, such as spectacular Winspit, excavations have left blue lagoons, while the slopes of the cliff-edge quarries are carpeted with wildflowers, and bats roost in the caverns. At Dancing Ledge, a large, quarried platform makes the perfect plunge pool.

As in other parts of Dorset, the local produce in this area is bountiful. Clavell's Farm or the Bere Regis rural farm shop are both recommended for their delicious breads and cheeses. While exploring inland, stop by the river Frome for a swim and enjoy a picnic, then walk through wildflower meadows and take in the superb views from Durston or Corfe Common.

For the best underwater wildlife, don't miss out on a trip to Kimmeridge Bay. The small beach has huge slate ledges with large rock pools that are rich in marine life, especially on spring tides when the bay can be empty of water during the afternoon. At higher tides, a unique snorkelling trail is in operation, and you can even collect a waterproof guide-sheet and route map from the visitor centre.

SECRET BEACHES

DURDLE DOOR & MAN O' WAR

Huge, ancient sea arch on dramatic coastline.
Often busy. Long steep, shingle beach –
undertow in surf conditions – with small
caves behind (good for sheltering from rain).
Man O'War beach on E side of Durdle Door
is more sheltered and quieter, with offshore
reefs for snorkelling and jumping.

Signed West Lulworth from A352, then
6 miles. Park in the massive visitor centre
car park and follow signs up hill (30 mins).
Or a shorter approach, park at Durdle Door
Holiday Park (turn R before West Lulworth and
continue up hill). There is a decent wooded
camping section here – the only one near the
beach for miles. Continue W on coast path
500m to Scratchy Bottom (50.6228, -2.2809)
to descend to a quiet section of beach. Or
continue W on beach to Bat Hole small sea
arch.

20 mins, 50.6217, -2.2767

2 STAIR HOLE, LULWORTH

Fantastic inland lagoon with sea caverns
and arches leading to sea. Amazing rock
formations and great swimming at high tide.
Tricky scramble down.

From Lulworth Cove car park (see Durdle
Door) bear R on the track by the coastguard
hut, just behind the visitor centre, 200m.
Cross rope barrier and scramble carefully
down scree slope. Best in calm, clear seas.
2 mins, 50.6180, -2.2524

3 MUPE BAY, LULWORTH

Remote, beautifully sheltered cove, with
good snorkeling at Mupe Rock beneath cliffs.

Walk around edge of Lulworth Cove (high
route via path or low route via beach) and
follow coast path heading E. Pass Fossil Forest
and old concrete lookout to find stairs down
to bay after 1 mile.
30 mins, 50.6187, -2.2225

4 WINSPIT, WORTH MATRAVERS

Rocky lagoon under cliffs with caves and
jumps. Huge old quarry caverns. Keep a look
out for rock samphire to forage.

Follow signs to Worth Matravers via
Langton Matravers (B3069 between Corfe
or Swanage). Park at the brilliant Square
and Compass (01929 439229, with mini
museum, see 25). Walk into village, past
green, and turn L (Winspit Rd, blue-painted
cottages) and continue down valley to sea
(1 mile), descending by waterfall to Winspit

rock platform. Lagoon on L with jumps from
rock table L. Old quarry caverns are near the
cliff edge both E and W. Continue on coast
path E ¾ mile to next valley bottom cove, to
Seacombe Cliff, a rocky platform with good
rock jumping ledges and caves (50.5894,
-2.0236), then pick up return path to village.
20 mins, 50.5843, -2.0332

5 WORBARROW BAY, TYNEHAM

Wide crescent of sand and shingle at the end
of a remote track through fields and woods,
beyond the deserted village of Tyneham.
Pondfield Cove is adjacent on L, with a sea
cave. Sunset views from the small headland.

Heading N from Lulworth Cove back to Wool/
A352 turn R towards East Lulworth (B3070),
then R (straight ahead) on entering the village,
at the army range warning sign (NB this road is
closed on army firing days). After 3 miles take
hard R down to Tyneham and follow footpath
signs to sea. (Pronounced 'Worbrough'!).
20 mins, 50.6170, -2.1844

6 DANCING LEDGE, LANGTON MATRAVERS

Great sea-level plateau hewn from cliff by
quarrymen, with rectangular plunge pool.
Several adjacent sea caves for exploring in
calm sea. Rock samphire to forage, too.

➔ Continue 1½ miles E along coast from Seacombe, or from Langton Matravers, turn L into Durnford Drove (signed Langton House) and park at road end. Footpath signed to Dancing Ledge. Tom's Fields camping (next L after Durnford Drove) is popular (01929 427110) though Acton Field, on next L, is often quieter and cheaper (01929 424184).
20 mins, 50.5917, -2.0046

7 CHAPMAN'S POOL, WORTH MATRAVERS
Grey-shingled crescent bay at bottom of wooded vale.
➔ Drive through Worth Matravers 1 mile W and park at Renscombe Farm.
20 mins, 50.5935, -2.0634

8 BROWNSEA ISLAND
NT-owned island, site of the first Scouting Association camp. Indigenous red squirrels thrive here, ornamental peacocks roam and there are huge flocks of waders from avocets to curlews.
➔ Brownsea Island Ferries (01929 462383) leave from Poole Old Town quay (£8.50, BH15 1BQ) or Bournemouth's Sandbanks (£5, BH13 7QN). From Branksea Castle pier bear L towards S beach – a mixture of shingle, sand and seaweed with woods behind. Sandier at

E end but deeper towards W. For deepest swimming bear L at memorial, along coastal path, to Pottery Pier and shingle beach.
20 mins, 50.6926, -1.9884

9 STUDLAND BEACH AND DUNES
Three mile long, unspoilt, NT-owned beach with dunes. The N stretch, most easily reached by chain ferry, has a wild, desert-island feel, appreciated by the naturist sunbathers at Shell Bay. Knoll Beach, to S, has a large car park, NT café and shop, and is favoured by families. A wealth of wild flowers, sika deer and rare heathers in dunes and heath behind. Try sea kayaking out to Old Harry rocks and sea arches.
➔ 4 miles N of Swanage or via the chain ferry from Sandbanks, Bournemouth.
5 mins, 50.6519, -1.9527

10 SEA KAYAKING AND COASTEERING
➔ Studland Watersports, Knoll Beach, Studland, BH19 3AX, 01929 554492, 07980 559143
➔ Second Wind, Lulworth Cove, DT3 6RY, 01305 835301
50.6461, -1.9504

11 MORETON FORD, FROME
A wide, gravel ford and shallow pool, lined with willows and tree swings. Popular with families – the long foootbridge is good for Pooh Sticks. Next to the church where Lawrence of Arabia was buried.
➔ Signed on L off the B3390, S of Tolpuddle. Turn L at Moreton Tea Rooms (well worth a visit – a regular winner of Dorset tea room of the year DT2 8RH, 01929 463647).
2 mins, 50.7047, -2.2763

12 WAREHAM BRIDGE, FROME
A popular spot for swimming, picnics and boating on a hot summer day.
➔ Wareham old bridge is in the centre of the town, off the A351. The downstream side is best for putting boats in the water but you can also walk and swim upstream to find a bit more tranquillity.
2 mins, 50.6839, -2.1095

13 SWINEHAM JETTY, FROME
The footpath passes along the shores of Swineham lake (you can book open water swimming sessions there) and arrives at a small jetty with ladder on the tidal Frome.

19

A circular walk returns upstream along the Frome's bank. Or swim or boat down then walk back.

→ Park at end of East St, Wareham (BH20 4NL) at East Walls junction, by dead ends signs. Contiue on foot 1km to reach jetty where river meets footpath. Swineham lake swimming bookings 07739960202.

20 mins, 50.6906, -2.0854

14 GREEN POOL, EAST CREECH

Set in wild, forested heath land, just to the S of the fee-charging 'Blue Pool'. Adjacent Kilwood has amazing wild garlic in spring.

→ From Stoborough Green (A351, S of Wareham) follow sign for Blue Pool/ Furzebrook (R at round about) and continue beyond ½ mile. On corner, just before East Creech farm camping and caravanning (01929 480519) find a bridleway on L leading through to Norden Heath. The green pool is just off the path on the L after 5 mins (350m), a bit muddy but very wild. Continue on the main path and bear R after the next pond to loop back via Kilwood nature reserve (50.6421, -2.0965), which has abundant wild garlic in late April/ early May.

5 mins, 50.6459, -2.0901

SUNSET HILL FORTS

15 FLOWERS BARROW, TYNEHAM

This coastal hill fort, set high above spectacular Worbarrow Bay, offers sublime sunsets and why not go naked moonlit swimming on the beach afterwards?

→ Continue a mile W from Worbarrow Bay (see 5). Or just stop at Worbarrow Tout headland and enjoy the view from there. You can access the barrow directly along the ridge top from Povington Hill picnic parking (50.6300, -2.1602). There's also a great view from the parking further along the ridge road (50.6346, -2.1364). This is army land, so it is only open on weekends and during August. Stay on marked paths.

30 mins, 50.6245, -2.1915

MEADOWS AND WILDLIFE

16 ARNE BEACH, WAREHAM

A pretty path through RSPB reserve heathland and ancient beechwoods (look out for deer), leads down to a remote peninsula, with a small sand and mud beach. Located on Poole Harbour lagoon, one of the world's largest natural harbours with flocks of wading birds.

6

→ From Wareham town centre, head S over the causeway to Stoborough and turn L, following signs (4 miles). Or hire a bike from Purbeck Cycle Hire (01929 556 601) near the station. It's a 20 min walk down to Shipstal Beach on a good wide path. Popular at weekends. Possible to swim, and best on a high tide. Watch for currents in the tidal channel.

20 mins, 50.6956, -2.0245

17 KIMMERIDGE LEDGE SNORKEL TRAILS

Small shingle beach with a huge expanse of shallow reefs and rock pools. Small visitor centre and marked snorkelling trails – collect your waterproof route map from centre (BH20 5PF, 01929 481044).

→ Continue on from Worbarrow, or head W from Corfe village via Church Knowle passing Clavell's Farmshop (BH20 5PE, 01929 480701). Clavell Tower on the cliff is a Landmark Trust property which can be rented. See also Clavell's farm shop/café (see 26).
5 mins, 50.6094, -2.1300

18 DURLSTON COUNTRY PARK MEADOWS

Superb cliff-top views and abundant wildlife. Open downland with amazing wild flowers, including yellow orchids, and 30 different species of butterflies, including the Lulworth skipper, which can be seen from end-June to early August. Interesting caverns at Tilly Whim on the cliff edge.
→ Follow brown signs up the hill S from Swanage
15 mins, 50.5955, -1.9568

19 CORFE COMMON ORCHIDS

Wonderful orchids in late April and May, and great views of Corfe Castle.
→ Heading S out of Corfe, turn L at end of village (B3069, Langton Matravers). After 100m find bridleway on R, and parking for 2 cars, and walk up onto the common.
10 mins, 50.6286, -2.0608

RUINS AND ANCIENT

20 CORFE CASTLE FROM KNOWLE HILL

Famous and iconic ruined castle approached from its wild side, with views over Poole Harbour.
→ From Church Knowle follow footpath from behind church up onto Knowle Hill and follow ridge E for a mile via West Hill to the castle.. When you get back, reward yourself with local fish from the New Inn (BH20 5NQ, 01929 480 357), good traditional pub in Church Knowle.
30 mins, 50.6409, -2.0659

21 TYNEHAM LOST VILLAGE

Tyneham was abandoned when the army took over the area as a firing range in 1943. The public telephone kiosk was installed outside the old post office, only a few weeks before the village was evacuated.
→ Open when the firing range is closed (weekends, August and Christmas). Follow directions as for Worbarrow Bay (see 5).
2 mins, 50.6228, -2.1685

22 ST ALDHELM'S CHAPEL

A beautiful Norman chapel situated on an exposed headland site and thought to have been built within an earlier Christian enclosure. The isolated chapel may also have

functioned as a lookout for Corfe Castle. According to one legend, the chapel was buil by the father of a bride who was drowned at sea on her wedding day.
→ As for Chapman's Pool but follow bridleway track to headland. Or combine with a visit to Winspit, 1½ miles E.
20 mins, 50.5796, -2.0567

WILD FOODS

23 SEA FISHING BY KAYAK

Be escorted to the best fishing spots and enjoy marine wildlife at close range on a half day or full-day sea-kayak fishing safari. Also kayak and snorkel tours and coasteering.
→ Studland Sea School, Beach Road, Studland BH19 3AP, 01929 450430
50.6463, -1.9503

24 FORAGE FOR A SEA FEAST

You can often find rock samphire along the cliffs around Dancing Ledge and Winspit.
→ Try your hand at marine foraging while coasteering, or try a land-based bushcraft day with Dorset Bushcraft (01202 460440).
50.5906, -2.0144

LOCAL FOOD AND PRODUCE

25 SQUARE AND COMPASS

The perfect quirky pub with home-brewed cider, pies and pasties, and an eccentric mini-museum of Jurassic curiosities. Sit inside by the fire or outside at tables hewn from rock.
→ Worth Matrvaerse, BH19 3LF, 01929 439229
50.5977, -2.0372

26 CLAVELL'S CAFÉ FARMSHOP

A family-run café and shop selling home-made seasonal produce from their Purbeck Isle farm, plus Kimmeridge Bay fish, Worth Matravers cheese and Purbeck ice cream.
→ Kimmeridge, Wareham, BH20 5PE, 01929 480701
50.6167, -2.1206

27 THE SCOTT ARMS, KINGSTON

Popular vine-clad village pub with roaring fires, leather sofas, big garden and superb views of Corfe Castle.
→ West St, Corfe BH20 5LH, 01929 480270
50.6164, -2.062

28 RURAL FARM SHOP, BERE REGIS

Food emporium set up to support local

oducers. Haven of artisan Dorset cheeses, eads, vegetables and free-range meats. elivery service within the local area.

→ Rye Hill Farm, Dorset BH20 7LP, 01929 472926
).7445, -2.2199

9 KNOLL BEACH CAFÉ, STUDLAND

ocal and organic food by the sea. The ajority of the food comes from the NT's state including venison and Red Devon eef, as well as foraged fruits and their mous seaweed soup.

→ Nr Swanage, BH19 3AX, 01929 450305
).6452, -1.9511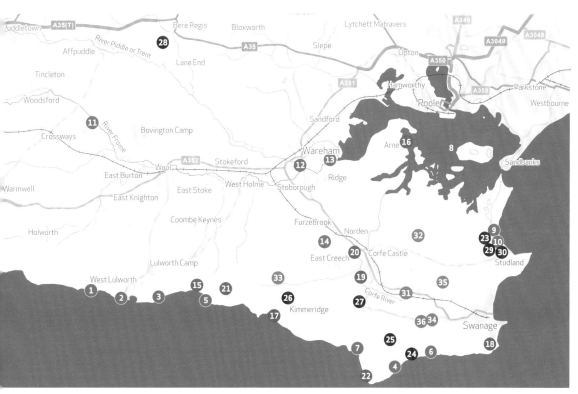

0 JOE'S CAFÉ, STUDLAND

each shack café with local organic and airtrade produce, including home-made ups and Purbeck ice creams.

→ South Beach, BH19 3AN, 07931325243
).6418, -1.9447

CAMP AND SLEEP

1 DOWNSHAY, WORTH MATRAVERS

njoy amazing vistas of glorious Dorset ountryside at this working dairy farm

and campsite. Pitches are often sloping so choose well. If you want to arrive in style, take the steam train to Harman's Cross and walk up to the site.

→ Haycrafts Lane, Swanage BH19 3EB, 01929 480316
50.6208, -2.0245 ▲

32 BURNBAKE FARM, CORFE CASTLE

Camp in the woods in the heart of the Isle of Purbeck and watch the kids make forest dens, splash in the stream and play tarzan on the rope swings. No bookings, no campfires.

→ Rempstone, Corfe, BH20 5JH, 01929 480570
50.6492, -2.0150 ▲🚻

33 STEEPLE LEAZE FARM, BRADLEY

Stay on this wildlife-friendly working farm set in a lovely, south-facing, wooded valley. Enjoy farm-reared meat, which you are encouraged to cook on your own campfire. Very basic facilities with no showers and no caravans allowed.

→ Luttons Farms, Steeple, BH20 5NY, 01929 480509
50.6282, -2.1271 ▲🔥

34 TOM'S FIELD, LANGTON MATRAVERS

Simple, traditional camping in four acres of unmarked grassy fields with some views. Can get busy but you can walk to the Square and Compass pub and down to Dancing Ledge for a morning swim.

→ Swanage, BH19 3HN, 01929 427110
50.6075, -2.0085 ▲

35 KNAVESWELL FARM, CORFE

Luxury Feather Down Farm tents on 150-acre, family-run dairy farm backed by woodlands and streams.

→ Corfe Castle, BH20 5JB, 01420 80804
50.6261, -1.9949

36 ACTON FIELD, LANGTON MATRAVERS

Camp amongst the wild flowers of this lovely tussocky and often steeply sloping site. Brilliant – if you can find a flat pitch. Simple facilities and you can head to Tom's field shop for supplies

→ E Acton Field, Langton Matravers, Swanage BH19 3HS, 01929 424184
50.6066, -2.0125 ▲

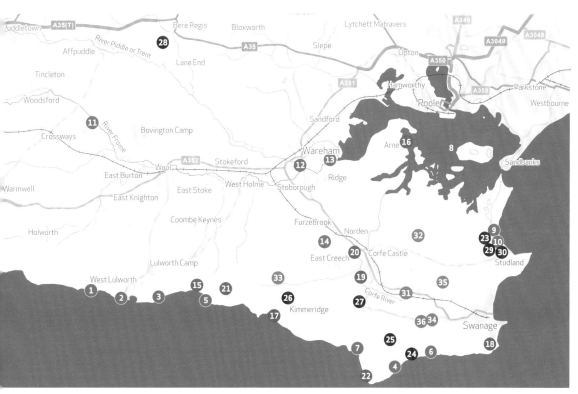

13

DORCHESTER & PORTLAND

Our perfect weekend

→ **Greet** the sunrise from Maiden Castle, Europe's largest Iron Age hill fort.

→ **Swim** beneath castle ruins at Church Ope Cove or explore caverns, reefs and sea stacks on the Isle of Portland.

→ **Visit** the Cerne Abbas Giant and discover the secret gatehouse ruin and holy well. Treat yourself to lunch at the New Inn.

→ **Scramble** down the smugglers' path from White Nothe through the undercliff to the hidden, wild beach below.

→ **Explore** the modern sculptures and rock-art installations in a dramatic cliff-edge setting at abandoned Tout Quarry.

→ **Wild swim** in the river Stour at Sturminster and laze on the grassy banks eating a picnic from Olives et al.

→ **Gaze out** over the beautiful, rolling landscape from Bulbarrow Hill, then walk among the ancient yews at Woolland.

→ **Cross** the Fleet lagoon at dusk and be amazed by the phosphorescence as night falls. Make a driftwood fire on Chesil Beach and wild camp.

→ **Join** the party and camp at Eweleaze. Enjoy cliff-top sunset views, campfire suppers and the site's own private beach.

From the lush pastures of peaceful Blackmoor Vale to the spectacular limestone caves and wild beaches of Portland, this part of Dorset has much to offer. Follow paths once trodden by smugglers, snorkel around sea stacks or spend lazy afternoons on the grassy banks of the Stour.

In the north, the slower stretches of the Stour are filled with yellow water lilies. This is Blackmore Vale, classic Dorset dairy country and where the novelist Thomas Hardy spent some of his happiest years. At Colber Bridge, a pretty white-painted, wrought-iron footbridge spans the Stour, just above Bather's Island, the site of the old river-swimming club. Up- and downstream are further places to dip, or launch a canoe if you are discreet

To the south, the great chalk uplands rise up to Cerne Abbas, site of Britain's largest chalk figure. It's not clear whether the naked giant pre- or post-dates the 10th-century Benedictine monastery, or if the monks would have approved. The abbey was destroyed but the elaborate, stone Abbot's Porch remains, and there is a small holy well – a quiet place for reflection.

Continue south via Maiden Castle, Europe's largest Iron Age hill fort, to Chesil Beach, nature's massive stone-grinding machine. Along its staggering 18-mile length, the pebbles range in size from pea gravel to fist-sized cobbles. To reach the wild central portions of the beach you must cross the Fleet marshes and lagoon, a journey completed under cover of darkness by many smugglers of the past.

The hard, white limestone of Portland rises up from the ocean in the far distance. The fine stone from its quarries was used to build prestigious buildings, including St Paul's Cathedral. Now the abandoned cliff-side quarry at Tout has been transformed into an inspirational sculpture park, with displays and installations carved from the rock faces all around.

Below Portland's cliffs, especially along the eastern shore, this limestone isle offers some of the most spectacular clear-water snorkelling in Britain and in its aquatic gardens you can spot orange wrasse, while pink anemones shelter among the kelp. There are strong currents offshore, so always stay close and keep away from Portland Bill, but on a hot summer day, this is a true paradise to explore.

10

SECRET BEACHES

1 CHURCH OPE COVE, EASTON
Pretty pebble cove with beach huts set beneath the ruins of castle and church.

→ From Easton on the Isle of Portland, take Church Ope Road, next to the Portland Museum, and follow path down to beach, under old archway, Rufus Castle ruins, then past those of St Andrew's chapel. Further S along the coast path you may discover the old sea-water baths below Pennsylvania Castle.
15 mins, 50.5377, -2.4282 🏖️⛪🏄

2 GORE COVE, CHESIL FLEET
The Fleet lagoon is the 10-mile-long lake behind Chesil Beach. Its water is warm, shallow and brackish, with phosphorescence at night. The adventurous can canoe or swim across to the most remote, central section of the beach.

→ Follow signs for Moonfleet Manor Hotel via East Fleet (from Chickerell, B3157, 3 miles W of Weymouth). Note the tiny chapel ruined by storms in 1824. Join the coast path via track on L, 200m before the hotel, and follow shore for about 15 mins N to reach the cove, or continue up the Fleet to Herbury Bay. There is also access to the shore via Langton Hive slipway (50.6308, -2.5577) 1½ miles down Coastguard Road, behind Langton Herring village, 4 miles N of Weymouth on B3157 (NB smugglers' tales at the Elm Tree Inn, DT3 4HU, 01305 871257). Chesil Beach N end can also be accessed directly from Abbotsbury, or the S end from Weymouth, Chesil Beach Centre.
20 mins, 50.6258, -2.5452 🐾🏖️🚤▼

3 SMUGGLERS' PATH, WHITE NOTHE
A precarious, zig-zagging smugglers' path descends 500 feet through the steep undercliff, a dense habitat created by huge landslips a century ago. At the bottom the flinty beach, backed by dramatic white, striated cliffs offers total seclusion. This path is reputedly the one described in *Moonfleet* by J. Meade Faulkner.

→ From Ringstead NT car parking area (see listing) continue beyond Burning Cliff/chapel another 15 mins to the abandoned brick watchtower. A stone marker indicates the Smugglers' Path down through the undercliff.
40 mins, 50.6252, -2.3241 ⚠️🏃⛪▼🐚

4 RINGSTEAD BAY & BURNING CLIFF
Quiet, remote family beach with fine pebble sand and offshore rock reef for snorkelling and exploration. Good café, serving mackerel and chips in the garden. At Burning Cliff see the tiny wooden chapel, then walk down to the wild bay below.

→ From Weymouth on A353 turn R for Upton, 1½ miles after Osmington Mills. Turn R again after ½ mile for toll road down to beach (café, toilets) or continue uphill to the grassland and free NT parking area (great sunset views) and walk to Burning Cliff (15 mins, look out for St Catherine's chapel, 50.6340, -2.3370,) and cliff path down to beach (wilder, more remote E end of Ringstead Bay, 15 mins more).
5 mins, 50.6312, -2.3532 🚤🏖️🍴⛪

RIVER SWIMMING

5 STOUR PROVOST, R STOUR
Tiny, peaceful village with pool below the old mill with machinery still intact.

→ Just off the B3092, S of East Stour. Park and walk down to bottom of Mill Lane.
2 mins, 50.9928, -2.2991 ⛪

6 COLBER BRIDGE, STURMINSTER
An open stretch of the Stour with grassy banks by decorative, white Colber Bridge. Water is a little weedy and slow, but clean and deep so perfect for long swims. Downstream is overgrown 'Bather's Island'.

→ Park in town car park and walk up hill to the High Street, over road and into The Row by the library and village hall. At end of the cul-de-sac (100m) pass through iron gate and follow footpath down the hill and straight over (150m) to find Colber Bridge on an open stretch of meadow. Long swims in either direction. Local museum has working mill and displays relating to country life in the past.
5 mins, 50.9280, -2.3105

7 CUTT MILL, HINTON ST MARY

Large weir pool by ruined mill.

→ At the N end of Hinton St Mary (B3092 N of Sturminster), just before village end, find unsigned, 'No Through Road' on L (Marriage Lane) ending at river after ¾ mile.
1 min, 50.9479, -2.3200

8 FIDDLEFORD MANOR MILL, STOUR

Mill pool and sluices by old manor set among meadows. A popular place for a swim on a hot day.

→ Signed Fiddleford Manor on L, a mile E of Sturminster Newton (A357). Free car park and free entry to the lovely 14th-century 'solar' with extraordinary ancient roof timbers.
5 mins, 50.9215, -2.2855

9 HAMMOON, RIVER STOUR

Secluded stretch of the Stour with grassy areas.

→ 1 mile W of Fiddleford turning (A357) take next L signed Hammoon (opp Okeford turning) and continue 1½ miles through village to bridge. Take footpath downstream 300m to bend and small beach.
5 mins, 50.9300, -2.2532

CAVES AND QUARRIES

10 CAVE HOLE & QUARRY, PORTLAND

Wonderful deep, clear waters for snorkelling and jumps; offshore stacks to explore. Peer down into one of the sea caves (Cave Hole) through a grate on the coast path, or descend on the iron ladder and swim in.

→ From Portland Bill lighthouse and car park head up the NE coast 300m, past café to Red Crane. To R is a popular inlet for jumping at high or low tide (50.5152,-2.4531). Continue on ¾ mile up coast to Cave Hole and Bob's Crane/Longstone Ope Quarry, and find an iron ladder below that allows easy entrance and exit to the sea, the sea cave and a little island stack. Also accessible from lighthouse road on track footpath, signed Longstone Ope Quarry.
20 mins, 50.5206, -2.4433

11 TOUT QUARRY SCULPTURES, PORTLAND

This abandoned stone quarry on the wild cliffs of Portland is now filled with quirky sculptures and stonework installations – including one by Antony Gormley – plus the remains of the quarry and its railway. Incredible views W over Chesil Beach.

→ Cross to Portland and drive up out of Fortuneswell on main road. At the first roundabout follow signs for Weston then turn R into industrial estate after ½ mile, signed Tout Quarry Park/Tradecroft. Turn R at end of cul-de-sac.
15 mins, 50.5512, -2.4467

SUNSET HILL TOPS

12 RAWLSBURY HILL FORT, BULBARROW

Rolling hills set with Iron Age ramparts and one of Dorset's finest viewpoints, both to the N from the lane along Bulbarrow, and to the SW from the hill fort itself.

→ As for Woolland (see 15) but turn L at Belchalwell Street, signed Bulbarrow and drive up and along the ridge until you reach the fort.
5 mins, 50.8512, -2.3316

13 MAIDEN CASTLE, DORCHESTER

Britain largest and most impressive hill fort,

14

3

241

over 1½ miles in diameter with multiple layers of high earth ramparts and the remains of a Roman temple.

→ Well signed from suburbs of Dorchester (S approach, A354). There is also a secluded approach from the bridleway near Winterborne Monkton (50.6913,-2.4797). 15 mins, 50.6947, -2.4702 🚶

14 CERNE ABBEY AND GIANT'S HILL

Better known for its well-endowed chalk man, Cerne Abbas village also has a beautiful gatehouse from the ruined medieval abbey, and a sacred well. Best food at the New Inn.

→ Take Abbey Street and, at the duck pond, turn right through arch for well or continue for gatehouse. New Inn, DT2 7JF, 01300 341274 5 mins, 50.8122, -2.4764 🅿🍴✝

TREES AND WILDLIFE

15 WOOLLAND CHURCH YEW

Pay a visit to this huge yew in Woolland churchyard. It dates from pre-Christian times and may be the oldest yew in Dorset.

→ From A357 E of Sturminster follow lanes to Okeford Fitzpaine, then Iberton and finally the tiny hamlet of Woolland (5 miles). In the woods of Bulbarrow Hill are more ancient yews. 1 min, 50.8622, -2.3192 ✝

16 PUDDLETOWN FOREST & HEATH

Spot grass snakes and newts at Rushy Pond (of Thomas Hardy fame) set in broadleaved woodland and ancient heathland. Running through the site is a well-preserved Roman road. By Hardy's cottage, so it can get busy.

→ Turn off A35 2 miles E of Dorchester, following signs for Higher Bockhampton and Hardy's Cottage (NT). 10 mins, 50.7288, -2.3906 🍴🚶

17 GREENHILL DOWN MEADOWS, HILTON

Isolated nature reserve with wildflower meadows, orchids, views and peace.

→ From Hilton (SW of Blandford Forum), follow the Knapp, then bridleway up hill NE for 1 mile. 25 mins, 50.8338, -2.3003 🚶⛰

SLOW FOOD

18 WINDSBATCH BAKERY, UPWEY

The 'baking birds', Lizzie and Bekki, create innovative breads and imaginative cakes, using ingredients, such as blackberries, picked in the local lanes or the best Dorset cheeses. Open Tuesday to Saturday mornings or at local farmers' markets.

→ Windsbatch Bakery, Friar Waddon Rd, Upwey, DT3 4EW, 01305 816378 50.6705, -2.4926

19 OSMINGTON MILLS WILD FISHING

Try fishing at dawn or dusk for mullet, bass, wrasse and pollack. Watercress can be harvested from the stream that runs down to the sea. Gutweed is common and, properly rinsed, can be dried, fried and sprinkled with salt – delicious as a snack with your beer.

→ Signed off A353 E of Weymouth. 50.6339, -2.3761 ▦

20 THE BLUEFISH CAFÉ, PORTLAND

Enjoy moules frites or local faggots at this small, family-run café in a 17th-century cottage at the end of Chesil Beach. The food is imaginative and seasonal.

→ 16-17A Chiswell, DT5 1AN, 01305 82299 50.5621, -2.4491 🚶

21 CRABHOUSE CAFÉ, WYKE REGIS

Oyster farmer and chef, Nigel Bloxham, serves excellent fresh seafood and Portland oysters from this quirky, wooden beachside cafe. Lovely views over Chesil Beach and the Fleet.

→ Ferrymans Way, Portland Road, Wyke Regis, DT4 9YU, 01305 788867 50.5852, -2.4730 📷

22 THE KIOSK, RINGSTEAD

A small beach café serving fish and chips, hot drinks and cream teas. You can often find a local fisherman's catch on sale.

→ Ringstead Bay Kiosk, DT2 8NG, 0130585242 50.6323, -2.3529 🅿🏊

23 THE SHIP INN, WEST STOUR

An independently owned pub serving local meat and fish, and vegetables from the family farm down the road.

→ Nr Gillingham, SP8 5RP, 01747 838640 51.0015, -2.3094 🅿

24 OLIVES ET AL, STURMINSTER NEWTON

Sit outside under a yellow umbrella and enjoy a top-class sandwich or choose from one of the 60 different cheeses and deli delights on offer.

→ North Dorset Business Park, Rolls Mill Way, DT10 2GA, 01258 474300 50.9196, -2.3207 🅿

25 BLACKMORE VALE INN, MARNHULL

Delightful inglenook-ed 17th-century pub. This was the disreputable Rollivers in

ardy's *Tess of the D'Ubervilles* and retains
omething of its character. Serves local ales
nd pies made with home-grown vegetables.
→ Burton Street, DT10 1JJ, 01258 820701
0.9743, -2.3243

CAMP AND SLEEP

6 EWELEAZE AND NORTHDOWN FARM

imple farm camping laid out over several
elds on two organic farms. Lovely sea and
alley views and access to private beach,
ith great rock-pooling. A farm shop sells
ome-reared meats and organic produce.
lorthdown Farm open July, Eweleaze August.
→ Osmington Hill, Weymouth, DT3 6ED,
1305 833690
0.6386, -2.4031

7 GREENFIELDS FOREST, MIDDLEMARSH

ow-key woodland camping on a small
amily-run farm with deer, chickens and
eese. Collect wood from the forest for your
ampfire and cook up the farm's venison
ausages, or catch a trout from the private
ake. There is also a shepherd's hut to rent.
→ A352, DT9 5QN, 01963 210060
0.8652, -2.4719

8 EAST SHILVINGHAMPTON, PORTESHAM

iafari tents with panoramic views, baby
joats to feed and home cooking.
→ Featherdown Farms, 01420 80804
0.6569, -2.5343

9 WOLVETON GATEHOUSE, CHARMINSTER

reat yourself to a week-end in this fairytale
jatehouse and climb up a wide spiral staircase
o turreted rooms. Jacobean fireplaces and
ots of history. Landmark Trust.
→ Dorchester DT2 9QN, 01628 825417
0.7291, -2.4570

0 STOCK GAYLARD, STURMINSTER

ocally made yurts set in ancient, wooded
arkland with deer. There is a lake, streams
nd you might hear nightingales in May.
→ DT10 2BG, 01963 23511
0.9123, -2.3952

1 SEA BARN FARM, FLEET

This is a big, holiday-park style site, but
here is a good camping field and the views
are amazing.
→ Sea Barn Farm, Fleet, Weymouth, DT3 4ED,
1305 782218
0.6242, -2.5301

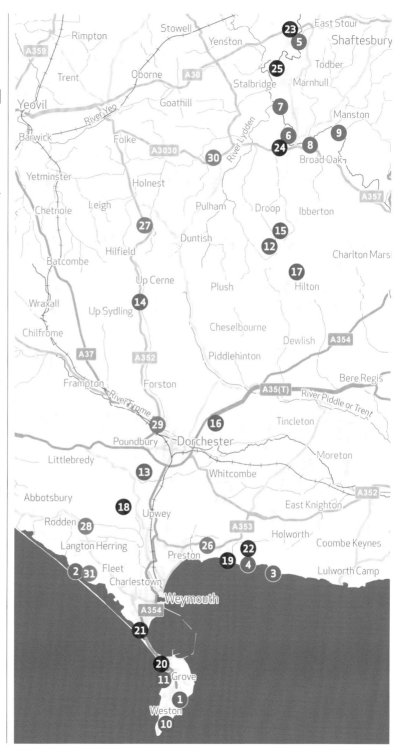

WEST DORSET

Our perfect weekend

→ **Wander** through great swathes of wild flowers and see unusual butterflies at Powerstock and Kingcombe meadows.

→ **Swim** at Hive Beach beneath the honeycomb-shaped cliffs and enjoy the freshest seafood from the brilliant beach-shack café.

→ **Seek out** the enchanting remains of St Luke's chapel, deep in ancient bluebell woods and still used for open-air services.

→ **Stock up** with picnic supplies at Felicity's farm shop, then head over to the secret beach of St Gabriel to find ammonites.

→ **Journey** deep into the sunken world of Hell Lane, one of Dorset's oldest holloways with green banks way over head height.

→ **Taste** real Jersey cream at Modbury Farm – the last place in Dorset to make cream in the traditional way.

→ **Watch** the sun go down over Chesil Beach from St Catherine's hilltop chapel or from nearby Abbotsbury Castle .

→ **Wild camp** at Brig's Farm with pizza from the wood-fired oven washed down with plenty of local cider.

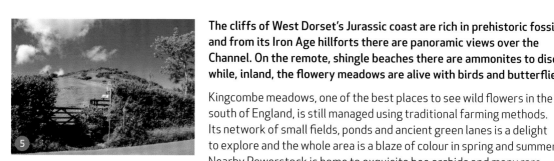

The cliffs of West Dorset's Jurassic coast are rich in prehistoric fossils, and from its Iron Age hillforts there are panoramic views over the Channel. On the remote, shingle beaches there are ammonites to discover while, inland, the flowery meadows are alive with birds and butterflies.

Kingcombe meadows, one of the best places to see wild flowers in the south of England, is still managed using traditional farming methods. Its network of small fields, ponds and ancient green lanes is a delight to explore and the whole area is a blaze of colour in spring and summer. Nearby Powerstock is home to exquisite bee orchids and many rare butterflies, while tiny Loscombe is the place to see snake's head fritillaries.

On the western side of the region are many hill forts, including Pilsdon Pen. For a long time, this was considered Dorset's highest point, until adjacent Lewesdon Hill was measured and found to be a few feet higher. Another nearby hill fort, Lambert's Castle was used as a signalling station by the admiralty in the early 19th century to warn of a possible French invasion by Napoleon's forces. Like Pilsdon, Lambert's Castle also has a single ditch and rampart, and was site of an annual fair from 1709. There was even a horse-racing track and parts are still visible in the south-west corner.

To the south are Dorset's ancient holloways, sunken lanes used by cattle drovers, now almost completely roofed over by a latticework of branches. None is more impressive than Hell Lane, a dark underworld with banks more than 4 metres high in places. Rising up out of the landscpe, the great rocky shoulder of Golden Cap is greensand, which is more resistant to erosion than the surrounding clay. On a clear day you can gaze out in every direction and there are views across Lyme Bay to Dartmoor.

There is incredible ecological diversity in Lyme Bay's clear, coastal waters. Around 300 species of plants and animals, including the pink sea-fan, the rare sunset coral, sponges and starfish have all been recorded here. Stretches of wild foreshore are, however, hard to access but a steep flight of steps, beyond ruined St Gabriel's chapel, leads down to one of the remotest parts – and probably the best place to find fossils.

SECRET BEACHES

ST GABRIEL'S MOUTH & CHAPEL

Visit the ruins of the old parish church of
St Gabriel and descend via steep wooden
steps to the secret beach, where there are
many ammonites. This is the only accessible
section between Seatown and Charmouth.

→ About a mile W of Chideock (A35), just after
the hill brow, turn L on unsigned lane, and L
again and park at NT Langdon Hill car park.
Head S through wood to Golden Cap (15 mins),
then descend R (W) via ruins of St Gabriel's
church (50.7284, -2.8485) and hamlet, to St
Gabriel's Mouth beach (15 mins). Top spot for
fossils. Also accessible from Stonebarrow Hill
(see 8).
10 mins, 50.7265, -2.8575

SEATOWN & GOLDEN CAP

Shingle beach and cliffs with a good pub
where you can eat fish and chips after a
swim. Head W to find fossils galore, to catch
sea bass or mackerel, or climb Golden Cap
for stunning views in every direction.

→ Turn off A35 at Chideock, 3 miles W of
Bridport. Anchor Inn (01297 489215). On
cycle route 2.
2 mins, 50.7220, -2.8234

3 HIVE BEACH, BURTON BRADSTOCK

Honeycomb cliffs, beach and seafood café
make this a favourite location for swimming
and exploring.

→ Turn R down Beach Road off B3157 3 miles
E of Bridport. Steep pebble beach – watch out
for undertow in rough seas. Café (DT6 4RF,
01308 897070).
2 mins, 50.6965, -2.7230

SUNSET HILL FORTS

4 EGGARDON, ASKERSWELL

Atmospheric hill fort with triple ramparts,
accessible via a quiet network of lanes.
Amazing panoramas.

→ 3 miles E of Bridport (A35) turn L signed
Askerswell/Maiden Newton. Continue for 3
miles, passing the Spyway pub.
2 mins, 50.7505, -2.6516

5 PILSDON PEN, BROADWINDSOR

Iron Age hill fort located at Dorset's second
highest point, enjoying stunning views over a
huge expanse of empty, rolling countryside.
Lewesdon Hill, highest point, is 1 mile away.

→ It's a short, satisfying walk to the top from
the layby on B3164 (between Broadwindsor

and Birdsmoorgate). A much longer walk
(about 4 miles) can be devised to take in
Lewesdon Hill too, or Bettiscombe Manor, site
of a legendary screaming skull. Pilsdon is also
on the Wessex Ridgeway and the Jubilee Trail.
10 mins, 50.8075, -2.8337

6 ABBOTSBURY CASTLE

A triangular and easily accessible coastal
hill fort commanding excellent views of
the Channel. Once part of the first line of
defence from Roman invasion.

→ 1 mile W of Abbotsbury (B3157) turn R
(signed Ashley Chase only) and park on L after
200m. See also Abbotsbury chapel (see 9).
2 mins, 50.6766, -2.6288

7 LAMBERT'S CASTLE, MARSHWOOD

Wooded early Iron Age hillfort with bluebells,
in spring, close to Pilsdon Pen. Used as a
signalling station in 1806 in case of invasion
by Napoleon and the site of the annual June
fair from 1709 to 1949. See if you can make
out the old horse-racing course.

→ On the B3165 between Axminster
and Thorncombe. The nearby Bottle Inn,
Marshwood, hosts a stinging nettle eating
championship on the second Saturday of June.
15 mins, 50.7878, -2.8921

11

24

8 STONEBARROW HILL, CHARMOUTH

After fossil collecting on Charmouth beach drive high up onto this wild common for wonderful sea-view picnics. You can also access the coast path here and walk to St Gabriel's Mouth (20 mins, see 1).

→ Heading E out of Charmouth (towards A35) and turn R after Charmouth Caravans, onto Stone Barrow Lane. Continue 1½ miles to the end.

5 mins, 50.7381, -2.8657 🚶

9 ST. CATHERINE'S CHAPEL, ABBOTSBURY

Set on a hilltop, this stone-vaulted 14th-century chapel was built as a retreat by monks from the nearby abbey. Wonderful sunsets over the Channel and Chesil Beach.

→ Follow the lane/path by Chapel Lane Stores from Abbotsbury on B3157 (15 mins), or park

at Abbotsbury beach car park (signed Sub-Tropical Gardens/Chesil Beach W on B3157) and walk from there (50.6593, -2.6244, 25 mins).

15 mins, 50.6617, -2.6060 ✝

RUINS AND ANCIENT

10 HELL LANE, SYMONDSBURY

One of the most impressive ancient holloways (sunken lanes) in Dorset, with walls up to 4 metres high. Runs from Symondsbury to North Chideock past Colmer's Hill with its distinctive nine-tree summit.

→ Start from behind the church at Symondsbury. To create a circular walk return via Axen Farm and the lily ponds.

20 mins, 50.7417, -2.7922 🚶

11 ST LUKE'S CHAPEL, ASHLEY CHASE

Enchanting fragment of a tiny 13th-century Cistercian chapel, still consecrated, above a small stream in remote woodland with spring bluebells. Only the west wall arch, three tombs, an altar and a wooden cross remain.

→ Continue 500m beyond Abbotsbury Castle hillfort (see 6) and at grassy area leave car and take track/byway on L. Follow for ¾ miles,

then take footpath over style into woods on F to find altar after 200m. Also accessible from Litton Cheney.

20 mins, 50.6893, -2.6272

12 KINGSTON RUSSELL STONE CIRCLE

Bronze Age stone circle with half of the 18 sarsen stones now lying flat flat. An impressively wild location with many neolithic remains.

→ From Abbotsbury turn off main road opposite the Ilchester Arms (Back Street) and follow lane 1½ miles out of village and up hill (in direction of Thomas Hardy's monument – also great for sunsets 50.6869, -2.5496). Take first L, park and follow bridleway track (not tarmac drive to Gorwell Farm) to the 'Grey Mare and her Colts' long barrow (50.6819, -2.5896, 10 mins) and then on to the stones (20 mins). Also accessible from Litton Cheney

30 mins, 50.6885, -2.5989 📷⛺🚶✝

MEADOWS AND WILDLIFE

13 KINGCOMBE MEADOWS

Patchwork of fields and unimproved grassland, broken up by thick hedges, streams, ponds, ancient green lanes and wooded areas alongside the Hooke stream.

3

Wild flowers and butterflies everywhere, especially spotted heath orchids in June.

➔ 1 mile NW of Maiden Newton (A356) turn L at the top of the hill to Toller Porcorum, then R in the village signed Hooke. After 1 mile look for Kingcombe Visitor Centre sign on R. There is a café here, also offering many courses, including wild food foraging.

15 mins, 50.7900, -2.6334

14 POWERSTOCK COMMON BUTTERFLIES

Marsh fritillary and wood white butterflies are found here, and there are wild daffodils, bluebells and bee orchids in season. Also roe and fallow deer.

➔ As for Kingcombe but continue through Toller Porcorum then R at T-junction (Hooke/Powerstock). Parking is next to old railway bridge. The disused railway line sections are particularly good for flowers, butterflies and grasshoppers in the embankments. Best in spring and summer.

10 mins, 50.7743, -2.6438

15 LOSCOMBE ORCHIDS & FRITILLARIES

Remote meadow reserve with stream and colony of exquisite snake's head fritillaries.

➔ 3 miles N of Bridport on A3066 turn R opposite the Half Moon Inn, Melplash, and follow signs to Loscombe (2 miles). The reserve gate entrance & car park is opposite a line of cottages. Boggy ground.

5 mins, 50.7785, -2.7073

16 FORDE ABBEY GARDENS

Splendid blooms all year, including crocuses and wild daffodils by the ponds in February.

➔ Chard, TA20 4LU, 01460 220231

50.8427, -2.9111

SLOW FOOD

17 MODBURY FARM, BURTON BRADSTOCK

The only remaining Dorset farm to make cream in the traditional manner. Stock up on home-reared beef, pork, honey and vegetables at this organic dairy farm. Sample their delicious raw milk and cream from the restored shippon (cow shed).

➔ Bredy Rd, Bridport DT6 4NE 01308897193

50.7053, -2.6837

18 THREE HORSESHOES, POWERSTOCK

An unpretentious, cosy rural pub serving excellent foraged, hunted and hung food. Convenient for Eggardon hill fort or Kingscomb, Powerstock and Loscombe meadows.

Dugberry Hill, Powerstock, Bridport,
6 3TF, 01308 485328
.7626, -2.6867

FELICITY'S FARM, MORCOMBELAKE
st off the A35 between Lyme and Bridport,
d artisan bread and cheeses, rare-breed
eats, organic veg and local tipples for sale.
agnificent Dorset views
Morcombelake, DT6 6DJ, 01297 480930
.7411, -2.8417

**HIVE BEACH CAFE, BURTON
RADSTOCK**
ceptionally fresh local fish, including crab
d scallops served in a simple tented café
ght on the beach. There is also a tempting
lection of home-made cakes and local
vington's ice cream.
Beach Rd, Bridport, DT6 4RF, 01308 897070
.6967, -2.7223

EVERSHOT BAKERY
r over 150 years there has been a
aditional bakery in Evershot. Try the spelt
d extra-slow-rise sourdough loaves for
ur picnic.

→ 18 Fore Street, DT2 0JW, 01935 83379
50.8386, -2.6062

22 HIX OYSTER HOUSE, LYME REGIS
Expensive but delicious local fish at Mark
Hix's seafood emporium.
→ Cobb Road, DT7 3JP, 01297 446 910
50.7224, -2.9411

CAMP AND SLEEP

23 BRIG'S FARM WILD CAMPING
12-acre smallholding nestled among hills and
winding lanes, 2 miles from the coast. Farm
eggs and vegetables are available for sale, as
well as local cider and meat. Friday night is
wood-fired pizza and salad night, and there
are Sunday lunches. August only.
→ Wootton Fitzpaine, Bridport, DT6 6DF,
01297 561267 / 07967 794038
50.7610, -2.9170

24 CRAFTY CAMPING, HOLDITCH
Bodkin, Fipple, Twybil and Bodger are just
some of the names of the handcrafted yurts,
tipis and shepherd's huts set in master
carpenter Guy Mallinson's woodland. Fish

for rainbow trout in the lake and join one of
Guy's many woodworking courses.
→ Canopyandstars.co.uk / Mallinson.co.uk.
Higher Holditch Farm, Chard, TA20 4NL,
01275 395447
50.8206, -2.9296

25 DOWNHOUSE FARM, HIGHER EYPE
A lovely quiet campsite with gorgeous views
just a hop, skip and jump away from Eype's
Mouth beach where you can swim, rock-pool
and sea fish. There are two fields with basic
facilities and a great café (open to non-
residents) serving up delicious cream teas
and home-grown produce.
→ Bridport, DT6 6AH, 01308 421232
50.7234, -2.7930

26 THE HUT, CHARMOUTH
Charming, spacious A-frame cabin with Aga,
woodburner and wonderful views of the
wooded valley. Very secluded, and the farm
shop is only 10 minutes away.
→ Sawdays.co.uk, Nettlemoor Farm, Fishpond
Bottom, Charmouth, DT6 6NW, 01297
678424
50.7741, -2.9094

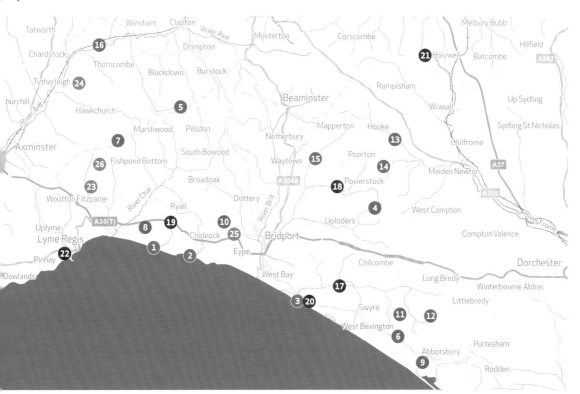

Grid References (Ordnance Survey)

Penwith & Scilly
1   SV 92356 16569
2   SW 35777 23587
3   SW 38181 21853
4   SV 90051 14271
5   SW 39324 22343
6   SW 35578 30862
7   SW 38971 35764
8   SW 44502 38871
9   SW 48044 35594
10 SW 38467 32502
11 SV 88624 16584
12 SW 36266 33602
13 SW 37173 21635
14 SW 43458 34420
15 SW 43274 24503
16 SW 40258 28838
17 SW 41858 29328
18 SW 42631 34939
19 SW 41218 27354
20 SW 38605 28016
21 SW 46873 38044
22 SW 51092 31139
23 SW 40906 25653

Lizard & Helford
1   SW 72108 14263
2   SW 76396 16699
3   SW 68444 13373
4   SW 66738 17902
5   SW 66159 20420
6   SW 55699 27918
7   SW 59293 26919
8   SW 80741 21162
9   SW 76388 26966
10 SW 73810 27309
11 SW 77356 26302
12 SW 74993 25299
13 SW 71143 22233
14 SW 63997 25863
15 SW 78350 25570
16 SW 73063 25737
17 SW 77222 27544
18 SW 59225 31278
19 SW 80341 23105
20 SW 78106 25380
21 SW 59951 26567
22 SW 72067 23908
23 SW 80768 21818

Roseland & Veryan
1   SW 84682 31568
2   SW 86352 31991
3   SW 84741 35675
4   SX 01350 40906
5   SW 95283 40792
6   SW 99369 40446
7   SW 87865 34781
8   SW 87075 32908
9   SW 80959 32745

10 SW 78999 32737
11 SW 76022 34253
12 SW 74935 37317
13 SW 76991 41495
14 SW 77394 37993
15 SW 83766 39656
16 SW 97355 41402
17 SW 79352 36263
18 SW 77884 30723
19 SX 00200 39402
20 SW 91292 38642

Fowey & St Austell
1   SX 03785 48063
2   SX 16584 51177
3   SX 08914 52461
4   SX 10350 50406
5   SX 11876 51031
6   SX 14784 50839
7   SX 01288 55036
8   SX 03076 55448
9   SW 95406 56897
10 SX 14378 51877
11 SX 12557 55971
12 SX 13742 51599
13 SX 12282 54823
14 SX 09826 63349
15 SX 13973 57168
16 SX 08822 63686
17 SX 10417 61379
18 SX 13669 56811
19 SX 06493 56740
20 SW 94808 54693
21 SW 99084 59639
22 SX 01127 53216

Tamar & Looe
1   SX 21044 50746
2   SX 32692 53926
3   SX 25648 51449
4   SX 24188 51453
5   SX 42058 49331
6   SX 36245 53703
7   SX 39210 52188
8   SX 42384 68083
9   SX 37773 55726
10 SX 28927 61203
11 SX 37412 71651
12 SX 45429 69518
13 SX 42364 72391
14 SX 41446 74399
15 SX 35708 72083
16 SX 37477 69179
17 SX 41801 48349
18 SX 34514 67501
19 SX 44180 48812
20 SX 42332 68486
21 SX 24311 54087
22 SX 43962 72699
23 SX 44838 61011

St. Agnes
1   SW 59605 42989
2   SW 72633 52126
3   SW 64195 44688
4   SW 77604 60980
5   SW 73423 52939
6   SW 69670 49570
7   SW 69062 48394
8   SW 71626 40832
9   SW 70994 50326
10 SW 68516 40789
11 SW 69910 50005
12 SW 36266 39837
13 SW 69301 45677
14 SW 73961 53339
15 SW 76522 60134
16 SW 76750 56439
17 SW 72155 51623
18 SW 58097 43303
19 SW 77424 60586
20 SW 69721 39890

Padstow & Bedruthan
1   SW 84324 66068
2   SW 84485 66707
3   SW 84867 70466
4   SW 91247 77124
5   SW 86020 76288
6   SW 85669 74297
7   SW 88899 75893
8   SW 92685 76900
9   SW 93697 80623
10 SW 96829 80612
11 SW 92619 78116
12 SX 00161 81007
13 SX 01386 69527
14 SX 05209 68260
15 SW 85050 72007
16 SW 85091 76136
17 SW 95778 79840
18 SW 89020 76266
19 SW 93434 81157
20 SW 82936 63085
21 SW 93617 79146
22 SW 92488 66152
23 SX 03944 71090

Tintagel & Bude
1   SX 04013 84135
2   SX 06630 89415
3   SX 12931 95475
4   SX 14252 96864
5   SS 18422 00168
6   SX 10841 91988
7   SX 07210 89594
8   SX 08096 88492
9   SX 13105 94423
10 SX 07855 90795
11 SX 20138 90758
12 SX 05022 87281

13 SX 05122 89003
14 SX 22391 97348
15 SS 20175 06775
16 SX 28761 89389
17 SX 11834 93455
18 SX 16698 99115
19 SX 12931 95475

Bodmin Moor
1   SX 11436 75903
2   SX 12641 75504
3   SX 09423 76711
4   SX 16368 72144
5   SX 22261 68658
6   SX 24940 72363
7   SX 25512 72066
8   SX 10428 72945
9   SX 12880 65265
10 SX 25180 74882
11 SX 25759 72448
12 SX 14552 80801
13 SX 10360 74383
14 SX 18739 66808
15 SX 26597 72030
16 SX 06611 67362
17 SX 20234 84510
18 SX 12966 77652
19 SX 14605 73252
20 SX 25817 71422
21 SX 10498 76839
22 SX 13921 83373

Hartland & Torridge
1   SS 21310 18012
2   SS 20145 09982
3   SS 35411 23744
4   SS 24726 27479
5   SS 22577 25878
6   SS 20160 11629
7   SS 38181 24268
8   SS 19967 13383
9   SS 22537 23647
10 SS 54032 06315
11 SS 48702 05744
12 SS 58212 26162
13 SS 54568 14133
14 SS 51782 16572
15 SS 31886 24859
16 SS 41113 05325
17 SS 22998 16996
18 SS 56048 11677
19 SS 19951 15153
20 SS 22685 25100

North Devon
1   SS 45495 44455
2   SS 45881 46113
3   SS 47682 46727
4   SS 56286 47892
5   SS 65489 49679
6   SS 67777 48996

7   SS 58107 47741
8   SS 68592 49187
9   SS 13322 46983
10 SS 42343 40211
11 SS 51405 47798
12 SS 44305 45571
13 SS 60114 48065
14 SS 12763 44877
15 SS 46772 46688
16 SS 46348 35059
17 SS 61093 40560
18 SS 47152 30261
19 SS 14245 43877
20 SS 69317 49368
21 SS 48707 37360
22 SS 49161 37313
23 SS 52541 47921

Southwest Dartmoor
1   SX 47721 67770
2   SX 56183 68856
3   SX 58228 70459
4   SX 59480 66075
5   SX 56653 73584
6   SX 55523 64713
7   SX 57468 63091
8   SX 64549 66910
9   SX 52149 58631
10 SX 52997 63514
11 SX 63852 57215
12 SX 64681 63480
13 SX 47569 69900
14 SX 64379 61742
15 SX 61609 61746
16 SX 63505 64433
17 SX 63249 62504
18 SX 60434 69943
19 SX 58534 73399
20 SX 55460 74796
21 SX 59119 66941

Northwest Dartmoor
1   SX 53248 85428
2   SX 56417 92116
3   SX 55448 83108
4   SX 60531 92439
5   SX 42804 90539
6   SX 61243 77188
7   SX 56478 89188
8   SX 50759 84475
9   SX 50324 81138
10 SX 47089 80430
11 SX 58223 78973
12 SX 60083 75405
13 SX 60276 85814

Northeast Dartmoor
1   SX 75998 77441
2   SX 74301 89942
3   SX 75132 78530

SX 65275 91224
SX 66237 83822
SX 72274 89668
SX 81079 82863
SX 77483 81589
SX 84402 86271
SX 78516 78517
SX 92253 85714
SX 80913 80831
SX 70149 80920
SX 66103 76338
SX 74635 78797
SX 65465 87380
SX 79655 88592
SX 66703 84066

outheast Dartmoor
SX 69713 71652
SX 69939 71324
SX 71073 70439
SX 70542 70174
SX 72613 72226
SX 71510 71163
SX 79070 63775
SX 83957 57380
SX 93584 64863
SX 78494 63755
SX 79985 62508
SX 73070 68511
SX 70590 69517
SX 84898 57192
SX 74382 66432
SX 73529 73161
SX 74921 67910
SX 94576 56601
SX 83923 62297
SX 80511 60316
SX 82733 57963
SX 67234 73161

outh Devon
SX 53101 47578
SX 57901 46958
SX 61408 47554
SX 64034 45495
SX 65605 43919
SX 66971 42405
SX 67432 41426
SX 69731 37475
SX 76179 36364
SX 73796 37944
SX 80202 37218
SX 81709 36917
SX 85045 47278
SX 88142 48568
SX 92250 53422
SX 55371 47983
SX 61944 47607
SX 69237 47244
SX 73605 43700

20 SX 73299 49671
21 SX 66761 39696
22 SX 81814 38450
23 SX 69445 41198
24 SX 51779 48449
25 SX 74125 39171

East Devon
1 SY 09785 85204
2 SY 16403 87919
3 SY 29835 90002
4 SY 08768 86890
5 SY 09109 92690
6 ST 27207 00047
7 SY 04002 84095
8 SY 24059 97379
9 SY 00006 99898
10 SS 97619 00067
11 SX 95973 99922
12 SY 04778 84359
13 SY 31689 92413
14 SY 25874 97497
15 SY 03355 87366
16 SY 13902 88360
17 SY 05702 89725
18 SY 07558 82006
19 SY 20752 88118
20 SX 93039 96099
21 SY 23027 89063

Central Exmoor
1 SS 73972 49775
2 SS 89813 49087
3 SS 90713 49346
4 SS 75278 48308
5 SS 75049 48970
6 SS 79318 45407
7 SS 72320 42316
8 SS 85589 33782
9 SS 79348 37462
10 SS 81642 36118
11 SS 85985 32672
12 SS 91943 25735
13 SS 89911 43567
14 SS 87545 41527
15 SS 70560 39111
16 SS 94781 48171
17 SS 84232 48187
18 SS 92218 39880
19 SS 88968 30293

Quantock & Blackdown
1 ST 14746 44006
2 ST 16718 44931
3 ST 28020 46528
4 ST 09799 13701
5 SS 98674 30148
6 ST 22514 13840
7 ST 11676 41099
8 ST 12753 39457
9 ST 16397 35948

10 ST 11032 15037
11 SS 99179 44100
12 ST 17541 40056
13 ST 09605 33527
14 SS 97838 42413
15 ST 14541 41385
16 ST 05235 21325
17 ST 13718 17194
18 ST 11101 39407
19 ST 16225 38276
20 ST 18397 31845
21 ST 14065 36732

Somerset Levels
1 ST 56417 31883
2 ST 54774 33821
3 ST 35181 37746
4 ST 42483 24846
5 ST 49843 17118
6 ST 52198 39161
7 ST 47983 32540
8 ST 35910 30518
9 ST 49371 16967
10 ST 42558 41017
11 ST 45629 43686
12 ST 44914 39634
13 ST 41493 26615
14 ST 41523 19986
15 ST 56307 37011
16 ST 45349 45658
17 ST 37559 12703

Mendip Hills
1 ST 29219 52429
2 ST 28060 59275
3 ST 61548 50982
4 ST 54727 51494
5 ST 59507 54935
6 ST 46707 53941
7 ST 47581 58225
8 ST 46823 58433
9 ST 47402 54423
10 ST 38193 58830
11 ST 52089 48438
12 ST 48199 54537
13 ST 48648 51374
14 ST 38757 55832
15 ST 45268 58994
16 ST 51873 49240
17 ST 50038 50771
18 ST 34113 50973
19 ST 50349 55517
20 ST 46363 53777
21 ST 55432 54624
22 ST 53909 52047
23 ST 47606 58681

Somerset Avon
1 ST 32728 66052
2 ST 23251 60635
3 ST 57492 59178

4 ST 51068 60637
5 ST 40338 65200
6 ST 78485 62516
7 ST 79195 64281
8 ST 62281 64179
9 ST 63229 64316
10 ST 53614 73281
11 ST 80613 60038
12 ST 68108 68776
13 ST 76517 61557
14 ST 47070 65404
15 ST 55372 74078
16 ST 55019 71790
17 ST 76839 67984
18 ST 76679 63403
19 ST 58149 58528
20 ST 60075 66075
21 ST 71077 67513
22 ST 79446 66127
23 ST 74374 60567
24 ST 56470 73267
25 ST 56398 72934
26 ST 58929 72346
27 ST 60019 63284

East Somerset
1 ST 80513 57681
2 ST 81439 42063
3 ST 80526 55412
4 ST 78157 50918
5 ST 76910 34531
6 ST 67187 47762
7 ST 63774 45939
8 ST 78380 29375
9 ST 82702 39123
10 ST 79175 43885
11 ST 80432 34571
12 ST 62933 25248
13 ST 66241 48369
14 ST 73500 57201
15 ST 73664 45790
16 ST 74183 48968
17 ST 74547 35120

East Dorset
1 ST 95777 00584
2 ST 99561 00049
3 SZ 03141 98971
4 ST 92279 03513
5 ST 96434 03019
6 ST 99942 19287
7 SY 98659 00260
8 ST 81718 22245
9 ST 88615 18744
10 ST 92536 20627
11 ST 85552 10700
12 ST 84545 12605
13 SU 02410 10280
14 SU 04098 19400
15 SU 03024 06744

Dorset Purbeck
1 SY 80522 80258
2 SY 82240 79841
3 SY 84355 79912
4 SY 97746 76063
5 SY 87050 79715
6 SY 99771 76886
7 SY 95609 77088
8 SZ 00916 88106
9 SZ 03440 83581
10 SZ 03603 82936
11 SY 80585 89488
12 SY 92360 87144
13 SY 93726 82917
14 SY 92171 83241
15 SY 86550 80551
16 SY 98366 88440
17 SY 90898 78862
18 SZ 01534 77309
19 SY 95796 80991
20 SY 95436 82359
21 SY 88177 80358
22 SY 96082 75542

Dorchester & Portland
1 SY 69751 70969
2 SY 61532 80820
3 SY 77171 80661
4 SY 75116 81338
5 ST 79105 21532
6 ST 78274 14329
7 ST 77616 16545
8 ST 80029 13599
9 ST 82302 14536
10 SY 68670 69073
11 SY 68449 72477
12 ST 76753 05795
13 SY 66886 88445
14 ST 66532 01514
15 ST 77631 07014
16 SY 72528 92204
17 ST 78949 03851

West Dorset
1 SY 39572 92226
2 SY 41973 91699
3 SY 49032 88789
4 SY 54128 94747
5 ST 41353 01214
6 SY 55667 86515
7 SY 37212 99072
8 SY 39008 93523
9 SY 57264 84845
10 SY 44199 93865
11 SY 55792 87927
12 SY 57790 87821
13 SY 55449 99128
14 SY 54701 97389
15 SY 50228 97897
16 ST 35948 05193

**Wild Guide:
Devon, Cornwall
and the South West**

Words and photos:
Daniel Start
Tania Pascoe

Research:
Jo Keeling

Editing:
Anna Kruger

Design and layout:
Oliver Mann
Marcus Freeman

Fact checking:
Sarah Jones

Proofreading:
Michael Lee, Candida Frith-
Macdonald, Marijka Pascoe

Distribution:
Central Books Ltd
99 Wallis Road
London, E9 5LN
Tel +44 (0)845 458 9911
orders@centralbooks.com

Published by:
Wild Things Publishing Ltd.
Freshford, Bath,
BA2 7WG, United Kingdom

guide

the award-winning
adventure travel series:

- South West England
- London & South East
- Lakes and Dales
- Scotland
- Wales
- Scandinavia
- Portugal

also available as an app for
iPhone and Android.

hello@wildthingspublishing.com

Photographs and maps. All photos © Daniel Start except: Cathy Warne p248 (St Luke's Chapel), Seb de Gange: p49 (cockles) p50 (crab) p50 (basking shark), p63 Justin Tiltman, p66 (Tregarsus) Brian Clint, p86 (Treyarnon pool) John Palmer, p95 Joe Brooks, p98 (Merlin's Cavern) Tor Udall, p118 www.tunnelsbeaches. co.uk/Neville Stanikk, p166 (Budleigh Salterton) Peter Taylor, p183 Richard Baker, p184 Julie Wright, p192 (Dundon Yew), p193 (Lovestruck) Jo Keeling, p196-197 Greg Fitchett, p50 Vicky's Bread, p74 Tree surfers, p82 (Jam pot), p90 Mighty-Oak.co.uk, p114 (Top and bottom) Vintage Vardos image courtesy of Sawday's Canopy & Stars, Fisherton Farm, Devon, (Fourth down) Jeffrey and Karina Griffin, Loveland Farm, image courtesy of Sawday's Canopy & Stars, p114 Dan the Fish Man (www.clovellyfish.com), p146 www. Powdermillspottery.com, p146 www.dartmoorstables.com, p154 (Long Barrow Windmill) www.sawdays. co.uk, p162 (Oyster Shack) www.visitbigburyonsea.com, p194 (Bartlett's Farm) www. gypsycaravanbreaks. co.uk, p248 Guy Mallinson / Crafty Camping www.mallinson.co.uk. The following reproduced by CC-BY-SA. **Geograph:** P54 (Treloan) Tim Green, p54 (Molunan) Chris Downer, p57(Enys) Rob Allday, p62 (Lantic) Roger Geach, p62 (Sea thrift) Rob Allday, p64 (Luxulyan) Rob Allday, p64 (Restormel) Chris Downer, p66 (Pont Pill) Derek Harper, p66 (Trelavour) Tony Atkin, p70 (Freathy) Derek Harper, p70 (Chapel) Derek Harper, p70 (Looe Island) Ewan Stevenson, p74 (Rame Head) Philip Halling, p82 Tony Atkin (South Wheal Francis), p82 (Wheal Coates cave) Helen Wilkinson, p94 (Treknow) Trevor Rickard, p98 (Treknow) Sally, p102 (Bearah Tor) Ken Ripper, p104 (Delford Bridge) Tony Aktin, p104 (Phoenix United) Tony Atkin, p106 (Bodmin Jail) Rob Fuller, p106 (Clether Well) Rob Purvis, p112 (Warren Tower) Tony Atkin, p122 (Battery Point) Grant Sherman, p122 (Bennett's Mouth)Roger Smith, p128 (Fogginton) Derek Harper , p129 (Fogginton) Jeff Collins, p129 (Cornwood Maidens) Richard Knights, p136 (Cowsic) Guy Wareham, p136 (Wheal Betsy) Richard Knights, p138 (Brent Tor) Chris Downer, p138 (Cranmere) Patrick Gueulle, p142 (Holwell) Mark Percy, p142 (Grimspound) Derek Harper, p146 (Nine Stones) Geoff Barker, p162 (South Huish) Martin Bodman, p176 David Croker, p177 (Culbone) Tony Atkin, p177 (Sillery) Anthony Parkes, p178 (Hurlstone Point) Exmoor Walker, p178 (Culbone Stone) Guy Wareham, p178 (Dunkery Beacon) Lewis Clarke, p182 (Steart Point) Lewis Clarke, p186 (Robin Hood's Hut) Des Blenkinsopp, p186 (Willet Hill) Barbara Cook, p190 (St Michael's Tower) Jim Champion, p193 (Westhay) Brian Robert Marshall, p198 (Gough's Cave) John Welch, p201 (Brent Knoll) Steve Ashman, p200 (Charterhouse) Rick Crowley, p202 (Velvet Bottom) Ken Grainger, p202 (Nine Barrows) Sharon Loxton, p202 (Aveline's Hole) William, p234 (At Adhelm) Philip Halling, p238 (Tout Quarry) Bob Ford, p242 (White Nothe) John Palmer, p246 (St Catherine's Chapel) Mike Searle, p246 (Pilsdon Pen) Eugene Birchall, St Luke's Chapel. **Flickr:** p42 (Men-a-Tol) Robert Moore, p138 (Pond Cottage) Landmark Trust / Lee Pengelly / www.silverscenephoto.co.uk, p143 Chris Popham / Tomorrow Never Knows, p144 Dave Evans / Snaps11, p152 (Berry Pomeroy) Warwick Conway, p201 (Cheddar Gorge) SanguineSeas / Adam Heath, p241 (White Nothe) Jim Champion / treehouse 1977. **Wikimedia:** p94 (Samphire) Jymm, p96 (Labyrinth) Simon Garbutt, p98 (Ladies Window) Nilfanion, p126 (Merrivale) Herbythyme, p202 (Brean Down) Geof Sheppard, p218 (Stoney Littleton) Rodw, p222 (Fontmell) Marilyn Peddle, p222 (Cursus) Jim Champion, p224 Marilyn Peddle, p234 (cave) Bob Embleton, p241 (Cerne Abbas) Pete Harlow, p242 (Tout Quarry) Simon Palmer. **Ordnance Survey:** maps contain data © Crown copyright and database right 2011.

Author acknowledgements: We would like to thanks Canopy and Stars, Sawday's, and the National Trust for ideas and information. heartfelt thanks to Marijka and Tony Pascoe, Ivan Pascoe, Emma Winterbottom, Michael Lee, Rose Start, Jack Thurston, Sarah Price, Jess Jackson, Owen Davies, Ciaran Mundy, John Foster, Tom and Tor Currie, Doodoo Tom-Baird, Aimee Tolhurst, Ruth Pratt, Toots Parkin, Fiona Smith, Dough King-Smith, Luke Hudson, Lucy Odling-Smee, John and Lucy Rouse, Olivier Geoffrey, Kate and Ben Porteous. This book has been made by an all star team. Extra special thanks to Anna Kruger whose has tirelessly shaped and crafted the words, to Oliver Mann whose layout and map makings skills have made everything beautiful and to Michael Lee and Sarah Jones for eagle-eyed checking.

Other books from Wild Things Publishing:

Wild Guide Wales	Wild Swimming Britain	Lost Lanes South
Wild Guide Scotland	Wild Swimming France	Lost Lanes Wales
Wild Guide Lakes & Dales	Wild Swimming Italy	Lost Lanes West
Wild Guide South-East	Wild Swimming Spain	Bikepacking
Wild Guide Scandinavia	Wild Swimming Sydney	France en Velo
Wild Guide Portugal	Wild Swimming Walks	Wild Running
Wild Garden Weekends	Hidden Beaches Britain	Wild Ruins
Islandeering	Scottish Bothy Bible	Wild Ruins B.C.